LOOKING LIKE A LANGUAGE, SOUNDING LIKE A RACE

LOOKING LIKE A LANGUAGE, SOUNDING LIKE A RACE

Raciolinguistic Ideologies and the Learning of Latinidad

Jonathan Rosa

OXFORD
UNIVERSITY PRESS

OXFORD
UNIVERSITY PRESS

Published in the United States of America by Oxford University Press
198 Madison Avenue, New York, NY 10016, United States of America.

© Oxford University Press 2019

Library of Congress Cataloging-in-Publication Data
Names: Rosa, Jonathan, author.
Title: Looking like a language, sounding like a race : raciolinguistic ideologies and
the learning of Latinidad / Jonathan Rosa.
Description: New York, NY : Oxford University Press, [2019] |
Includes bibliographical references and index. |
Identifiers: LCCN 2017028685 (print) | LCCN 2017043926 (ebook) |
ISBN 978-0-19-063474-2 (updf) | ISBN 978-0-19-063475-9 (online course) |
ISBN 978-0-19-085175-0 (epub) | ISBN 978-0-19-063473-5 (softcover : acid-free paper) |
ISBN 978-0-19-063472-8 (hardcover : acid-free paper)
Subjects: LCSH: Linguistic minorities—United States. | Group identity—United States. |
Latin Americans—Ethnic identity. | Hispanic Americans—Ethnic identity. |
Anthropological linguistics—United States.
Classification: LCC P119.315 (ebook) | LCC P119.315 .R68 2018 (print) |
DDC 306.44/973—dc23
LC record available at https://lccn.loc.gov/2017028685

Hardback printed by Bridgeport National Bindery, Inc., United States of America

For my parents, whom I miss infinitely, and yet whose presence is always with me.

For my parents, whom I miss infinitely, and yet whose presence is always with me.

CONTENTS

FIGURES

TABLES

ACKNOWLEDGMENTS

When I entered the doctoral program in the Department of Anthropology at the University of Chicago in 2003 and simultaneously began working with organizations and schools throughout the city, I quickly learned that many of the insights that most captivated me in my formal graduate studies were also theorized, enacted, and contested in community-based efforts toward transforming institutions that systematically reproduce various hierarchies and forms of marginalization. My dissertation and now this book are indebted to actors, ideas, and experiences I encountered across these contexts.

Staff, students, families, and community members associated with New Northwest High School generously allowed me to participate in their everyday lives for several years, and they have continued to think with me about how their experiences unsettle prevailing conceptions of language and identity. I am especially grateful for the time I spent with Dr. Baez, Yesi, James, and Rigo, who emerge as key thinkers throughout the pages that follow.

My research within the high school and its surrounding communities was deeply informed by my participation in various initiatives of Chicago's Puerto Rican Cultural Center. It was through the PRCC that I first learned about longstanding Mexican-Puerto Rican interrelations in Chicago, which became an important focus of my research. José López, the director of this inspiring organization, taught me to see race and colonialism as intertwined historical problems that are continually rearticulated and demand to be resolved. I am yet another person whose work is a testament to José's intellectual brilliance and unselfish commitment to nurturing future generations of scholar-activists dedicated to imagining and enacting political possibilities.

My mentors at the University of Chicago taught me semiotic tools for denaturalizing social and linguistic categories, on the one hand, and interrogating formations of power, on the other. Susan Gal, Michael Silverstein, and Kesha Fikes profoundly shaped the approach to racial and linguistic category-making that characterizes my work. Their careful attention to questions of perspective, context, and conditions of possibility continues to anchor my thinking. In addition to my dissertation committee members, I also received helpful guidance and feedback from many other professors at the University of Chicago, including Cathy Cohen, Melissa Harris-Perry, Judith Farquhar, John Kelly, Stephan Palmié, and Jessica Cattelino. They are joined by formal and informal mentors beyond U of C, including Frances Aparicio, Bonnie Urciuoli, Gina Pérez, Mary Bucholtz, Charles Briggs, Renato Rosaldo, Mary Louise Pratt, Cally Waite, Lisa Smulyan, Diane Anderson, Donna Jo Napoli, K. David Harrison, and Stanton Wortham. Arlene Dávila and Ana Celia Zentella have provided incredible mentorship over the years, a great deal of which contributed to the completion of this manuscript.

Many friends and colleagues provided critical feedback and support during the writing of the dissertation and book, including Adrienne Lo, Angela Reyes, Elaine Chun, Netta Avineri, Lily Chumley, Jacqui Lazú, Gustavo Rivera, Lucia Cantero, Tehama Lopez Bunyasi, Hilary Dick, Sonia Das, Micaela Díaz-Sánchez, Falina Enriquez, Daniel Nieves, Laurence Ralph, Michael Ralph, Simon May, Amy Cooper, Michael Rodríguez-Muñiz, Teresa González, Uri McMillan, Anthony Ocampo, G. Cristina Mora, H. Samy Alim, O. Hugo Benavides, José Del Valle, and Greg Thompson. Elizabeth Todd-Breland always reminded me of my core insights. Nelson Flores is my raciolinguistic partner in crime. Vanessa Díaz is a constant sounding board and source of encouragement. Focused writing meetings and equally focused irreverence with Christopher Loperena became a key source of productivity and joy during the final stages of this project. Yarimar Bonilla's ride-or-die support over the years, coupled with intense but loving critique, have taught me that friends can become family.

The Department of Anthropology at the University of Massachusetts Amherst reinvigorated my investment in the potential for the discipline to become a critical site of community collaboration and contributor to justice efforts. I am especially grateful to UMass and Five College colleagues, including Emiliana Cruz, Jacqueline Urla, Mari Castañeda, Joseph Krupczynski, Alberto Sandoval-Sánchez, Ginetta Candelario, Sonia Nieto, Jason Irizarry, Whitney Battle-Baptiste, Amanda Walker Johnson, Julie Hemment, Jane Anderson, Bob Paynter, Art Keene, Krista Harper, Sonya Atalay, Betsy Krause, Ventura Perez, Jen Sandler, Lynnette Sievert, Laura Vandenberg, Korina Jocson, Antonio Martínez, Wilson Valentín-Escobar, Benjamin Bailey, Donal Carbaugh, Gloria Bernabe-Ramos, Jose Ornelas, Laura Valdiviezo, Theresa Austin, Sonia Alvarez, and José Hernández. I also received a great deal of support from the UMass Centers for Research on Families and Latin American, Caribbean, and Latino Studies.

Joining the faculty at Stanford allowed me to finish the book in the company of an incredible, interdisciplinary community of scholars. I have received tremendous support from colleagues and mentors, including Guadalupe Valdés, Arnetha

Ball, Dan Schwartz, Tomás Jiménez, John Rickford, Paula Moya, Jennifer DeVere Brody, Daniel Murray, Ramón Antonio Martínez, Jennifer Langer-Osuña, Antero Garcia, Ray McDermott, Bryan Brown, Ari Kelman, Brigid Barron, Roy Pea, Kabir Tambar, Miyako Inoue, Martin Carnoy, and Leah Gordon.

My high school, undergraduate, and graduate student mentees, collaborators, and friends continually push my thinking. Thanks especially to Carlos Rosado, Sunny Trivedi, Brendon MacKeen, Moises Lopez, Christa Burdick, Sela Kenen, Vanessa Miranda, Krista Cortes, Eduardo Muñoz-Muñoz, Teresa Pratt, Sharese King, Casey Wong, Davíd Albán Hidalgo, Andrea Flores, Alicia Pérez, Rocio Hernández, Bernardo Vélez, and Xavier Burgos.

My brother and sister have been there for me in every way possible throughout this process. Despite our deep sense of self-reliance, it gives me an immeasurable amount of peace to know that I can rely on you for anything. Gil and Vanessa, your books are next!

David Flores has been with me through each step of this project, alternately celebrating my progress and prodding me to finish. Your partnership and insights have contributed to this manuscript in infinite ways, including your design of the beautiful, provocative cover art. I could ask for no greater champion for this book or me than you.

I have received generous feedback on sections of this manuscript from various audiences, including the Department of Anthropology at Stanford University, Institute for Latino Studies at the University of Notre Dame, Institute of/for the Global South at Fordham University, Advanced Research Collective at CUNY Graduate Center, Social Science Matrix at University of California Berkeley, New York Linguistic Anthropology Working Group, New England Consortium for Latina/o/x Studies, the Seminar in Borderlands/Latino Studies at the Newberry Library, Department of Anthropology at Hamilton College, Comparative American Studies Program at Oberlin College, Department of Social and Cultural Analysis at New York University, Kira Hall's wonderful students in two graduate seminars at the University of Colorado Boulder, and University of Chicago Workshops on Semiotics: Culture in Context, Reproduction of Race and Racial Ideologies, US Locations, and Politics, Communication, Society.

I am grateful to the editorial team at Oxford University Press, particularly Hallie Stebbins and Hannah Doyle, for a smooth and supportive publication process from beginning to end. I am also appreciative of the warm, supportive mentoring Laura Ahearn has provided as editor of the series in which this book appears, Oxford Studies in the Anthropology of Language.

This research was supported by generous funding from the Ford Foundation, National Science Foundation, Wenner-Gren Foundation for Anthropological Research, Woodrow Wilson Foundation, Social Science Research Council/

Mellon Mays Graduate Initiatives Program, Center for Applied Linguistics, Social Sciences Division at the University of Chicago, Center for the Study of Race, Politics, and Culture at the University of Chicago, and Office of Multicultural Student Affairs at the University of Chicago.

Sections of Chapters 3, 4, and 5 were published in "Standardization, Racialization, Languagelessness: Raciolinguistic Ideologies across Communicative Contexts," in *Journal of Linguistic Anthropology* (vol. 26, no. 2); "From Mock Spanish to Inverted Spanglish: Language Ideologies and the Racialization of Mexican and Puerto Rican Youth in the United States," in *Raciolinguistics: How Language Shapes Our Ideas about Race*, edited by H. Samy Alim, John Rickford, and Arnetha Ball (New York: Oxford University Press, 2016); "Nuevo Chicago?: Language, Diaspora, and Latina/o Panethnic Formations," in *A Sociolinguistics of Diaspora: Latino Practices, Identities, and Ideologies*, edited by Rosina Marquez and Luisa Martín Rojo (New York: Routledge, 2015); and "Learning Ethnolinguistic Borders: Language and Diaspora in the Socialization of U.S. Latinas/os," in *Diaspora Studies in Education: Toward a Framework for Understanding the Experiences of Transnational Communities*, edited by Rosalie Rolón-Dow and Jason G. Irizarry (New York: Peter Lang Publishing, 2014).

TRANSCRIPTION, CODING, AND ORTHOGRAPHIC CONVENTIONS

[Simultaneous talk by two speakers, with one strip of talk above the overlapping talk at the moment of simultaneity
=   Interruption or next utterance following immediately
...   Noticeable pause (untimed)
<u>underline</u>   Emphatic stress or increased amplitude

Transcript line numbers are provided only when they are referred to in the main text.

Throughout the book I use the term "Latinx" (a gender nonbinary alternative to Latina, Latino, and Latin@) to refer to US-based persons of Latin American descent. I use "Latino" or "Latina" in direct quotations and when referring specifically to self-identified male-identified or female-identified persons, respectively. I occasionally use "Hispanic" and variants thereof such as "Hispanicization" in similar panethnic and diasporic ways, particularly when engaging with literature that uses this terminology or research participants who use it. To the extent that these shifting usages signal confusion, debate, and anxiety about the relationship between forms of communication and categories of identity, well, that's the point!

"Inverted Spanglish" usages are bolded, italicized, informally transcribed for nonlinguists, phonetically transcribed in brackets, and then parenthetically transcribed as they might be produced with conventional Spanish phonology, written with Spanish orthography, and translated into English. For example:

numerow trace [numɜ˞ɹoʊ treɪs] (Spanish, [numeɾo tɾeɪs], "numero tres," number three)

Self-identified Mexican and Puerto Rican students are coded using the abbreviations "Mex" and "PR," as well as generation cohort with respect to (im)migration and grade year in school. For example:

Pedro (PR, Gen. 3, Gr. 10)
Name (Self-ascribed identity, (im)migration cohort, grade year)

Generation 1: born and raised outside of the US mainland until the age of 12 or older

Generation 1.5: born outside of the US mainland, but raised within the US mainland before the age of 12

Generation 2: born and raised within the US mainland by parents who were born and raised outside of the US mainland

Generation 3: born and raised within the US mainland by parents who were born and raised within the US mainland

I use the phrase "US mainland" to distinguish between the continental United States and its territories and possessions. Puerto Rico is a US Commonwealth; thus, someone born in Puerto Rico is born "outside of the US mainland." This allows for a unified designation for people born in Puerto Rico or any other location in Latin America.

For students whose parents are from different Latinx subgroups, the parent who corresponds to a given group is abbreviated in brackets as "m" for mother and "f" for father following the name of the group. For example:

Miguel (PR[m]/Mex[f], Gen. 2, Gr. 10)
Puerto Rican mother/Mexican father

LOOKING LIKE A LANGUAGE, SOUNDING LIKE A RACE

INTRODUCTION

MAKING LATINX IDENTITIES AND MANAGING AMERICAN ANXIETIES

In February 2010, as I was nearing the end of several years of Chicago-based fieldwork focused on language, race, and Latinx identities, the *Chicago Sun-Times* ran a series of stories titled "Nuevo Chicago" ("New Chicago"), "How Young Hispanics Are Reshaping the Region."[1] The stories frame the experiences of "young Hispanics" growing up in Chicago as "two cultures finding a happy medium in the mainstream":

> In high school cafeterias, college dorms, Loop offices, and River North nightclubs, a new generation of Latinos is rising, pushing toward success and often seamlessly weaving together elements of their heritage into the mainstream culture.

The stories suggest that "emphasis on language and identity seem to go hand in hand," and point to examples of young Latinx Chicagoans whose "multiple national identities" give them a unique perspective. One boy "thinks of himself as Mexican" even though he "was born in Chicago and speaks fluent English without an accent. . . . Like many young Latinos, [he] identifies strongly with his parents' home country even while growing up in the United States." A young Latina in one of the stories said that she used to be embarrassed because she felt different from her White peers, but during "her senior year in high school, she began embracing her Latino identity." After this change in perspective, she was no longer ashamed, and now she is "very proud [to be] Mexican."

After foregrounding these multicultural, coming-of-age Latinx success stories, the tone of the report begins to shift:

> Overwhelmingly U.S. born, bilingual and optimistic about the future—though lagging in education levels and facing a

stubborn teen pregnancy rate—Latinos are the largest and youngest minority group in the United States. . . . While Hispanic women and other groups have increased their bachelor's degree attainment rate, the rate for males has remained stable at 10 percent, the lowest of any group. . . . Latino men are less likely to start or finish college because of family pressure to work and gang activity. . . . Coupled with the fact that Hispanic women have the highest rate of teen pregnancy of any group, both males and females end up having trouble staying in school.

In one moment, Latinxs are "bilingual," "optimistic about the future," and "seamlessly weave together elements of their heritage into the mainstream culture," while in the next they struggle with gangs, teen pregnancy, and educational underachievement. Dávila (2008) and Chavez (2008) characterize this narrative dynamic as "Latino spin" and "Latino threat," respectively. Dávila argues that seemingly contradictory representational tropes associated with Latinxs, such as "illegal, tax burden, patriotic, family-oriented, hard-working, and model consumer" (2008:1), should be understood as efforts to reproduce normative American racial, class, gender, and sexual ideals rather than empirical representations of Latinxs' fundamental character. While Dávila explores whitewashing through "Latino spin," Chavez tracks racialization through "Latino threat" narratives that position Latinxs as an abject Other population in need of careful management. Importantly, both "Latino spin" and "Latino threat" narratives often frame language shift from Spanish to English as a sign of progress, which reflects how seemingly contradictory representations contribute to the overdetermination of Latinx identities and linguistic practices as part of broader projects of population management. These popular discourses demonstrate how conceptions of Latinx difference—the stereotypical characteristics associated with US-based (im)migrants from Latin America and their descendants—are closely linked to a set of anxieties and ideologies surrounding race and language.[2] I argue that the co-naturalization of language and race is a key feature of modern governance, such that languages are perceived as racially embodied and race is perceived as linguistically intelligible, which results in the overdetermination of racial embodiment and communicative practice—hence the notion of *looking like a language* and *sounding like a race*. Thus, race, language, and governance must be analyzed collectively.

The ethnoracial[3] status of Latinx identity is widely debated in both scholarly and popular discourses, often from the perspective of spectrum-based racial logics that problematically imagine Latinxs as an intermediary "brown" population located between Blackness at one end and Whiteness at the other, or as a phenotypically heterogeneous group that is better understood ethnically (i.e., stereotypically defined culturally or nationally) than racially (i.e., stereotypically defined physically). The former logic is anchored in white supremacist histories of Indigenous erasure and anti-Blackness through which some groups and bodies come to be positioned as desirable for their perceived mixed-race status and proximity to Whiteness; the latter logic is anchored in white supremacist colonial management schemas that homogenize and differentiate populations in varying ways.[4] Thus, historical power formations, rather than objectively similar or different bodies, organize processes of phenotypic homogenization and differentiation. There is infinite phenotypic heterogeneity within Indigenous, Black, Asian, and White populations, so Latinxs are not a magical, "cosmic race"[5] that will usher in a newly mixed-race American future in relation to imagined pasts consisting of bounded racial categories that never were.

Spectrum-based racial logics also tell us very little about how populations come to be positioned in particular historical, political, and economic circumstances. Imbricated, ongoing American histories of Indigenous genocide and containment, African enslavement and subsequent African American societal abjection, Asian and Latinx (im)migrant labor exploitation, detention, and deportation, and contemporary Islamophobia cannot be understood by locating populations on a binary Black-White racial spectrum. However, rather than moving beyond a Black-White binary, which is often a convenient way in which to reproduce anti-Blackness, we must understand this binary as but one racial logic among many, albeit a very powerful one that is tied to consequential histories of colorism of which Latinxs are certainly a part (Fergus, Noguera, and Martin 2010). An alternative approach to racial assemblages seeks to understand the linked modes in which racialized populations inhabit various historical, political, and economic positionalities as they orbit around Whiteness in shifting, yet colonially patterned, ways.

Regardless of perceived phenotypic heterogeneity, semiotic ideologies recruit linguistic practices and various signs of difference to homogenize Latinxs as racial Others. Crucially, I approach race and language not as objectively observable or embodied phenomena in the first place, but rather as historically and institutionally constituted subject formations that are rooted in the rearticulation of colonial distinctions between normative Europeanness and Othered non-Europeanness that emerged through the contested production of modernity as an ideology and power formation that is global in its scope (Bauman and Briggs 2003). From this perspective, perceptions of bodies and communicative practices are colonially conditioned constructions of reality rather than unmediated reflections of preexisting differences or similarities. While I am interested in how bodies and linguistic practices are perceived, parsed, and experienced in everyday interactions and modes of identification, I argue that we must attend to the historical and institutional conditions of possibility for such intersubjective phenomena in order to understand how they reproduce, disrupt, and reconfigure racial categories and linguistic varieties. Insofar as Latinx identities are produced as part of a US settler colonial history and broader histories of European colonialism, we must continually attend to the ways that these forms of coloniality shape perceptions of Latinx bodies in relation to an imagined phenotypic spectrum from Blackness to Whiteness, and Latinx communicative practices in relation to an imagined linguistic spectrum from Spanish to English. Indeed, these spectra hinge on the reproduction of anti-Blackness and the erasure of Indigeneity, and as such should be interrogated as racialized colonial logics rather than empirical rubrics within which bodies and linguistic practices can be objectively situated. The fact that millions of people are perceived from some perspectives as Indigenous, Afro-Latinx, White, Asian, and/or some combination thereof, yet self-identify as "Hispanic," "Latino," or "Spanish," is a reflection of the constructed nature of these categories on the one hand, and of the need to interrogate their historical and contemporary reproduction on the other. The same could be said for people who might identify as monolingual English users or English-dominant, yet who often engage in practices that could be classified as bilingual or multilingual. The inability to apprehend the role of coloniality in shaping these modes of perception and identification leads to the indictment of individuals and populations as suffering from racial and linguistic denial, rather than the indictment of colonialism as a historical and contemporary power formation that profoundly circumscribes desirable and possible subjectivities. Thus, I am interested in the ways that the rearticulation of colonial logics surrounding race and language figures centrally in the creation of Latinx as particular coordinate within a broader assemblage—note, not a spectrum!—of racial categories and language varieties.

This book explores the joint perception, construction, and naturalization of racial categories and language varieties in the context of a predominantly Latinx Chicago public high school and its surrounding communities. I demonstrate the ways that Latinx difference is ambivalently imagined as the cause of and solution to stereotypical urban challenges such as educational underachievement, gang violence, and teen pregnancy.[6] These ambivalences are tied to tensions involved in the emergence of Latinx panethnicity as part of wider patterns of ethnicization and racialization, as well as the reproduction of these patterns in conjunction with the management of socioeconomic class, gender, and sexuality. I examine how broad, racialized and panethnic identity formation processes are negotiated locally in Chicago through historically situated interrelations among knowledge economy on the other. Media portrayals such as the *Chicago Sun-Times* story mentioned previously typically frame these disparate outcomes as products of a racialized culture of poverty created within the home and the hood or as meritocratic rewards for individual strivers, respectively. Neither of these explanations remotely reflects how schools and mainstream institutions more broadly are structured by systematic forms of racial and class exclusion that characterize the fundamental nature of the US liberal democratic project, its settler colonial underpinnings, and the modes of governance required to maintain the image of its political legitimacy.

For the principal of NNHS, racial and class exclusion, along with intersectional forms of gender and sexual marginalization, were primary foci of her administrative project. A brief ethnographic interlude will help to demonstrate this. In March 2010, I attended a meeting of the NNHS Local School Council,[22] whose participants included students, teachers, parents, administrators, and community members. A few minutes before the meeting was scheduled to begin, Dr. Baez, the school's principal, entered the cafeteria space in which the meeting was held. After observing that no one other than the council members was present at the meeting (that is, no one from the public showed up), she went upstairs to the school library and recruited an adult English as a Second Language (ESL) class to attend the meeting. She returned with a small crowd of approximately 25 adults. The ESL class participants sat in the last two rows of chairs that were set up for the public audience. Dr. Baez encouraged them to move up to the front two rows and partake of the refreshments that were stationed along the wall. The formal meeting opened with the reading of the previous meeting's minutes. Because the ESL class participants almost exclusively composed the audience for this meeting, several members of the Local School Council initially expressed confusion about whether the meeting should be conducted in English or Spanish. With a council whose members were all self-identified English-Spanish bilinguals, it was possible to consider using either language or a combination thereof. Dr. Baez intervened, stating that everyone should feel comfortable speaking English and Spanish at the meeting and that the ESL class should see this as an opportunity to practice their English. Thus, Dr. Baez disrupted the normative terms of English language learning by orienting it in relation to legitimate participation in a formal meeting rather than rote classroom learning; she also disrupted normative expectations of monolingual English language use in the Local School Council meeting by stipulating both normative English-Spanish bilingualism and egalitarianism among the elected council members and the adult ESL class participants. Dr. Baez recognized processes of institutional exclusion and used her position of authority to performatively enact a counter-hegemonic otherwise.

There were two main topics for this meeting: the upcoming Local School Council elections that would take place in April 2010 and the 2010 US Census. For Dr. Baez, these topics were closely related. Drawing on a range of English and Spanish language practices, she explained to the audience that they should seriously consider running for positions on the Local School Council, such as parent representative (if they had children who attended NNHS) or community representative (if they lived within the school's neighborhood boundaries). She said that as members of the Local School Council, they would be able to join the school in helping students to overcome the obstacles that stand in the way of their educational success, such as gang participation and pregnancy.[23] For those who were uninterested in running for a position on the Local School Council, Dr. Baez provided instructions for how to vote in the Local School Council election. She told audience members that they would need two forms of identification. When Dr. Baez noticed that this prompted whispers among audience members, she clarified that even a paper indicating participation in the ESL class could count as identification. She suggested that both voting for in the Local School Council election and filling out the 2010 US Census form are important ways to improve the community. She said that the Latino population is on the rise and that this population must be counted in order to secure resources for the school and the community. Dr. Baez reassured the audience that "las personas sin papeles," or people without papers,[24] would not be at risk of attracting the attention of US immigration authorities by participating in the Census.[25]

Those who are unfamiliar with the variety of US Latinx[26] experiences might not think that there was anything particularly noteworthy about this meeting. In contrast, I saw it as characteristic of the unique panethnic Latinx relationships that I had consistently encountered in Chicago since I began living in the city and working in its schools in the fall of 2003. Dr. Baez, a Puerto Rican woman who was born on the island (and thus a US citizen by birth) but raised in Chicago from the age of 4, had closely interacted with Mexicans in Chicago—citizens and noncitizens alike—throughout her life. In fact, she is a mother to MexiRican children (i.e., children of Puerto Rican and Mexican parentage). Dr. Baez immediately understood the potential anxieties of unauthorized migrant audience members at the Local School Council meeting when issues of identification and Census participation were raised. She also drew on a range of English and Spanish linguistic practices to communicate with audience members and fellow Local School Council members. Interactions like these have been taking place in Chicago for the better part of a century.

I am interested not only in the ways that Dr. Baez's multilingual, panethnic, and political sensibilities reflect Chicago's unique Latinx and broader social histories, but also in the embodied knowledge that informed her savvy signaling of mainstream institutional allegiance and simultaneous contestation of normative expectations about a school such as NNHS. Despite Dr. Baez's awareness of stark inequality within Chicago and throughout the United States, she promoted participation in liberal democratic political rituals such as elections and the Census, which are legitimated through ideologies linking normative civic behavior to the equitable distribution of rights and resources. She also invoked stigmatizing tropes of gang membership and teen pregnancy, which are commonly used to frame Latinx educational underachievement as a behavioral problem rather than as a structural phenomenon. Yet, Dr. Baez deployed these normative scripts while concomitantly facilitating a political dialogue among Local School Council members and adult ESL students that challenged structural hierarchies of language use, citizenship status, educational credentials, and socioeconomic class. To make sense of this situation, we must attend to the classic linguistic anthropological distinction between the denotational text and interactional text—both what is said and what is done, or better, what is done by or through or while saying something.[27] Dr. Baez communicatively invoked normative scripts while enacting a counter-hegemonic otherwise.

Such an analysis is also required to understand Dr. Baez's overall vision for NNHS students. In one of our initial conversations, she explained: "When people look at these students they see them as gangbangers and hoes [whores]. . . . I want them to see Young Latino Professionals."[28] I was struck by the ideologies of race, class, gender, and sexuality invoked in this formulation, questions surrounding the forms of embodiment and communication associated with a Young Latino Professional, and, importantly, the ambiguity in the location of the problem within the students themselves versus society's recognitions of them. I conceptualize this administrative effort as an intersectional mobility project—following the crucial Black feminist insight that intersectionality is not simply about understanding a given individual's multiple identities, but rather the interlocking systems of domination that fundamentally structure particular populations' everyday experiences of marginalization (Collins 2000). The administrative effort toward transforming recognitions of students as gangbangers and hoes into Young Latino Professionals rejected the figured opposition between assimilation and distinctive cultural identity maintenance as the exclusive possibilities for intergenerational (im)migrant trajectories of socialization—the notion that Latinxs must either assimilate to normative American Whiteness through a disavowal of their Latinidad or maintain their cultural authenticity while accepting a subordinate racial and socioeconomic status. The racialization of NNHS students meant that assimilation to Whiteness was not an option for them, regardless of their phenotype or other conventional signs of race. Moreover, NNHS students' access to any sort of professional class was profoundly limited if not altogether foreclosed. Thus, Dr. Baez's notion of professionalism differs from a conventional economic definition of the term. She was not merely distinguishing between modes of labor, that is, a professional as opposed to a service sector laborer. For Baez, Young Latino Professionals are not necessarily Latinxs who hold jobs in privileged sectors of the formal economy, but rather Latinxs who graduate from high school and become normatively economically self-sustaining to any degree. What might sound like a dramatically low bar is in fact a radical goal in the context of endemic intergenerational poverty and a deeply inequitable urban school district with a roughly 50% graduate rate. Further, as I explore in Chapter 1, the effort to forge the category Young Latino Professional simultaneously rejects and reinscribes normative gender and sexual scripts. Importantly, the intertwined ideologies of race, class, gender, and sexuality that compose the figures of gangbanger, ho, and Young Latino Professional pose difficulties for any effort to divorce these figures from one another. The co-constitution of these figures creates a double-bind in which recognition of a young professional as Latino might involve the joint recognition of their stereotypical, racialized essence as a gangbanger or ho.[29] I approach Dr. Baez's intersectional mobility project of shaping recognitions of students into Young Latino Professionals as part of a broader effort toward resolving this double-bind through the deployment of counter-hegemonic institutional strategies which challenge an educational structure that systematically fails students like those at NNHS. Similar to the Local School Council meeting, Dr. Baez draws on scripts that invoke normative stereotypes while simultaneously contesting structures of institutional inequity through her broader educational project, which ultimately resulted in a graduation rate at NNHS that hovered around 98% during the years in which I conducted fieldwork there. The ingenuity of this kind of strategic simultaneity is a central component of Latinx responses to exclusion that is too often overlooked. Throughout this book, I analyze how Latinxs challenge exclusion by contesting ethnoracial, geopolitical, and linguistic borders.

Multiculturalism, Assimilation, and Exclusion

The Local School Council meeting at NNHS and media discourses surrounding the 2010 US Census include references to Latinx marginalization, the rising US Latinx population, the segregation of Latinx students in US schools, and the language practices that play a central role in defining Latinx identities. These issues pertaining to implications and perceptions of Latinx difference are managed in everyday affairs through a projected negotiation between assimilation and multiculturalism.[30] My analysis of multiculturalism builds from Povinelli's characterization of liberal multiculturalism "as an ideology and practice of governance, a form of everyday affective association and identification, and a specific discursive incitement across the variegated contexts of national and transnational life" (Povinelli 2002:6). This approach involves a focus on multicultural difference as the product of liberal democratic governance rather than preexisting group essences, and a consideration of the practice of multicultural inclusion as the very mode through which such political orders legitimately reproduce marginalization. Povinelli shows how liberal multiculturalism requires "subaltern and minority subjects . . . to perform an authentic difference in exchange for the good feelings of the nation" (2002:6). For US Latinxs, this performance of difference produces a double-bind that requires them to signal their difference constantly without ever overstepping the shifting boundaries of what constitutes tolerable difference in a given context.[31] Thus, institutional affirmations of multicultural diversity must be interrogated based on the ways in which they circumscribe, domesticate, and commodify difference (Shankar 2015; Urciuoli 2016). In a similar line of examination, the mantra of "diversity and inclusion" can be understood as part of a normative project that seeks to present the superficial appearance of racial diversity while leaving white supremacist institutions and structures fundamentally unchanged (Ahmed 2012).

However, the politics of multiculturalism as they pertain to Latinxs in the contemporary United States have taken on a distinctly *postmulticultural* quality. The widespread racialization of Latinxs as "illegal," border militarization, and the corresponding rise of a massive deportation and detention regime that systematically targets Latinxs as "impossible subjects" (Ngai 2004) demonstrate the legitimation of Latinx exclusion.[32] Márquez theorizes the United States, as well as Latinxs' marginalized and stigmatized positionality therein, as a "racial state of expendability" (2012a:476). This expendability responds to anxieties that the rapidly rising US Latinx population will fundamentally redefine American identity, authorizing widespread efforts toward Latinx management, containment, and eradication.

The alleged threat that Latinxs pose to Americanness heightens the demand for ways to identify and manage Latinx difference and results in alternately celebratory and ominous framings of this population. At times, Latinxs are characterized as another in a long line of American immigrant groups possessing a range of ethnic differences that are to be celebrated in the nation's multicultural melting pot. In contrast, Latinxs are often described as a highly racialized, culturally distinctive, and stubbornly unassimilable group that must be managed carefully to prevent it from undoing the nation's cultural fabric. These framings simultaneously position Latinx as a distinctly American category *and* as a diasporic concept that potentially redefines Americanness by linking it to Latin America in newfound ways; the regimentation of signs of Latinidad becomes

class exclusion. These forms of exclusion position Latinx and American as frictive, often incommensurable categories. In Povinelli's (2002) analysis of Australian multiculturalism, Indigenous subjects' dilemma is precisely the inability to reconcile the paradoxical reality of such incommensurability. For Povinelli, the facade of the multicultural project is revealed when it is clear that there are no real opportunities for inclusion; she powerfully demonstrates the various ways in which the Indigenous subject is left trapped. This dilemma is where my study begins. I locate the negotiation of the projected tension between multiculturalism and assimilation in relation to a range of contexts and actors within NNHS and its surrounding communities, with the broader goal of analyzing the semiotic creation of a US Latinx social category and the signs that index it.[40] To do so, I carefully track the intersectional creation of Latinx panethnicity—an overarching category-concept that encompasses Latin American national groups—in this local Chicago scene and broader scales to which it is linked.

Orientation to an emergent, intersectional Latinx panethnic category involves multidirectional trajectories of socialization. I show how the experiences of generations 1.5, 2, and 3 Mexican and Puerto Rican students involve modes of socialization that redefine ethnoracial, geopolitical, and linguistic borders.[41] This remapping of borders is linked to *axes of differentiation* (Gal 2012) involving stereotypes and ideologies whose interrelations I analyze throughout the book[42]:

> Chapter 1: gangbangers/hoes vs. Young Latino Professionals; neighborhood high schools vs. selective enrollment/application-based schools
> Chapter 2: Mexico/Puerto Rico vs. United States; Latinx/Hispanic vs. American
> Chapter 3: Mexican vs. Puerto Rican; ghetto vs. lame
> Chapter 4: bilingual vs. monolingual; English Language Learner vs. mainstream student
> Chapter 5: Spanish vs. English: Inverted Spanglish vs. Mock Spanish
> Chapter 6: gang-related graffiti vs. non–gang-related tagging; street kids vs. school kids

Collectively, these axes of differentiation demonstrate how Latinxs learn to be—and sound like—themselves in highly studied ways. While the binary presentation and operation of these categories is central to the modes of exclusion with which they are associated, the reconfiguration and rejection of such binaries is central to the story of creativity in the face of marginalization that this book hopes to tell. I suggest that the ingenuity of panethnic, diasporic category-making and the deployment of polyvalent expressive practices show how a deep, shared awareness of oppressive circumstances inspires everyday actions.[43]

Category-Making in American High Schools

As institutions charged with the responsibility of (re)producing legitimate US citizen-subjects, public schools occupy a unique structural position within American society. In particular, public high schools come to be viewed as institutional last chances at shaping individuals on the cusp of American adulthood. These naturalized conceptions of education obscure the normative ways in which US public schools, as governmental institutions, participate in the creation of the very forms of difference that they purport to manage and overcome.[44] In their analysis of the educational production of categories, Varenne and McDermott (2003) analyze the powerful role that the hegemonic and co-constitutive notions of success and failure play in structuring schools as distinctly *American* institutions. Schools simultaneously legitimate meritocratic imaginings of the United States as an exceptional nation in which individuals get what they deserve by means of a neutral sorting system and confirm presumptions about the truth of particular groups' inferiority. Note that these ideologies are reflected in discourses that frame educational outcomes as straightforward successes and failures. To grasp the concepts of success and failure not as fundamental truths about individuals or schools, but as categories central to the "structuring powers of America" (2003:213), Varenne and McDermott demonstrate the contradictory ways that educational practices such as standardized testing, tracking (i.e., placing students into separate cohorts based on academic performance), and the identification of learning disabilities collaborate to establish and naturalize US notions of difference.

Building from this focus on the denaturalization of difference and school-based linguistic ethnographies that aim to situate interactional and institutional structures in relation to broader political and economic processes, this book takes up questions about language, schools, and the production of ethnoracial categories.[45] I follow Eckert (2000) in identifying a schoolwide axis of differentiation and tracking the ways that students construct and contort their presentations of self by manipulating stereotypes about social categories. Similar to Eckert, the paramount categories of difference among students and administrators within NNHS become linked to socioeconomic class trajectories. Eckert shows that schools are staging grounds for life, in which relational identities position students either in alignment with or opposition to schools' efforts toward socialization. In the broader scheme, the institutional powers of schools tether these negotiations of identity to the socioeconomic class trajectories into which students are sorted. Thus, in the canonical studies of Eckert, as well as of Willis (1977) and Bourdieu and Passeron (1977), high schools are key sites for the reproduction of socioeconomic stratification.

NNHS is distinct from the educational contexts analyzed in these previous accounts. This book presents an ethnographic study of a school that is actively trying *not* to reproduce economic stratification by sorting students into successes and failures. The principal of NNHS recognizes that her school is already positioned as a failure in the context of the hierarchy of Chicago Public Schools. She attempts to overcome this positioning by creating what I describe as an *intersectional mobility project*. That is, the principal acknowledges her students' shared racial and class marginalization and suggests that her school must find a way for *all* students to become defined as institutional successes. Unlike the schools that Eckert and Willis describe, students at NNHS are managing their markedness with respect to class *and* race. Thus, the primary axis of differentiation for NNHS students—Mexican vs. Puerto Rican—involves categories that are anchored by spatial, racial, and class exclusion. Students come to understand that they are participating in an intersectional mobility project. As a result, stereotypes surrounding the paradigmatic categories of Mexican and Puerto Rican become infused with racialized and gendered notions of "ghetto" and "lame," which allow students to identify and deride what they imagine as one another's class-negative and class-positive characteristics.[46] That is, students' notions of "ghetto" and "lame" are intertwined with the principal's explicitly stated administrative project of transforming them from gangbangers and hoes (i.e., ghetto) into Young Latino Professionals (i.e., lame). Importantly, NNHS students' inhabitance of shared, marginalized socioeconomic positions means that regardless of whether they identify as Puerto Rican or Mexican, they often draw on similar material resources as they construct and enact these categories.

As with Eckert (2000) and Mendoza-Denton (2008), I show how language and other semiotic practices tie school-based identities to various social figures and positions outside of school. Similar to Mendoza-Denton's study of gang-affiliated Latina youth in California, I am interested in situating linguistic practices alongside clothing styles, musical tastes, and modes of embodiment, among other symbolic realms.[47] I also follow Mendoza-Denton in demonstrating how local scenes uniquely instantiate and reconfigure broader social relations. In Mendoza-Denton's case, girls affiliated with *Norteña* (North) and *Sureña* (South) gangs stereotype one another as US-oriented/English-dominant (*Norteñas*) and Mexico- or Latin America-oriented/Spanish-dominant (*Sureñas*); these geographical, behavioral, and linguistic distinctions also map onto "the semiotics of the body and the circulation of material artifacts" (2008:294). To make sense of these distinctions, Mendoza-Denton introduces the notion of "hemispheric localism" through which her research participants "not only . . . display historical continuities in terms of group formation and political thought in the Mexican-US borderlands, but by 'taking sides' as a Norteña/o or a Sureña/o . . . interpret and stancefully deal with the world around them (2008:87)." Like Mendoza-Denton, I show how students' stereotypes about and enactments of Puerto Rican and Mexican identities situate Chicago's local (im)migration history in relation to the broader creation of diasporic and panethnic Latinx identities. I argue that this (im)migration history uniquely positions Chicago as a producer of emblems of Latinidad that are composed of elements associated with the nation's most populous Latinx subgroups (i.e., Mexicans and Puerto Ricans). Thus, Chicago becomes a ritual center for imagining and experiencing Latinx diaspora and panethnicity.

I approach students' engagements with categories such as Mexican, Puerto Rican, and Latinx in terms of the models of personhood with which they become stereotypically associated. I follow Wortham's (2006) lead in tracking the ways that students' enactments of these models of personhood change over the course of their educational careers in a given school context. In NNHS, these changes involve the creation of increasingly rigid discursive borders between Mexican and Puerto Rican categories as students move from their freshman to senior year. I argue that this reflects students' uptake of and resistance to the administrative category of "Young Latino Professional," which erases Mexican-Puerto Rican difference. Importantly, these increasingly rigid discourses of difference take shape alongside consistently intimate interrelations between Mexican and Puerto Rican students. I build from Eckert, Mendoza-Denton, and Wortham by focusing on the institutional creation and experience of identities that mediate local concerns and national anxieties. The fraught construction of Latinx identities reflects NNHS administrators' and students' efforts to transform their local participation in a national ritual of educational socialization and stratification. The following section links the construction of Latinx identities on these local and national scales.

Latinx Panethnicity

Between 2000 and 2010, when I conducted my preliminary and formal fieldwork, the US Latinx population grew from 35.3 million to 50.5 million.[48] This 43% growth made Latinxs 16.3% of the total US population,[49] accounting for 56% of the overall US population growth during the first decade of the 21st century.[50] Latinxs are projected to compose one-third of all US children by 2035 and nearly one-third of the overall US population by 2050.[51] It is crucial to understand these shifting contemporary and future demographics in terms of the historical, colonial relationship between the United States and Latin America.[52] Since at least the beginning of the 19th century, Thomas Jefferson, John Adams, John Quincy Adams, and James Monroe advocated US control of the entirety of "Spanish America" (González 2001:32). This culminated in the 1823 Monroe Doctrine, which stated that European powers should no longer pursue colonies in the Americas.[53] US interventions following Spanish rule in Mexico and Puerto Rico are prime examples of US efforts toward supplanting European influence in the Americas. Shortly after Mexico achieved independence from Spain in 1821, the US sought to incorporate territories from an independent Mexico. The subsequent Mexican-American War (1846–1848) ended with the creation of the Treaty of Guadalupe Hidalgo and transferred 55% of Mexico's prewar territory to the United States (González 2001). This is similar to the sequence of events in Puerto Rico. At the end of the 19th century, Puerto Rico experienced increased autonomy from Spain. Following the 1898 Spanish-American War, however, Puerto Rico became a colony of the United States. This colonial relationship between the United States and Puerto Rico exists to this day, albeit in modified form, with Puerto Rico officially designated as a US commonwealth or unincorporated territory. The US geographical expansion throughout the 19th and early 20th centuries, and the corresponding colonial and economic empire built by American political leaders and multinational corporations, "laid the basis for and helped to spark the massive Latino immigration after World War II" (González 2001:xiii).

This "massive Latino immigration" to the United States contributed to debates about how best to measure this population in demographic terms. In particular, Hispanic community leaders complained that they were unable to make claims for government resources because they had no way of demonstrating the size of the Hispanic population. Until the 1980 Census, Hispanics were counted as White, rendering them indistinguishable from Italians, Irish, and other European immigrant groups (Mora 2014). By 1980, the US Census Bureau had instituted a panethnic demographic category based on "Spanish/Hispanic origin or descent." Importantly, this category was positioned as "commensurate with, though not officially equal to, race" (Mora 2014:118). The Census question about "Spanish/Hispanic origin or descent" was (and continues to be) separate from the race question, yet the Census Bureau frequently presents these data in ways that position "Hispanic" as both an ethnic and racial category. This means that a given individual can identify as Hispanic and as any race on the Census. Yet, racial data are often reported as "White (non-Hispanic)," "Black (non-Hispanic)," etc. These questions and the data they generate are framed in similar ways to this day. The main change is that "Latino" is added to the question on ethnicity, which now reads, "Is this person of Hispanic, Latino, or Spanish origin?" It becomes important to track the ways that Latinxs are positioned in relation to race and ethnicity. As Urciuoli explains, "race and ethnicity are both about belonging to the nation, but belonging in different ways" (1996:15). Each of these concepts is defined in relation to the potential for assimilation and class mobility. Whereas ethnic difference (as experienced by Italians, Irish, and other European immigrants) becomes legitimately American, racial difference is defined in opposition to the nation. When one is racialized as non-White in the US context, one's potential to be American or contribute to Americanness can perpetually be called into question.

In the Chicago context, Mexicans began arriving in the early 20th century, following the Mexican Revolution and recruitment by railroad companies (Cruz 2007).[54] By the 1920s, Mexicans had started their own social service organizations and built their own churches in the city. Yet, during the Great Depression nearly half of Chicago's Mexican population was forcibly repatriated. The population began to increase again in the context of the "Bracero Program" (1942–1964), a wartime US labor recruitment strategy that brought four and a half million Mexican workers to the US, including thousands who came to Chicago. Puerto Ricans entered the US mainland en masse beginning in the late 1940s as part of the US program "Operation Bootstrap," which sought to decrease the island's poor population so as to facilitate its industrialization (Briggs 2003). Puerto Ricans were the first ethnoracial group to migrate to the United States en masse by airplane, largely to cities such as New York, Philadelphia, and Chicago. US citizenship was imposed on all Puerto Ricans beginning in 1917 by way of the Jones Act, which immediately allowed 60,000 Puerto Ricans to fight for the United States in World War I (De Genova and Ramos-Zayas 2003). Amaya (2007) refers to this as nonconsensual citizenship and compares it to the 60,000 Mexicans on whom US citizenship was imposed in 1849, following the end of the Mexican-American War and the signing of the Treaty of Guadalupe Hidalgo.

Shortly after the end of my fieldwork in 2010, there were 1,561,000 Mexicans and 190,000 Puerto Ricans in the greater Chicago area (out of an overall population of 9,185,000), composing 79.2% and 9.6% of the Chicago-area Latinx population, respectively.[55] This made Chicago the city with the nation's third largest population overall, fifth largest Latinx population, fourth largest Mexican population, and fourth largest Puerto Rican population.[56] Previous studies of Mexican-Puerto Rican interrelations in Chicago and elsewhere have looked at issues such as labor (Padilla 1947), political mobilizations (Padilla 1985), contradictory discourses of difference (Pérez 2003), and histories of shared experiences (Fernández 2012). De Genova and Ramos-Zayas (2003) present the most extensive ethnographic account of Puerto Ricans and Mexicans in Chicago, yet they do not focus specifically on interactions and interrelations between these groups. Meanwhile, sociolinguistic studies of Latinx panethnic intrarelations have generally focused on issues such as dialect leveling among varieties of Spanish (Zentella 1990; Ghosh Johnson 2005; Otheguy and Zentella

2012), language socialization (Zentella 2005), and identities and linguistic practices of Latinxs with parents from different Latinx subgroups (Flores-González 1999; Aparicio and Chávez-Silverman 1997; Rúa 2001; Chabram-Dernersesian 1999, 2009; Potowski and Matts 2008). In fact, Chicago's "urban pluralingualism" (Farr 2011) makes it a frequent focus of research on language and Latinx identities (Farr 2004).

This ethnography takes its cue from Ricourt and Danta (2003) and Rivera-Servera (2012) in approaching intra-Latinx relations as a matter of convivencia diaria (living together daily) and frictive intimacy. Ricourt and Danta's study of a panethnic group of adult Latinas and Rivera-Servera's analysis of queer Latinidades provide instructive models for approaching the complexly interwoven everyday lives of Latinxs from various national backgrounds. Two important points of departure in my study are (1) my focus on generations 1.5, 2, and 3; and (2) my focus on enregistered English and Spanish language practices as potential indexes of US Latinx panethnicity, such that it becomes possible to investigate processes of being/doing Latinx in Spanish *and* English. Of course, it is also important to disrupt hegemonic language ideologies that equate English language use with stereotypical signs of inclusion and assimilation into American society, such as access to upward socioeconomic mobility—a measure that fundamentally misunderstands the nature of language, racism, and capitalism within the United States as a settler colonial and imperial formation. As of 2010, Puerto Ricans and Mexicans were classified as having the highest rates of English language proficiency among any Latinx subgroups, at 80.5% and 61.6%, respectively.[57] Yet, in the same year they also had the second and third highest poverty rates, at 22.6% (Puerto Ricans) and 22.3% (Mexicans).[58] These poverty rates are striking evidence of the similar forms of socioeconomic marginalization experienced by Mexicans and Puerto Ricans. Such ethnoracial and class dynamics also demonstrate the importance of challenging preconceived notions about language, citizenship, national identity, and societal exclusion.

Entering New Northwest High School

I established a relationship with NNHS through my work with the Puerto Rican Cultural Center in Chicago's Humboldt Park community area. After meeting with the school's principal, I was officially hired by Chicago Public Schools as an AVID (Advancement Via Individual Determination) tutor. This nationwide program was introduced to Chicago Public Schools in 2003. AVID is a non-profit organization that provides study skills support and seeks to increase college preparedness for students from groups traditionally underrepresented in higher education. All NNHS students were required to participate in AVID classes. This means that every classroom in which I worked was composed of students who demonstrated varying levels of academic achievement.

During the 2007–2008 and 2008–2009 school years, I worked closely with 10 teachers and their students in grades 9 through 12, tutoring approximately 30 students individually each day (and interacting with many others). Through my work in these classrooms I was able to identify potential key participants and set up interviews. I conducted formal, in-depth interviews with: (1) 10 freshmen, 10 sophomores, 10 juniors, and 10 seniors, who were evenly distributed among Mexicans and Puerto Ricans as well as among girls and boys; (2) 4 African American students; (3) 10 teachers; (4) 2 school administrators; and (5) 2 school support staff. In many cases, I interviewed students and teachers in their homes. Outside of school, I tutored students in their homes, helped them to complete school projects, went to get haircuts with them, went out to eat with them, helped them to find jobs, chatted with them on the phone, exchanged cellular text messages, and brought them to the college classes that I was teaching. Additionally, I attended various school events, such as soccer games, pep rallies, Local School Council meetings (I was elected to the Local School Council as a community representative in 2010), and the prom.

My work in NNHS was also informed by my preliminary field experiences in several other predominantly Latinx and African American high schools and community organizations in Chicago. Through these preliminary experiences I learned about the stereotypes surrounding different schools, neighborhoods, and ethnoracial identities in Chicago. It was also through these preliminary field experiences that I learned about and became interested in NNHS. Additionally, I lived four blocks away from the school. This allowed me to walk to and from the school with students each day, and to accompany them to local restaurants and stores. These interactions with students outside of school played a crucial role in helping me to understand what was going on inside NNHS. Had I not lived near the school, I might not have ever seen the Mexican and Puerto Rican flags juxtaposed in storefronts, apartment windows, and cars; nor would I have encountered the Mexican and Puerto Rican food items sold side by side on the shelves at the Walgreens and Cermak Produce stores near the school. These Mexican-Puerto Rican panethnic displays are particular to the Near Northwest Side of the city. Living nearby the school allowed me to participate alongside other Puerto Ricans and Mexicans in the mundane panethnic interactions that are a central part of everyday life in this context.

As a third-generation Puerto Rican born and raised in Western New York, I alternately occupied insider and outsider ethnoracial positionalities while conducting this fieldwork. Students, school employees, and community members frequently assumed that I was Puerto Rican—often explicitly stating as much—primarily based on stereotypes about my physical features or language use (I describe these stereotypes in detail throughout the book). In other situations, I was asked about my race and nationality. For example, the principal of NNHS asked whether I was Puerto Rican during our first meeting. Many of my interactions with Puerto Rican students and school employees unfolded as Puerto Rican in-group conversations. There were some Puerto Ricans with whom this was not the case, most notably a few members of the school's security personnel and members of the principal's support staff. In the former case, I discovered that some of the security guards (many of whom were Puerto Rican men) communicated almost exclusively with fellow security guards, students, and administrators, but not with teachers or support staff such as myself; in the latter case, I perceived that my gender and relatively youthful appearance made it difficult to break into the close-knit circle of middle-aged Puerto Rican women who constituted the principal's administrative support staff. Likewise, my Puerto Ricanness neither facilitated nor hindered my ability to establish relationships with Mexican students and school employees in straightforward ways. In some interviews with Mexican participants, it was initially difficult to elicit stereotypes about Puerto Ricans. In these cases, I would get the ball rolling by providing examples of such stereotypes and jokingly self-deprecating. I frequently used my knowledge of Puerto Rico and Mexico, as well as stereotypical Puerto Rican and Mexican cultural practices, to initiate conversations with students about where they and their families were from. I constantly used different varieties of English and Spanish to navigate a bilingual cultural context in which students and school employees made use of expansive linguistic repertoires consisting of a range of English and Spanish language practices that I describe and analyze throughout the book.

My apparent age also seemed to play a role in how teachers viewed me. I informed every teacher in whose classroom I tutored that I was a doctoral student conducting a study focused on language and identity in NNHS and sought their consent for participation. Every teacher agreed to participate, but only a couple of them seemed to take me particularly seriously as a researcher and educator. The few who did occasionally asked me for curricular advice or turned to me when students stumped them with a tough question. In the vast majority of classrooms, however, I was treated like the other tutors. Almost all of the tutors were Latinx undergraduate college students in their late teens and early 20s; many of them attended a university where I had taught several courses. Unlike most teachers, students regularly acknowledged and expressed interest in my research, frequently asking how my "book," which they also jokingly referred to as my "homework," was coming along. Gender norms played a significant role in shaping my interactions with students outside of school. Whereas my interactions with most male-identified students involved stereotypical academic (e.g., tutoring and working on various school assignments) and nonacademic (e.g., going out to eat, getting haircuts at local barbershops) activities, my interactions with many female-identified students primarily involved stereotypical academic activities and took place under their parents' supervision. This characterization of my position in the school and the community should give readers some sense of how I went about collecting the data that I analyze throughout the book.

Inside New Northwest High School

NNHS opened in the fall of 2004 and served a full freshman, sophomore, junior, and senior student body for the first time in the 2007–2008 academic year, with a total of roughly 1,000 students. In the 2007–2008 and 2008–2009 school years (the period during which I conducted fieldwork in the school on a near daily basis), the principal and her support staff were predominantly Puerto Rican. The teachers and teachers' aides were more or less evenly distributed among Whites (non-Hispanic), Puerto Ricans, and Mexicans; there were also three Asian teachers, as well as an African American teachers' aide and an African American librarian. The security staff was mostly Puerto Rican, whereas the lunchroom and janitorial staff were Mexican, Puerto Rican, and African American. The student body was roughly 45% Mexican, 30% Puerto Rican, 15% other Latinx, 7.5% African American, and 2.5% multiracial.

Most students' careers at NNHS began during the summer before their freshman year, when they participated in a transition program that introduced them to high school level mathematics and English classes. The presumption was that by the end of elementary school many students were already performing below grade level and were in need of additional support in these core subjects. The six-week summer program was administered by a small group of ninth-grade teachers. During the regular academic year (from September to June) the school day officially began at 8:00 a.m. and ended at 2:45 p.m. The school served free breakfast to all students who arrived before 7:40 a.m. as part of the Chicago Public Schools breakfast program, but only a few freshmen and sophomore students participated in the breakfast program. Based on their families' incomes, nearly all students qualified for free meals in the breakfast and lunch programs. Monday, Tuesday, Thursday, and Friday of each week were generally structured as "regular" (i.e., full-length) school days. The school used block scheduling, with a 25-minute division (i.e., homeroom) and four 90-minute classes each day. Most Wednesdays were either "Student Development" or "Professional Development" days. During these "half-days" (as most people in the school referred to them), classes were shortened to 27 minutes. On Student Development days, students took a 75-minute Student Development class at the end of the day. Whereas there was a relatively standard set of math, science, English, social studies, and elective courses, students were free to choose from a range of Student Development courses, including music, dance, drama, and leadership. Teachers designed Student Development courses based on their skills and interests, but students also pitched courses that the school then created and integrated into the set of available options. Professional Development days were similar to Student Development days, but at the end of these days the staff met for Professional Development workshops that consisted of team-building exercises, presentations from outside experts, and dialogues about educational best practices. Importantly, unlike most other neighborhood high schools, NNHS's combination of Student Development Wednesdays and block scheduling on Mondays, Tuesdays, Thursdays, and Fridays paralleled the structure of the city's most prestigious selective enrollment high schools. In Chapter 1, I describe the crucial distinction within Chicago Public Schools between selective enrollment schools and neighborhood schools such as NNHS.

Chapter Overview

The chapters in Part I focus on the creation of a racialized Latinx panethnic category by analyzing NNHS's complex project of transforming students into Young Latino Professionals (Chapter 1), the ways that this project shapes students' ideas about and identifications with ethnoracial categories (Chapter 2), and the stereotypes that become central to the embodiment and enactment of Latinidad in this context (Chapter 3). Together, these chapters provide a thickly described ethnographic account of the school-based creation of Latinx ethnoracial categories.

Chapter 1, From "*Gangbangers and Hoes*" to "*Young Latino Professionals*": Intersectional Mobility and the Ambivalent Management of Stigmatized Student Bodies, focuses on the school administration's overarching goal of transforming students. It analyzes the contradictions teachers and administrators face as they simultaneously work to validate and transform students' modes of self-making. The chapter begins by describing the anxieties surrounding violence, pregnancy, and poverty that are associated with Latinx youth socialization in the Chicago context. I go on to show how these racial, class, gender, and sexual anxieties are heightened within the context of an open enrollment neighborhood high school. I argue that the transformation of students into Young Latino Professionals, which I formulate as an intersectional mobility project, becomes an ambivalent negotiation that alternately locates the problem within the students themselves and outsiders' perceptions of them.

Chapter 2, "*I Heard that Mexicans Are Hispanic and Puerto Ricans Are Latino*": Ethnoracial Contortions, Diasporic Imaginaries, and Institutional Trajectories, unpacks the relationship between the principal's project of creating Young Latino Professionals and students' investment in their Puerto Rican and Mexican identities. I track the contradictory ways in which race and ethnicity are conceptualized in the context of NNHS and demonstrate how these contradictions are systematically linked to broader forms of ambivalence surrounding interrelated processes of racialization and ethnicization. I argue that "Mexican" and "Puerto Rican" are not merely straightforward identities that students bring with them to school; instead, I show how students respond to the erasure of Mexican-Puerto Rican difference within the school's project of socialization by twisting and turning these categories through practices I describe as "ethnoracial contortions."

Chapter 3, "*Latino Flavors*": Emblematizing, Embodying, and Enacting Latinidad, shifts from the previous chapter's analysis of the ethnoracially contested construction of Latinx identities to demonstrate how emblems of Latinidad are made recognizable in everyday life. In particular, I focus on the ways in which qualities attributed to objects, practices, and bodies are mapped onto one another in the contemporary fashioning of a racialized, panethnic Latinx category. By analyzing interrelations among forms of emblematicity associated with a range of cultural concepts, from hairstyles, clothing, and language, to food, dance, and music, I track the complex semiotic operations that connect the creation Latinx things to the embodiment of Latinx people. These processes allow actors within NNHS to experience and enact Latinx identities. I conclude the chapter by pointing to the close relationship between conceptions of Latinx identity and "Spanishness" as a cultural and linguistic quality, laying the groundwork for the second half of the book.

The chapters in Part II draw on the ethnographic and analytical framework crafted in the beginning of the book to situate processes of ethnoracial category-making as crucial counterparts in relation to which language and literacy are understood and practiced in NNHS and its surrounding communities. In particular, these chapters analyze the mechanisms at work in a profound redefinition of bilingualism as disability (Chapter 4), students' emergent strategies for escaping their linguistic marginalization and voicing Latinx identities (Chapter 5), and the semiotic operations through which students' literacy practices become criminalized (Chapter 6).

Chapter 4, "*They're Bilingual . . . That Means They Don't Know the Language*": The Ideology of Languagelessness in Practice, Policy, and Theory, analyzes the ways that the ethnoracial constructions and contortions detailed in the first half of the book map onto the school's approach to and ideas about students' language use. I argue that these ideas and anxieties produce a profound transformation in which bilingualism comes to be equated with Limited English Proficiency and in which students designated as English Language Learners are positioned alongside special education students as second-class educational figures. I show how this situation can be productively understood in relation to a racialized ideology of "languagelessness," which frames US Latinxs as illegitimate users of any language. The double stigmatization that results from standardizing forces surrounding English and Spanish demonstrates how languagelessness operates in powerful ways to racialize students as linguistically inferior across contexts.

Chapter 5, "*Pink Cheese, Green Ghosts, Cool Arrows/Pinches Gringos Culeros*": Inverted Spanglish and Latinx Raciolinguistic Enregisterment, builds from the preceding analysis of the stigmatization of Latinx students' English *and* Spanish language practices to demonstrate some of the creative ways that they attempt to fashion linguistic escape routes from modes of discrimination. Students feel pressured to signal their intimate knowledge of Spanish, but they seek to do so without calling into question their ability to produce what is perceived as unaccented English; they are faced with the task of producing Spanish and English simultaneously without being understood to possess an accent. I argue that students combine emblematic Spanish lexical items and English phonology as part of the broader enregisterment of "Inverted Spanglish" usages that differ from what has been previously described as "Mock Spanish." I suggest that "Inverted Spanglish" is a linguistic icon of US Latinx panethnicity and a parodic take on the school-based category of Young Latino Professional.

Chapter 6, "*That Doesn't Count as a Book, That's Real Life!*": Outlaw(ed) Literacies, Criminalized Intertextualities, and Institutional Linkages, demonstrates how students' literacy skills are not simply erased within the school but also criminalized. Students write their identities in complex ways, highlighting the competing forces that require them to signal simultaneously their alignment with and opposition to the school's project of socialization. Previous analyses of school-based socialization in urban contexts characteristically distinguish between "school kids" (who graduate and become upwardly socioeconomically mobile) and "street kids" (who never finish school and become part of the racialized American underclass). In contrast, I show how NNHS students draw on various literacy practices to construct and signal school kid and street kid identities concurrently.

Collectively, the chapters of this book explore the indeterminate ways that semiotic practices simultaneously reproduce existing relations and entail unforeseen futures and, by extension, how language and race are dynamically co-naturalized. Analyses of semiotic indeterminacy and naturalization demand careful attention to context, scale, and perspective and undermine any universalizing claims about the fundamental nature of a given racial category or language variety. In NNHS and its surrounding communities, this involves the creation and enactment of Latinx identities that are both deeply anchored in long-standing local histories and continually renegotiated in contemporary circumstances. While the analysis that emerges throughout the book focuses on particular people and places, the broader goal is to provoke discussions about the potentially global co-naturalization of language and race, such that we might interrogate the forms of governance through which people come to *look like a language* and *sound like a race* in various societal contexts. Insofar as this dynamic interrelation between race and language is understood as a colonially constituted phenomenon, we might also consider anticolonial and decolonial possibilities for unsettling normative forms of governance, institutionality, identity, and expressivity. I hope to demonstrate how schools and their surrounding communities can become key sites for both the rearticulation and contestation of these colonially organized racial and linguistic power relations.

Through my engagement with the rearticulation and contestation of power relations, I seek to present neither a romantic portrayal of triumphant individuals who transcend the profound marginalization that constrains their everyday lives, nor a pathological account of victims of structural inequality who are unable to do anything beyond reproducing their own disparity.[59] Too often, urban ethnographers attempt to move beyond this structure/agency binary by focusing on the most sensationalized situations, providing broad reading publics with a glimpse into hyperexotic worlds, whether precarious domestic ghettoes or peculiar foreign elsewheres, rather than exploring the deep embodied knowledge cultivated within mundane everyday life. Even if inadvertently so, such narratives cannot help but contribute to the replication of the very forms of stigmatization that they purport to combat. These analyses are often problematically heralded for their readability, canonized in introductory anthropology courses, and circulated widely among scholarly and popular audiences alike. This deep resonance is derived from the ways that many of these studies reinforce preexisting assumptions about imagined ghettoes and jungles rather than subjecting common-sense notions to critical scrutiny. *Looking like a Language, Sounding like a Race* is my attempt to disrupt troublesome raciolinguistic legibilities and demonstrate an alternative approach to the analysis of structural inequality. Rather than seeking to make objectified racial groups and their linguistic practices intelligible to outside audiences, I seek to denaturalize the categories, differences, and modes of recognition that condition everyday life in particular neighborhood and institutional contexts. By emphasizing the production of racial categories and linguistic varieties through interrelations among institutions, actors, and ideologies, I show how contingent processes rather than naturally occurring cultural essences structure these contexts. Thus, this examination of the co-naturalization of language and race becomes a potential vantage point from which to imagine alternative theoretical and practical approaches to understanding communication, identity, and the governance thereof.

LOOKING LIKE A LANGUAGE

Latinx Ethnoracial Category-Making

1

FROM *"GANGBANGERS AND HOES"* TO *"YOUNG LATINO PROFESSIONALS"*

INTERSECTIONAL MOBILITY AND THE AMBIVALENT MANAGEMENT OF STIGMATIZED STUDENT BODIES

In the spring of 2009, as I was finishing my second year of fieldwork in New Northwest High School (NNHS), the *Chicago Sun-Times* reported that 508 Chicago Public Schools (CPS) students had been wounded by gunfire over a 16-month period between 2007 and 2009.[1] On March 10, 2009, with one-fourth of the 2008–2009 school year remaining, the CPS student homicide total reached 27, already surpassing the total of 26 from the previous school year.[2] By May, the total reached a record-breaking 36.[3] This made Chicago the city with the nation's highest youth homicide rate, surpassing New York and Los Angeles.[4] These statistics were cited frequently in local, national, and international news coverage, with some commentators going so far as to refer to Chicago as "Beirut by the lake." Racist, revisionist monikers such as "Beirut by the lake" and "Chi-Raq" naturalize violence in the Middle East, and obscure the foundational role of violence in the creation and reproduction of the US by exceptionalizing urban contexts such as Chicago.[5]

On one Monday morning in the fall of 2007, the daily announcements at NNHS included a moment of silence in honor of one of the school's former students who was shot and killed over the weekend. The killing took place near the school, and several students in the 11th grade classroom in which I was working traded stories about the details.[6] A group of girls in the back corner of the classroom discussed whether the deceased student had been precariously trying to associate himself with two rival gangs. They named the different gangs in the area: MLDs (Maniac Latin Disciples), YLOCs (Young Latin Organization Cobras), Cobras (Insane Spanish Cobras), Devils (Almighty Latin Devils), etc.[7] One girl, Vanessa (PR, Gen. 1.5, Gr. 11), reported that the boy who was killed did not properly quit one gang before associating himself with another; in order to earn the right to do so, he would have needed to receive a "violation"—a severe beating—from members of the gang that he was quitting. She suggested that his failure to do so cost him his life.

When I asked these girls about their affiliations with gangs, they sought to demonstrate their in-depth knowledge without identifying themselves too closely with any gang in particular.[8] Vanessa described a male friend of hers who was an incarcerated gang member; she opened her school planner to show me that she had marked the date of his release, which was scheduled to take place later that school year. She emphasized that he was not her boyfriend, and explained that many girls whose boyfriends are gang members either "rep" (represent) for the boys' gangs or join an affiliated female gang; Vanessa was "not into that." She went on to say that girls often allow boys to "run the train" on them, which involves having sex with multiple male gang members, in exchange for their protection. Such moments confronted me with narratives of race, class, gender, and sexuality that resonate with long-standing, pathologizing stereotypes about urban youth of color. Rather than simply disavowing these stereotypes in favor of more optimistic representations—after all, no student was reducible to these stereotypes in straightforward ways—I am interested in analyzing the historical, political, and economic dynamics out of which they emerge, as well as their fraught institutional consequentiality.

In this chapter I explore how interconnected binary gender stereotypes about Latino criminality and Latina promiscuity became central components of the anxieties surrounding race, class, gender, and sexuality that structured NNHS's project of youth socialization.[9] While mainstream schools often operate as normative institutions directed toward the inculcation of social hygiene among their students, perceived threats of criminality, pregnancy, and socioeconomic marginality heightened the stakes of managing student bodies in the context of NNHS. I describe how efforts toward managing student bodies cohered in an explicitly stated administrative project of transforming students from "gangbangers" and "hoes" into "Young Latino Professionals." I analyze the construction of these figures and show how neither domination nor emancipation emerged as a straightforward result of this project of transforming students. Instead, administrators, teachers, support staff, and students occupied shifting roles that demonstrated and produced profound ambivalence about where and how to locate the problem: could it be discovered in or on students' bodies, or in the societal stereotypes that surrounded them? This ambivalence allowed students to be imagined simultaneously as the causes of and solutions to school failure and inequality more broadly, and underscored the precarious circumstances surrounding the creation of Latinx identities in NNHS.

Chicago and the Creation of Educational Alternatives

In the fall of 2004, the inauguration of NNHS was celebrated on the Near Northwest Side of Chicago. One of only two schools built on the Northwest Side in the past 30 years, the construction of NNHS was widely understood as an effort to offset overcrowding at nearby Old Northwest High School (ONHS).[10] In 2003–2004, Old Northwest High had an enrollment of 1,979 students, despite being designed for only 1,300 students. With the opening of New Northwest High, which had an enrollment of 267 ninth-grade students in 2004–2005, the enrollment at Old Northwest High dropped to 1,773—a decrease of 206 students. In its initial year, NNHS served only ninth-grade students. It added an additional class during each subsequent year; 2007–2008 was the first year that NNHS had a "full" student body of nearly 1,000 students.

The press conference held during the opening of the new school reflected its contested position with respect to actors and discourses on various political scales. Whereas community organizers described the school's opening as a triumphant victory gained through decades of struggles with the city, Mayor Richard M. Daley characterized the $35 million school as a shining example of the progress made possible by his (then) year-old educational reform plan, "Renaissance 2010." Dr. Baez, the principal of NNHS since its opening, appreciated the mayor's interest in the school, but was also quick to point out that NNHS is not part of the mayor's Renaissance 2010 educational reform plan. She emphasized that the creation of NNHS was made possible by long-standing local struggles. These struggles included protests organized by ONHS students and the Logan Square Neighborhood Association,[11] as well as the efforts of elected officials such as State Senator William ("Willie") Delgado and Alderman Regner ("Ray") Suarez. Still, Mayor Daley was on hand for NNHS's first graduation ceremony in June 2008, which reinforced the image that the school was an important part of his reform plan.

It is no mistake that these competing origin narratives would emerge in relation to NNHS. While years of community-level efforts toward the reform of ONHS were met with limited results, the school came under newfound scrutiny in the midst of President George W. Bush's and Mayor Daley's educational reform plans, No Child Left Behind (NCLB) and Renaissance 2010, respectively. According to figures from the 2003–2004 academic year,[12] ONHS students were designated[13] as 98.3% racial minorities (93.6% Hispanic: 51.3% Mexican, 34.1% Puerto Rican, 7.9% other Hispanic), 90.9% low income, and 15% Limited English Proficient.[14] Based on the school's academic performance, it continually failed to make adequate yearly progress in accordance with NCLB. In its inaugural year (2004–2005), NNHS students were designated as 99.2% minority

(91.8% Hispanic: 49.1% Mexican, 37.8% Puerto Rican, 4.9% other Hispanic), 92.1% low income, and 15% Limited English Proficient.[15]

Situated as they are, just west of areas undergoing rapid gentrification (from east to west), NNHS and ONHS present a picture of the segregation for which Chicago and US cities more broadly are notorious.[16] NNHS is located in the northwest corner of the Humboldt Park community area. During the period of my fieldwork, Humboldt Park was primarily populated by almost equal numbers of African Americans (47.7%) and Latinxs (48%), but segregation patterns and neighborhood school attendance boundaries positioned NNHS in a predominantly Latinx area.[17] While Mexicans slightly outnumbered Puerto Ricans, Humboldt Park was and continues to be recognized by many as the center of Chicago's Puerto Rican community.

During the years leading up to and following the opening of NNHS, I worked closely with several Mexican and Puerto Rican youth who either graduated from or were pushed out of its counterpart, ONHS.[18] Whereas community organizers presented their case for an alternative to ONHS by focusing on overcrowding, these former students—graduates and pushouts alike—unanimously described the fears they experienced during their first few days at ONHS. One of these former students, Elizabeth, remembered a gang fight breaking out on the first day of her freshman year.[19] After seeing a gun slide across the floor of one of the school's hallways during this fight, some students left the school in fear and never returned. She also remembered countless female students who left school after they became pregnant: "if you got popped, you dropped."[20]

Luis was pushed out of ONHS because gang members, who wrongly claimed that he was a member of a rival gang, threatened to kill him. After leaving ONHS in the second week of his freshman year, he did not reenroll in another school for a year and a half. Luis' experiences are not uncommon. In 2005, Chicago's graduation rate was 51% (the national average was 70.6%); among the students who were pushed out, the majority left during their freshman year.[21] This was actually a 9.5% improvement from 1995. When broken down by race, the national dropout rates in 2007 were 27.5% for Latinxs and 21% for African Americans, compared with 12.2% for Whites.[22] Violence, pregnancy, and dropping out were some of the primary challenges that the creators of NNHS sought to address and overcome. These challenges point to the stakes of education in urban high schools such as NNHS, whose hypersegregated student bodies are often 100% low income, Black, and Latinx. Reflecting on these challenges, it was with much pride and excitement that the principal of NNHS reported that the graduation rate for the school's first two graduating classes was just over 98% both in 2008 and 2009. How did NNHS—an open enrollment neighborhood high school—achieve this normatively defined success in the context of a broader school district whose graduate rate was 51%?

Transforming Latinx Identities

My first meeting with Dr. Baez, the principal of NNHS, took place in the fall of 2007. During this relatively informal get-together, she explained to me that one of her long-term goals as principal was to create a new kind of Chicago public high school:

> Two things I tell people we are not about are fundraisers and dropping students out; we will graduate you. We are not a . . . brand name school, let's put it like that . . . there's the brand name schools that people go to, those [selective enrollment] schools . . . and then there's the generic schools, and we fall in the category of neighborhood generic schools; but I do believe that this generic school can do just as well as the brand name, that it serves just as good a purpose. So I don't have to buy brand name clothes. . . . I can buy generic clothes and people will think they're brand name. That's the same thing with students. I believe that we don't have to have our young adults from our community attend a college prep school outside of their community . . . that we can in fact make our neighborhood school a college prep school . . . if we're committed.

Dr. Baez draws on economic metaphors to distinguish between "brand name" and "generic" schools as a way of framing the structure of CPS. While CPS has a number of categories for its high schools, such as "Career Academy," "Military Academy," and "Charter," for the purposes of this book the most relevant distinction is between "neighborhood" schools (i.e., "open enrollment" schools) and "selective enrollment"/application-based schools.

Neighborhood high schools are open to all students who live within a given school's attendance boundaries. In contrast, acceptance to the city's selective enrollment high schools is based on an application and entrance exam. CPS frames its selective enrollment schools as institutions geared toward providing opportunities for the city's most academically successful students. From many other perspectives, however, these schools are intended to keep middle-class families in the city (Lipman 2008). Such perspectives suggest that without elite public educational options, middle-class families would continue to relocate to the suburbs or send their children to private schools. To provide these elite public educational options, selective enrollment schools become distinct from neighborhood schools in almost every way, including the quality of their facilities, the amount of training and experience of their teachers, and student demographics. The result is that CPS students from particular demographics—middle-class, White, Asian—are dramatically overrepresented in selective enrollment high schools.

Meanwhile, student demographics at dozens of neighborhood high schools are almost exclusively low income, African American, and Latinx. As opposed to selective enrollment schools, many CPS students, teachers, and families view neighborhood schools as undesirable, last-ditch options. Several NNHS students reported that their eighth-grade teachers often warned them that if they did not work harder and take school more seriously they would end up at one of the neighborhood high schools in the surrounding area. From these perspectives, attending a neighborhood high school is seen as a punishment. One NNHS student whose experiences I describe throughout this book, Jimmy (PR, Gen. 3, Gr. 12), succinctly voiced this perspective when he explained, "I ended up at NNHS because I couldn't get in anywhere else." Unlike Jimmy, many other NNHS students never even filled out the application for selective enrollment schools at the end of elementary school. These students' experiences are frequently overlooked or ignored in popular discourses surrounding school choice.

As an alternative to this open enrollment/selective enrollment framework, application-based charter schools are often presented as open enrollment opportunities that make the high-quality education associated with selective enrollment schools available to students who might not be able to gain admission to these institutions. Many of these charter schools admit students on the basis of a blind lottery. In practice, however, the students who apply to these charter schools are often those who are least at risk of underachievement or being pushed out. This self-selecting system can be very misleading. It produces charter schools with ethnoracial and socioeconomic student demographics that are generally similar to nearby neighborhood schools, but in many cases the students in these charter schools were the highest achievers in their previous schools. Thus, selective enrollment schools and application-based college preparatory charter schools are similar in that they attract students who would otherwise contribute to the normatively defined academic success of the neighborhood schools near where they live. Of course, many low income, racially minoritized students benefit academically from the opportunities offered within these nonneighborhood schools. The point, however, is that by taking the highest academic achievers, these schools make it exceedingly difficult for neighborhood schools to meet achievement standards. Because they serve many high-performing, low income, racially minoritized students, application-based charter schools are often invoked in educational discourses that suggest that all students are provided with the opportunity to succeed academically and that the failure to do so is mostly a result of individual choices (whether on the part of students, teachers, parents, or principals).[23]

Dr. Baez regularly noted that NNHS takes in many of the students who are dropped by the application-based charter school that is located just a few blocks away. She also suggested that these charter schools are not generally equipped to serve special needs students or those designated as English Language Learners. From Dr. Baez's perspective, application-based charter schools are smaller versions of selective enrollment high schools, and neither of these educational frameworks is designed to serve the vast majority of CPS students.

On September 24, 2009, US District Judge Charles Kocoras removed the CPS Desegregation Consent Decree that structured the student selection process in selective enrollment schools for nearly 30 years. As such, CPS no longer considers race as an admissions factor for magnet and selective enrollment schools. The Desegregation Consent Decree required a race-based lottery in order to achieve integration. It stipulated that White students, who make up only 9% of CPS students, were allowed up to 35% of the spots in magnet and selective enrollment schools.[24] When broken down by race, the percentages of students in selective enrollment high schools (SEHS) at the time of my fieldwork, compared with the overall district-wide percentages, are telling: White students in SEHS—23%, White students overall in CPS—8%; Asian students in SEHS—12%, Asian students overall in CPS—3%; Latinx students in SEHS—22%, Latinx students overall in CPS—38%; African American students in SEHS—38%, African American students overall in CPS—49%.[25]

These numbers highlight the irony of a national educational reform policy titled "No Child Left Behind." The neighborhood/selective enrollment framework of CPS, which is similar to urban districts throughout the nation, structurally identifies those who will likely be left behind before students even step foot into a classroom. This structure, which often removes the highest achieving students from many communities, poses numerous challenges to efforts toward creating high-performing neighborhood schools.

In broader terms, educational reform plans that are presented as efforts to increase "school choice" (e.g., George W. Bush's NCLB and Mayor Richard Daley's Renaissance 2010), are part of the neoliberal shift toward educational privatization.[26] Some aspects of these efforts identify substantive challenges in urban education, such as the detrimental effects of overcrowded schools and the benefits of smaller schools that allow for more personalized instruction. However, "school choice" becomes a deceptive discourse in that it suggests that educational underachievement is an isolated issue that can be addressed simply by providing students with a wider range of educational options from which to choose. This overshadows "how job, wage, housing, tax, and transportation policies maintain minority poverty in urban neighborhoods, and thereby create environments that overwhelm the potential of education policy to create systemic, sustained improvements in the schools" (Anyon 2005a:66, 2005b). For Lipman, "there is a striking relationship between evolving educational differentiation in Chicago Public Schools and the stratification of labor" (2008:279); this differentiation hinges on distinctions among schools by the varying degrees of selectivity in their enrollment processes. While the relationship between schooling and economic stratification is a long-standing scholarly concern (Willis 1977; Bourdieu and Passeron 1977), the stakes of this relationship become heightened in the context of the racialized economic restructuring that corresponds to efforts toward making Chicago a "global city." It is within the context of this inherently inequitable educational structure that Dr. Baez's analogy of "brand name" and "generic" schools must be understood. She attempted to prove that the distinction between these schools, like that between "brand name" and "generic" goods, could be cosmetic rather than substantive.

The effort toward making a "generic" school into a "brand name" school would seem to suggest that Dr. Baez was merely attempting to recreate a selective enrollment educational environment in the context of her open enrollment neighborhood school. In other instances, however, she articulated a vision of education that moves beyond the way that schooling is typically carried out in neighborhood *and* selective enrollment situations:

> You know, what people have to see is that we are still living in old ideas, old ways, and there's a general way of things, but society has changed, and it's not the same. So you cannot just go about business as usual or you become obsolete. So you have to make adaptations all the time. . . . I think this new generation does not understand and they don't know about history, the struggles to help them to be where they are, and they don't understand that it was through the civil rights movement, it was through the hardships that they have a public education . . . we also live in a generation right now with young adults, you know, you can talk about kids not getting pregnant [in the broader population], but the reality is that we have young adults, especially in the Hispanic community, that are pregnant. You can have low numbers [in the broader population], but in this neighborhood . . . us alone, we have at least 25 [pregnant students]. As soon as we drop down to 24, there's another one. And so you have to have avenues for them, because they're working, they're trying to support their family, just all the baggage at home. So when they cannot make it, I mean we should have a flexibility, like a college, where you can sign up for this class this period, or this class another period, or an evening class. Run it

like a college. Then it would [allow students to] make an adjustment, so that all students could go to school. So instead of seeing a night GED program as a program for failed students, it should be seen as an option. So what we have is a partnership. Por ejemplo, si están involved in gangs, o los niños quieren pelear (For example, if they are involved in gangs or the kids want to fight), okay, they can't be here for safety reasons. But we don't just dismiss them. Because if we don't pay now we pay later, with jails. So we provide alternatives for them to come back in the evening [program] because we have a partnership with Malcolm X [College].[27] And then we also have GED classes in the evenings for parents, also run by Malcolm X [College]. So we don't like to see them out there [on the streets]. In most schools, they just drop out . . . 18 days [of absences] and they are dropped.

Dr. Baez suggests that many schools are out of touch with the challenges that students are facing and that students are out of touch with the historical struggles that have sought to secure educational opportunities for low income, Black, and Latinx populations. She explains that a typical school schedule centered on weekday mornings and afternoons might not be the best option for some students. Invoking recurring themes, she gives examples such as students who are pregnant and those who are involved in gangs. Dr. Baez thinks that these students should be presented with a range of educational opportunities analogous to those offered at public institutions of higher education. These opportunities consist of more flexible scheduling during the regular school day, as well as evening options. This is part of Dr. Baez's broader vision of a school in which all students can learn. Her goal was to make NNHS an institution uniquely capable of serving not only students with an established record of mainstream academic success but also those who might otherwise fall through the cracks.

Dr. Baez described many students who had left NNHS for a range of reasons (e.g., homelessness, pregnancy, incarceration) and were welcomed back into the school when they wanted to return. One such student, Laura (Mex[m]/ Brazilian[f], Gen. 2, Gr. 11), told me that she was 14 when she left NNHS. As a freshman, Laura became involved in a romantic relationship with a man who was seven years older than she. Laura was out of school during one of the two years that she lived with him. She said that he wanted to have a baby with her, but that she went to a community clinic by herself to obtain birth control.[28] After agreeing to her mother's request that she return home, Laura went to NNHS to speak to Dr. Baez about her situation and the possibility of returning to school. She said that Dr. Baez told her that she would give her a chance only if she agreed to be more careful: "Me dijo, 'Tú sabes que muchos hombres solo quieren meterlo, y ya' " ("She told me, 'You know that many men only want to have sex and that's it'"). Laura appreciated that Dr. Baez spoke to her "woman to woman." She graduated in June 2010. Laura's path from leaving school to graduating corresponded to Dr. Baez's broader vision for the entire school. She candidly explained to me that turning her "generic" neighborhood school into a "brand name" college preparatory school would require students to experience a transformation: "When people look at these students they see them as gangbangers and hoes [whores] ... I want them to see Young Latino Professionals."[29]

This administrative outlook demonstrates that in the context of a neighborhood school such as NNHS, the distinction between cosmetic and substantive pedagogical efforts is by no means straightforward. In fact, the principal's project of transforming students—and recognitions of them—from "gangbangers" and "hoes" into "Young Latino Professionals" invokes many historical and contemporary intersectional mobility efforts.[30] In some ways, the creation of the category "Young Latino Professional" can be understood in relation to a long-standing African American politics of respectability, which emphasizes respectable presentation of self as a pathway toward societal inclusion and transformation.[31] In an analysis intraracial class politics in Chicago, Pattillo (2007) examines the history of complex linkages and fissures among African Americans of varying class positions. While in-group efforts toward intraracial economic uplift among African Americans, such as those Patillo describes, are by no means new phenomena, there is some question as to how these efforts might work in relation to the contemporary creation of Latinx as an identifiable social category.[32] In what ways are the attempts to transform stigmatized Latinx identities analogous to makeover tropes that circulate widely in contemporary US popular culture?[33] I analyze some of the school-based practices geared toward this transformation's achievement, the recognitions it seeks to reconstitute, and the cultural figures through which it operates. I argue that in their efforts to coordinate such a transformation, NNHS administrators grappled with the management of Latinidad, an ethnoracial concept whose complex definition, practice, and embodiment were difficult to manage within the institution's limited grasp. Moreover, I frame the creation of the category of Young Latino Professional as an intersectional mobility project that seeks to drive a wedge between the projected tension between assimilation and cultural identity maintenance (i.e., multiculturalism).

Of course, the figures of gangbanger, ho, and Young Latino Professional comprise many constitutive ideological elements. Gangbanger and ho are gendered as masculine and feminine, respectively. They are associated with deviant sexuality, teen pregnancy, criminality, and educational underachievement. They are also classed as economically illegal, illegitimate, and/or impoverished. Finally, they are often racially stereotyped in relation to Blackness and Latinidad. Yet, race, class, gender, and sexuality play disparate roles in the logics of this transformation. What *kind* of raced, classed, gendered, and sexualized Latinx is associated with each of these figures? In what ways do densely interwoven ideologies pose difficulties for any effort to distinguish these figures from one another? The co-constitution of these figures creates a double-bind in which recognition of young professionals as Latinxs involves the joint recognition of their potential essence as gangbangers or hoes. I approach Dr. Baez's intersectional mobility project of shaping students into "Young Latino Professionals" as an effort toward resolving this double-bind through the creation of a new social category. Dr. Baez's notion of professionalism should not be understood in terms of straightforward economic distinctions between modes of labor associated with the informal versus formal economy. For Baez, Young Latino Professionals were not only people who could become self-sustaining to any degree through participation in the formal economy, but also civic-minded people who were interested in contributing to community uplift more broadly. In many ways, her notion of professionalism was infused with a Deweyan commitment to education as/for civic engagement and democracy (Dewey 1916). Young Latino Professional is a concept that seeks to combine upward socioeconomic mobility with the maintenance of one's ethnoracial and cultural identity.

It is also possible to give a queer reading to the ways that the notion of Young Latino Professional potentially disrupts normative race, class, gender, and sexual stereotypes. On the one hand, the shift from binary gendered categories such as "gangbanger" and "ho" to the promotion of Young Latino Professional, which deploys the masculine form "Latino" as an umbrella concept, could be seen as the reproduction of masculinity as the default model of personhood. On the other hand, the rejection of stigmatizing stereotypes associated with "gangbangers" and "hoes" in favor of the all-encompassing category Young Latino Professional potentially presents the possibility for constructing gender nonbinary, nonheteronormative Latinx identities. Gangbanger and ho are conventionally constructed not only as binary gender concepts but also as heternormative. As an emergent local category, Young Latino Professional did not necessarily stipulate normative gender and sexual identities in this way. Later in this chapter, I examine the ways that students and school employees reproduced and contested these gender and sexual norms.

The sociocultural resources directed toward the effort to transform students from gangbangers and hoes into Young Latino Professionals demonstrate the perils of the multicultural embrace of difference in this context. In urging the students to become very particular kinds of Latinxs, the school's staff simultaneously sought to validate *and* transform students' modes of self-making; that is, students who were presumed to be Latinx by nature needed to learn to be *themselves* in highly studied ways in order to become Young Latino

Professionals. Yet, these analyses of identity management shed light on the meaning of everyday life within NNHS only through a consideration of the various perspectives that inform the creation of the category of Young Latino Professional. These matters of perspective and recognition are the focus of the following section.

Negotiating Multiple Perspectives and Recognitions

In the winter of 2010, a member of the NNHS class of 2009 used the social networking website, Facebook, to create a group called "YOu know YOu went 2 NNHS When. . . ." This prompted many former and current NNHS students to become members of the group and to make jovial and provocative statements about the school. Examples of students' posts include:

You know you went to NNHS if a bullet hole in the lunchroom window didn't surprise you.
You know you went to NNHS if your VALEDICTORIAN dropped out of college.
You know you went to NNHS when the principle would go to McDonalds in the morning just to tell them not to serve the students breakfast lmfao [laughing my fucking ass off] BITCH
you know you went to NNHS if you had a baby before your senior year
you know you went to NNHS if you ever wondered why people who couldn't even speak english were gangbanging at everyone
You know you went to NNHS if your principal couldn't stay still
You know you went to NNHS when 26 dumbasses got arrested in one day and at the same time over gang shit.
You know you went to NNHS when the teachers were after you to help you graduate.
You know u go 2 NNHS when making it thru senior year without a kid is a surprise . . . .
Yu know yu go to NNHS wen there is no such thing as a football team [a]nd yet we have a big ass field!!!
You know you went to NNHS when ONHS feels that we[']re in some kind of competition and feels the need to make up their own "you know you went to ONHS when" because we[']re waaay better than they are :) NNHS ROCKS!!!

As students sought to one-up each other's posts in terms of being humorous, outrageous, and insightful, membership in the group grew to nearly 300 in the week after it was created. After learning about this Facebook group, Dr. Baez printed out more than 100 pages of comments and highlighted those that she saw as a problem. She was concerned not so much with students' perspectives on the school, but with their presentation of those opinions in a public forum.

Dr. Baez was especially quick to meet with NNHS alumni who participated in this group and had become employed by the school as tutors. As graduates of NNHS who were attending college, these tutors seemed to be following the path toward becoming Young Latino Professionals. Wilson (Dominican, Gen. 2, first year in college) is the former NNHS student who posted the comment: "You know you went to NNHS if your VALEDICTORIAN dropped out of college[.]" He was making reference to the school's first valedictorian, Jacob (PR[m]/Mex[f], Gen. 2, leave of absence from college). Both Wilson and Jacob graduated in June 2008 and began attending DePaul University in the fall of 2008. Dr. Baez and others told me that during his first semester, Jacob used his college loans to help his mother pay for rent, heat, light, and groceries. Shortly thereafter, he was unable to pay for his books and tuition and was compelled to leave school for this reason. Wilson successfully completed his first year at DePaul. On one level, then, his comment signaled an effort to one-up the person designated as the school's top student. For Dr. Baez, however, this was an insensitive comment that poked fun at someone's hardships and suggested that even the best NNHS students are academically inept. This contrasted with Wilson's strong advocacy for NNHS. He characterized the school as place with a lot of opportunities, helpful policies (such as the uniform policy, which I describe and analyze in detail later in this chapter), and support that pushes students to go to college. Dr. Baez told Wilson that in many places of employment he would lose his job for voicing opinions in the way that he did in the Facebook group. She was similarly concerned with videos that students created with their cellular phones inside the school and then posted on publicly accessible websites such as MySpace and YouTube. These examples show how the perspectives of students, alumni, and a broader Internet-viewing public became linked in recognizing NNHS students and the school overall. Dr. Baez anticipated these multiple recognitions, particularly negative portrayals of NNHS such as those articulated by Wilson and others, and sought to curtail and counteract them.

Many teachers suggested that Dr. Baez was overly concerned with these matters, which they considered to be trivial. In most cases, these were liberal White teachers of varying ages who said that Dr. Baez was too focused on raising her own profile and outward appearances in general. They pointed to the example of a documentary film crew that followed the school and Dr. Baez throughout the 2007–2008 school year. This led to the creation of a film that focuses primarily on women elementary school principals in the Chicago area. The film, which aired on PBS, was also released as an educational DVD containing a 25-minute "mini-documentary" focused specifically on Dr. Baez's multipronged effort toward ensuring NNHS students' educational success. The opening scenes of the film survey the neighborhood surrounding NNHS, with Puerto Rican folkloric music as the soundtrack. There are images of people walking in front of a colorful mural and into a restaurant called "La Isla" [The Island] that advertises "PUERTORICAN FOOD." These images are juxtaposed with views of students in their uniforms walking along run-down streets toward the school. As statistics flash on the screen stating that nearly 100% of the school's students come from low income Latinx families, time-lapse footage shows how in a typical day the school transitions from the serenity of a janitor waxing the floors alone to the boisterousness of hundreds of students traversing its hallways. The film combines interviews with students, teachers, and staff, as well as scenes that focus on school life inside and outside the classroom. The overarching theme is Dr. Baez's commitment to helping all NNHS students graduate. While some teachers felt that this was grandstanding, Dr. Baez welcomed the positive portrayal of NNHS. Many high school principals would appreciate this positive publicity, but it plays a particularly important role in the context of a CPS neighborhood high school.

As discussed at the beginning of this chapter, CPS high schools are a frequent target of stigmatizing stereotypes and negative local media coverage (often focusing on issues of violence), and at times these narratives reach national and international audiences. This negative attention can have powerful effects. The controversy surrounding a widely publicized, predominantly Latinx CPS neighborhood high school in which Dr. Baez was previously employed as part of the administrative support staff illustrates this point. During the mid- and late-1990s, the *Chicago Sun-Times* and other mainstream Chicago newspapers ran misleading cover-page stories with titles such as "Public School's Pathetic Use of Poverty Funds" and "Classes Infused with Politics" (Ramos-Zayas 2003). These reports alleged that the school was using public funding to promote anti-American sentiments among students and to support Puerto Rican "terrorist" activities against the United States. This media coverage led to the resignation of the school's principal and the Chicago School Reform Board's rejection of the replacement principal selected by the Local School Council. Dr. Baez sought to avoid a similar fate for herself and her school by carefully constructing an educational project—emblematized by the category of Young Latino Professional—that delicately balanced the embrace of cultural difference with the push toward assimilation. Moreover, she welcomed positive promotion of NNHS via media such as the documentary film described earlier in order to preempt negative attention that could be directed toward the school at any moment. Practices that teachers recognized as contributing to Dr. Baez's unnecessary self-promotion could be understood from another perspective as important counterbalances to potential criticisms of the school that might be waged by mainstream Chicago media outlets. As with the case of the high school described earlier, media coverage can play a powerful role in prompting CPS to target particular schools for restructuring. The example of Dr. Baez's promotional efforts shows how teachers and CPS officials, as well as media outlets and their consumers on various scales, become interested audiences for educational projects carried out within NNHS and other schools.

An additional element of the positive promotion of NNHS to the city of Chicago involves the relationship between the school and various political leaders. Not only did Mayor Daley take an active interest in the school, but also State Senator Willie Delgado, City Clerk Miguel del Valle, Alderman Ray Suarez, and Alderman Ariel Reboyras. Each of these elected officials visited the school on various occasions and addressed students and families at important events such as graduation. Relationships with figures including Delgado and Suarez made the school a part of a citywide network of Latinx professionals. NNHS was the site for and subject of events that were advertised by the "Chicago Latino Network," which characterizes itself as "the eSource for New Generation Latinos":

> The Chicago Latino Network in its 10th year is the leading online resource for over 46,000 acculturated Latinos in the Chicagoland area looking for content that reflects their unique lifestyle, issues, and culture. This niche market of early influencers, who enjoy higher education and income levels (with significant disposable income), has been that untapped, oftentimes overlooked, and certainly elusive and mysterious market. The Chicago Latino Network has managed to not only market effectively to this niche community, but also to bring light to these successful professionals and entrepreneurs, while disseminating valuable information and resources.[34]

This rich self-description suggests that there is an audience of "acculturated Latinos...with significant disposable income" who might take interest in NNHS. From Dr. Baez's perspective, such relationships could provide role models and employment opportunities for NNHS graduates. While few Latinxs who grew up in the neighborhood surrounding NNHS have become adults with "significant disposable income," a self-titled Latino professional community is certainly one audience with which a category such as Young Latino Professional resonates strongly.

However, parents of NNHS students with whom I spoke were not so much interested in the school's professional connections as they were in what they considered to be more fundamental aspects of education such as the school's ability to ensure the physical and emotional safety of their children. Jimmy's (PR, Gen.

3, Gr. 12) mother attended the previously described high school that became the topic of negative media coverage. She told me she was glad Jimmy would not have to attend a school like that and mentioned Dr. Baez by name in describing her appreciation of NNHS, which she succinctly characterized as a "beautiful, safe school." Karina's (Mex, Gen. 3, Gr. 10) father expressed similar laudatory praise for NNHS. He explained that Karina's older sister, an 11th-grade student at the application-based charter school located a couple of blocks away from NNHS, should have attended NNHS instead:

> She got hurt really bad at school from playing lacrosse, so she had to have surgery and stay out of school for several weeks.[35] When she went back the kids and one of her teachers had started talking all these rumors about how she was out of school because she was a ho and that she was pregnant. I mean it was bad for her. I went to the school to talk to someone about it but the assistant principal told me that he only had a minute. I said okay and I started to tell him what happened and then all of a sudden he told me, "minute's up," and he just got up and left. I'm not going to say what I wanted to do to him, but I never seen anything like that before. They got no respect. And then, I go over there to NNHS for Karina for report card pick-up and the people from the school are there all nice, you know, talking to me about Karina and telling me if they can help me with anything. It's like night and day.

Despite the application-based charter school's reputation for academic rigor, Karina's father claimed that the school was less interested in providing an inviting environment for students and parents. He was interested not only in the school's academic performance but also in its respect for the population it serves. It is no coincidence that he felt more comfortable within NNHS. At report card pick-up, Dr. Baez moved throughout the school talking with parents in English and Spanish. This included holding the front door of the school open to welcome them inside, and also talking to them about their children's grades and encouraging them to follow up with the teachers. When I asked Dr. Baez about Karina's father's experience at the nearby application-based charter school, she suggested that the school's leaders are not from the community and that they do not have a full understanding of how to relate to students' and families' needs. For Dr. Baez, parental support for the school's efforts was crucial. She explained that her students' parents might not have a lot of material resources, but they want the best for their kids and they know how to recognize when a school wants what is best for them as well. When she reported to me that, "parents are pleased," it was apparent that she respected the importance of making parents feel welcome within the school and clearly communicating the school's goals to them. In some ways, Dr. Baez sought to empower parents to talk with teachers about their children. Ultimately, she aimed to create a mutually reinforcing relationship between the modes of socialization taking place in the school and at home. Note also the ways in which Karina's father invokes the idea that NNHS is a context in which Karina is not confronted with stigmatizing gender and sexual stereotypes that her sister faced at the nearby charter school.

The investment in parents' perspectives was also connected to the way that residents of the neighborhood surrounding the school became an important part of the audience for efforts toward making NNHS into a successful neighborhood high school that would provide Latinx students with a strong education. Structured essentially as a large two-story atrium that allows passers-by to view its immaculate hallways, classrooms, and offices, the $35 million school certainly stands out in an economically marginalized neighborhood whose other large buildings are almost exclusively run-down or vacant factories. As opposed to other neighborhood high schools, which many residents describe as prison-like structures, NNHS is often simply described by neighborhood residents as "beautiful." Students walking to and from the school are immediately recognizable because of their uniforms. The first graduation, which was held under a pavilion on the neatly trimmed, bright green field next to the school, in many ways became a community celebration of the accomplishments of students who resided nearby. Crucially, Dr. Baez wanted elementary school students in the community to know that NNHS is a school for everyone.

Parents, students, alumni, community members, elected officials, Latinx professionals, CPS officials, media outlets, Chicago residents, broader media publics, and online publics were all part of the audience for NNHS's project of social transformation. Dr. Baez's project of creating the category of Young Latino Professional was profoundly shaped by these viewpoints. The following section further explores some of these viewpoints by presenting an account of two specific school-based policies geared toward transforming students into Young Latino Professionals, and demonstrates their fraught reception from the perspectives of NNHS students, teachers, police, and residents of the surrounding neighborhood.

Latinx Uniformity?

In material and pedagogical terms, the strategies that Dr. Baez employed in her attempts to facilitate the transformation of her students from gangbangers and hoes into Young Latino Professionals reveal the trouble with redefining Latinx identity. In this section I highlight two of these strategies: (1) the enforcement of a strict uniform policy and (2) the principal's staunch opposition to academic tracking (i.e., the separation of students into academic performance groups, such as honors, mainstream, and remedial). From many perspectives, these practices would be mutually exclusive, with uniforms and antitracking positioned as conservative and progressive pedagogical approaches, respectively. I argue that the apparent contradiction reflects competing claims about the nature of Latinx identity—it is alternately positioned as the cause of and solution to underachievement and school failure. Are uniforms necessary because there is a problem with Latinx students' appearance or society's perceptions of them? Should academic performance tracking be opposed because it separates students in damaging ways or because all Latinx students are prepared to take honors courses? I will show how Latinx identity is negotiated at once as a site of institutional stigmatization and possibility.

The uniform policy, a central strategy in these efforts, provides for a useful case study. Students were required to wear a NNHS polo shirt or sweatshirt to school each day, and the student identification cards that were scanned upon entry each morning needed to be visible throughout the day (they were provided with lanyards for these cards).[36] Polo shirts were to be tucked in at all times. Only solid black or brown shoes could be worn, and the shoelaces had to match the color of the shoe. Pants were to be worn with a belt at the waist; skirts and dresses had to reach the knee. Jeans were prohibited. Body and facial piercings were not allowed, with the exception that girls could wear earrings.[37] Girls could not wear "extreme heavy makeup," and no one could have "haircut or eyebrow designs." In a somewhat humorous transgression of the haircut design prohibition, two boys came to school one morning in the fall of 2007 with "graphics" in their hair (i.e., shapes, words, and designs created by using a straight razor). After these students were directed to the office, Dr. Baez asked a student in the school who was a well-known barber to retrieve the necessary equipment from his car and to remove the graphics by providing these students with short haircuts know as "fades."[38] She paid the student barber his going price of $5 per haircut. Reflecting on the incident, a Puerto Rican teacher joked that the boys ended up getting really good haircuts, "with lining and everything."[39]

Dr. Baez pointed to the practical and symbolic importance of these policies focused on students' clothing and bodies. Practically, the uniforms made it difficult for students to conceal weapons or signal gang affiliation through their clothing. It is possible to signal gang affiliation sartorially by wearing particular colors, having any piece of clothing on the left or the right side of one's body (e.g., letting the slack of one's belt hang to the left or right, wearing a bandana out of the left or right side of one's back pocket, throwing any article of clothing over one's left or right shoulder), piercing one ear/eyebrow or the other, shaving designs into one's hair/eyebrows, lacing a particular number of eyelets in one's shoes, and having tattoos. This list is by no means exhaustive, but I hope it gives readers some sense of the number of minute ways that high-stakes identities could be signaled in this context.

Symbolically, wearing the uniform was an opportunity for students to present themselves in a "professional" manner on an almost daily basis. Dr. Baez argued that baggy shirts and/or sagging pants for boys and too tight and/or revealing clothing for girls contributed to negative perceptions of her students. She strictly enforced and adhered to this policy. She also wanted her teachers and general staff to be viewed as professionals. She went so far as to explain to me that she would not even wear jeans in public on the weekend, for fear of running into a teacher and giving them fodder for gossip or an important official who might think less of her.[40]

First thing each morning and throughout the school day, Dr. Baez, her assistants, and security guards could be seen and heard in the hallways examining students' dress and reminding them to tuck in their shirts. She reprimanded teachers who did not enforce the policy and sent students home if they did not follow it. Most students were relatively indifferent with regard to the uniform policy inside the school. In fact, many students underwent clothing-based makeovers inside *and* outside of school. Jimmy (PR, Gen. 3, Gr. 12) is one such example. Although he was a huge fan of hip-hop music, he had long since ceased to wear the sort of baggy clothing often stereotypically associated with participants in the broader cultural practices that surround this genre of music at the time. Jimmy told me that his decision to stop wearing baggy clothing was based on a conversation he had with his older sister (who was in her mid-20s) at the beginning of high school. When Jimmy and his sister walked by someone on the street whose tight clothing Jimmy began to ridicule, his sister challenged his ideas about styles of dress. She explained to him that no self-respecting girl would want to be with someone who dressed "ghetto." She said she knew that Jimmy thought tighter clothes would make him look "gay," but that fitted clothes that matched his figure would make him look mature.[41] He took her suggestion to heart and stopped wearing baggy jeans and "hoodies" (hooded sweatshirts). Instead of shopping at hip-hop clothing stores in the mall, Jimmy began shopping at stores such as Old Navy, Aeropostale, and American Eagle. He said that he laughed when he looked at his old XL and XXL-sized clothes, which he now felt were far too big for him. Thus, Jimmy grappled with sartorial signs of queerness and heteronormative masculinity, as well as the racial and class-inflected ways in which these signs were institutionalized inside and outside of NNHS.

There were aspects of the uniform policy that some students found annoying or objectionable, such as the constant surveillance, but there was certainly no widespread opposition. Many students, particularly boys, reported that the uniform made them feel safer walking to and from school than they would if they were wearing everyday clothes. They said that gang members were much less likely to "check" them (i.e., confront them about their gang affiliation) when they were in uniform.[42] Meanwhile, many teachers relaxed the policy inside their classrooms. For example, the policy prohibited students from wearing coats, jackets, or sweaters inside the school, but teachers would sometimes allow such practices inside their classrooms, especially if students pleaded that they were cold. Periodically, students would meet in their regular classroom at the beginning of the period and then travel as a group to the library, computer lab, or auditorium for a range of activities. Before leaving the classroom, where untucked shirts often went unchecked, teachers frequently reminded students to tuck in their shirts and take out their identification cards. NNHS teachers not only voiced disagreement with but also mobilized in opposition to the uniform policy. Specifically, many of the younger White teachers wanted to dress less formally in the school. They claimed that it was not within Dr. Baez's authority to stipulate their attire. At the end of the 2008–2009 school year, as my fieldwork period drew to a close, several of these teachers sought to join NNHS's Local School Council in order to change this policy.

A second school policy that sought to reshape students' experiences was anti-tracking, or what some educational scholarship has called "detracking" (Rubin and Noguera 2004). That is, the principal very loudly and clearly opposed academic performance tracks. She argued that an educational culture of low expectations too often prevented students from achieving their full potential and that all of her students were honors and Advanced Placement caliber[43]:

> I believe that in everything we do here, we are not selective of certain students, in terms of . . . can they succeed . . . sometimes these students have this view that they cannot be anything; for example, they don't believe that if you're a special education student that you can get "A's" and that's not true. So what we try to do is really transform lives to see, for them, the bell to click, so it's not about teaching the subject, but rather the student is the subject . . . a lot of times teachers want to bring their own agenda and we have to kind of put them on check . . . this is not about you, this is about the students . . . because they come in with their stuff, their prior knowledge, and want to have the kids think like them, as opposed to, why don't you get to know who these students are and try to work with them. . . . NNHS is not business as usual, because I don't

accept the idea, come, don't come . . . you know, you're late, too bad. . . . I mean, so what? . . . No, no. If you have not done your job in contacting those parents, and you know that is your job, that's part of . . . who you're supposed to be, so . . . if you have never made an attempt to reach out to those parents, that had you done it parents could have intervened, don't blame the parents. If you did not bring them in, then you have no right to fail that child.

From Baez's perspective, not only was it important to treat *all* students as honors students, it was also crucial to hold teachers accountable for students' success. It is important to distinguish between Dr. Baez's use of "teacher accountability" and the contemporary conservative discourse of "educational accountability." The deployment of the discourse of "educational accountability" approaches school failure not as a systemic problem but as a problem with individual teachers, students, parents, principals, and schools. In contrast, Dr. Baez saw urban public school failure as an endemic problem.

Several teachers shared experiences of being called to Dr. Baez's office in order to account for the number of students who failed their classes. They were required to produce phone logs and other records to demonstrate that they had made sufficient efforts to reach out to students and parents. Baez explained that as a parent of former CPS students, she understands that the parents are frequently uninformed about what is happening with their children in school:

Most of the time parents are doing the best they can, but our job is to help those parents to be better parents, inform the parents of what's going on so they can intervene. . . . Maybe part of what has made me think this way is that my daughter was attending one of the more successful CPS high schools and had seventy-two cuts in her two classes right before and after lunch. I've worked in CPS for thirty-two years now and always had a phone at my desk and I received not one phone call from that school . . . my daughter's no angel, but the school has to take blame, too. Instead, the kids and the parents get blamed . . . and at times I educate the parents. During report card pick-up the parent tells me I'm going to go upstairs (to talk to the teacher) and I tell them to ask questions of the teachers . . . ask them why they weren't contacted; I'm not siding with either one, parents or teachers, they both need to be accountable, but I'm here for that student.

By reclaiming the notion of accountability from its deployment as a neoliberal scapegoating of teachers and schools, Baez sought to make educational achievement a multiparty effort that involved collaboration among students, parents, teachers, and administrators.

Baez also described the importance of the AVID (Advancement Via Individual Determination) program at NNHS.[44] This nationwide program was introduced to CPS in 2003. In most schools, it serves as a college-bridge program for particular students from backgrounds underrepresented in higher education. At NNHS, however, *all* students were required to participate in AVID. Dr. Baez wanted each one of her students to have the opportunity to participate in this program, so NNHS initiated a school-wide AVID program when the school was opened. In addition to AVID, most NNHS students took one or more honors or Advanced Placement classes throughout their high school career. Students were generally encouraged to take these classes, and, unlike in most schools, there were few selective restrictions placed on registration. The notion that all students should take AP courses is extremely rare in a low income, racially minoritized neighborhood high school setting. Participation in these courses was intended to make college enrollment a part of students' future plans from the beginning of their freshman year through graduation. Despite these efforts, Dr. Baez noted that although 65% of the first graduating class enrolled in college, only 30% finished the first year of college and remained on track to begin the second year. This included the school's first valedictorian; as described earlier, he left college within the first month after facing difficulties with his financial aid. This said, AVID continually reminded students of their progress toward graduation and greatly facilitated seniors' college application process.

In addition to the emphasis Dr. Baez placed on the importance of AVID, she argued that the language and learning abilities of her students were often underestimated and misunderstood, which led to their overclassification as English Language Learners (ELLs) and Learning Disabled (LD). For example, she claimed that many students who might be considered ELLs understood and spoke more English than the official language assessments reflected. Moreover, she pointed to particular students' rapid English language learning in immersion settings as evidence of the benefits of mainstreaming. Based on this thinking, she promoted the mainstreaming of many students who would likely be sheltered if they attended a different high school.[45] There were a few self-contained classrooms for students classified as severely and profoundly handicapped or ELLs, but some teachers questioned the school's methods for identifying and serving these students. They claimed that the principal's ideological perspective prevented her from recognizing the substantive differences among students and the accommodations that these students needed.

Many teachers openly voiced their opposition to the antitracking policy. They said that because students were placed into higher caliber courses regardless of their demonstrated ability, the policy prevented the school from having "real" honors and Advanced Placement classes. When teachers raised this concern at a staff meeting early in the 2008–2009 school year, Dr. Baez explained that it was the teachers' responsibility to present challenging material in such a way that all students could succeed. Disgruntled teachers argued that it was impossible to accommodate students with dramatically varying skill levels in the same classroom, and claimed that this arrangement was to blame for the school's poor standardized test scores and brief placement on academic probation. Additionally, a few top-performing students complained that some classes were slow-paced and insufficiently challenging. For these teachers and students, detracking was tantamount to economic redistribution. This is not by chance because educational and economic stratification are closely linked. The process of leveling the academic playing field meant that even in Advanced Placement and honors classes, high-performing students sat alongside lower performing students. Yesi (PR, Gen. 1.5, Gr. first year college), one such high-performing student, attributed her score of 2 on the Advanced Placement Chemistry exam (which was not high enough to earn college credit) to the fact that her teacher had to spend too much time working with students who were not prepared for the exam. Students in this class joined together, with their teacher's approval, to write letters to Dr. Baez expressing their frustration with this situation. For Dr. Baez, however, allowing as many students as possible—particularly those who were not commonly understood as high achievers—to take honors and Advanced Placement courses was what mattered most. Exposure to these courses might encourage these students to raise their academic self-esteem and view themselves as future college students. Providing increased access to lower achieving students meant that high-achieving students such as Yesi had to relinquish the educational privileges (e.g., small class sizes, increased teacher attention, and exclusive access to honors/Advanced Placement courses) to which they had become accustomed in their previous educational experiences. Yesi's eventual matriculation to one of the nation's top liberal arts colleges and the majority of her lower achieving classmates' enrollment in college demonstrate the potential collective benefits of detracking.

What can these policies tell us about the project of transforming students and creating a new social category of Young Latino Professional? In some ways, a uniform policy is a very familiar, quasi-Catholic project of social and educational control in which students must learn discipline in conjunction with the privatization of identity. That is, in Catholic terms, a religious identity is not something to be displayed outwardly; good public behavior should signal private Catholic piety. But what happens when the identities involved are ethnoracial and thus not so easily privatized? That is, in what ways does the fact of Latinidad, to adapt the Fanonian (1967) formulation, elude attempts at privatization and redefinition?[46] Whereas the Catholic educational project takes as its problem "youth" as a universal age cohort in need of particular socializing efforts, the problem at NNHS was with youth who were associated with stigmatizing racial, class, gender, and sexual stereotypes. And yet the radical egalitarianism at NNHS, exemplified by the opposition to tracking, demonstrated the potential for these students to graduate at remarkable rates. What interests me most here is the way in which these policies reflect the profound ambivalence and contradiction that structure the socialization of Latinx youth. To navigate this complex terrain, Dr. Baez was required to carve out a very delicate bureaucratic path not only among teachers, students, parents, and city officials, but also among the overdetermined figures of gangbangers, hoes, and Young Latino Professionals.

Power Struggles

NNHS's uniform and antitracking policies, both of which were spearheaded and overseen by Dr. Baez, are just two examples of the broader ways that the principal played a profound role in shaping everyday school life. The ability of the principal to strongly influence school life is a common characteristic of neighborhood schools. This is distinct from the role of the principal in charter schools, which are often overseen by a board of directors, and in selective enrollment schools, which are frequently guided by empowered parents and assertive Local School Councils. Local School Councils (LSCs) were created through the 1988 Chicago School Reform Act, which had been promoted by the city's first Black Mayor, Harold Washington, and was passed shortly after his untimely death. The creation of LSCs secured unprecedented levels of control for parents and communities (Todd-Breland 2018). Elections are held annually in order to select an LSC for each Chicago public school. LSCs consist of parents, teachers, community residents, a student representative, and the school's principal. LSCs not only oversee schools' discretionary funds but also have the power to hire and fire principals. While the newfound power to hire principals contributed to the continued increase of the number of African American principals, it also dramatically increased the number of Latinx principals (Shipps 2006). These increases meant that the race of the principal selected by an LSC was much more likely to correspond to the predominant race of students within the school. The previous system, which allowed the CPS central office to appoint principals, frequently placed White principals in schools whose student bodies were almost exclusively African American and Latinx. Dr. Baez was particularly attuned to these patterns. Her 1998 doctoral dissertation investigated local school communities' preferences for leadership that corresponds to their "ethnic" identity.[47] In the dissertation, she asks:

> Are ethnically identifiable groups of people more likely to prefer and select school leaders that mirror the ethno-political and social background of their children? And do these ethnically identifiable groups of people perceive that having a school leader that represents their ethnicity to be the most effective means of educating their children as demonstrated by higher student achievement, attendance, and deportment?

She utilizes statistical and survey data to analyze how "Hispanic leadership leads to fewer Hispanic students being placed in special education programming, more in honors courses, less disparity in discipline, and a higher proportion of students graduating." These were the very issues on which she set her sights as principal of NNHS. Baez highlights her dissertation research participants' comments about the importance of language, culture, and community accountability in the selection of a school's principal, as well as their belief that a principal whose "ethno-political and social background" differs from that of the community would not feel accountable in the same way. In the conclusion she argues that these "ethnocentric" preferences are a product of social inequality and that we should look forward to a future when "we see ourselves as mutually accountable."

Although small in stature, inside NNHS Dr. Baez was an iconic figure who could be invoked simply by uttering pronouns such as "she" or "her." If there is an apparent slippage between my references to "the school's project of socialization" and "the principal's project of socialization," it can be attributed to Dr. Baez's profound influence on the school's educational approach. As described earlier, Dr. Baez framed her perspective in terms of knowledge that she gained from a combination of more than 30 years of employment with CPS, university training that earned her a doctorate in education, her experiences as a parent of students who attended CPS, and her experiences as a Puerto Rican woman who came to Chicago from the island at the age of 4 and who learned English after entering CPS.

Several teachers at NNHS called these qualifications into question. Specifically, they suggested that Dr. Baez's limited classroom teaching experience prevented her from becoming an effective principal. Dr. Baez was aware of these criticisms. For Baez, being a "short Latina woman" posed a threefold challenge to her ability to attain teachers' respect. In Smulyan's study of the "balancing acts" that are required of female principals, the normative Whiteness and masculinity associated with these leadership positions "creates conflicts for women principals, both in their interactions with their varied constituencies and in their evaluations of themselves as school leaders" (Smulyan 2000:25). Dr. Baez's leadership style, which juxtaposed authoritarianism with discourses of egalitarianism, was cause for concern among teachers who sought increased autonomy. The opposition of some teachers to the uniform policy, as described earlier, was evidence of their frustration with Dr. Baez's unwavering commitment to a specific definition of professionalism. One teacher claimed that Dr. Baez was obsessed with cosmetic issues such as students' uniforms, staff attire, and the cleanliness of the school. Delpit (1995) attributes these conflicting perspectives to teacher education programs and broader educational philosophies that are disconnected from the politics of urban education. In fact, the vast majority of the teachers who talked to me about their opposition to Dr. Baez had grown up in predominantly White suburban communities and had limited experience working in educational contexts similar to NNHS. One such ninth-grade social studies teacher, Mr. Thomas, earnestly questioned why the students should have to wear such formal clothes to school each day. Mr. Thomas contrasted the relaxed sartorial rules he experienced in his suburban high school with what he perceived as the arbitrary, unnecessarily restrictive policies at NNHS. For Dr. Baez, these "cosmetic" concerns were symbols of the school's fundamental stability and productivity. In an era of educational reform that required the identification and restructuring of "problem" schools, the ability of a given school to signal its stability is paramount. This also helps to explain the practical importance of the symbolic transformation of students into Young Latino Professionals.

Simultaneous Interpellations

Competing ideas about Latinx identity complicate the figures of the gangbanger, ho, and Young Latino Professional and serve to map out the precarious sociocultural field in which Dr. Baez sought to coordinate her project of transformation and recognition. In a seemingly straightforward sense, the enforcement of the uniform policy reproduced the very ideas about students that Dr. Baez attempted to transform. As in all Chicago Public Schools, there were police officers on duty at NNHS at all times during school hours—a patrol car was always parked very conspicuously in front of the entrance to the school—and students began each day by passing through metal detectors. The constant surveillance of students' clothing was a reminder of their criminalization and the ubiquitous threat of incarceration.

NNHS was also part of the Chicago Police Department's "Students First Safe Passage Pilot Program." The main features of this program were increased police patrol at the end of each school day and the installation of what students called "blue light cameras" around the school. These cameras, with their flashing blue lights, have been prominently attached to lampposts in the city's most highly criminalized neighborhoods since 2003. The blue light cameras, which are linked to one another as part of a larger citywide network of more than 10,000 cameras, constitute a surveillance program that makes Chicago the "most closely watched U.S. city."[48] In addition to these blue light cameras, NNHS was equipped with 75 security video cameras at its opening. This is virtually unprecedented for a CPS high school. Yet, these cameras were not nearly as much a concern for students as were their face-to-face encounters with Chicago police officers. Students reported countless negative experiences with police officers throughout their lives. These experiences generally involved police stopping students, questioning them, and then frisking them when they were traveling in a car or walking. I was struck by the similar ways that students talked about being harassed by police and gang members. In the neighborhood surrounding NNHS, I often observed multiple police cars setting up checkpoints and aggressively monitoring passing cars, frequently pulling people over, asking them to step outside, and then pushing them against their vehicles while frisking them. These police encounters were a naturalized aspect of NNHS students' everyday lives. Insubordination and other behaviors that might merit in-school or out-of-school suspension in more privileged educational contexts are potential grounds for arrest in particular CPS neighborhood schools; this made the notion of the "fashion police,"[49] a common popular cultural trope, all too real in this context.[50]

The naturalized relationship between race and criminality dramatically heightened the stakes of presentations of self at NNHS. This reinscription of governmental surveillance produced a context in which questionable pants or untucked shirts were all it took to blur the lines between Young Latino Professionals, gangbangers, and hoes. Even if students were recognized as Young Latino Professionals in a given moment, contrasting ideas about Latinxs made it difficult to distinguish between acceptable and problematic manifestations of this identity. For low income Latinx students in urban schools, there is no straightforward way to perform the role of Young Latino Professional without potentially being perceived as a gangbanger or ho. The signaling of professionalism achieved by the uniforms did not simply dispel the ideological presumption that young, low income Latinxs are gangbangers and hoes by nature. In fact, the uniform policy prompted students to play with articles of clothing that could simultaneously associate them with the figure of a gangbanger, ho, and Young Latino Professional. For many normatively masculine presenting students, Dickies pants were a desired brand. Jeans, sweatpants, and shorts were prohibited. Although Dickies clearly met school uniform criteria, they were also widely associated with "gangster style." Was a Latinx student in Dickies a gangbanger or a Young Latino Professional? The uniform policy also refocused attention to other potential signals of gangbanger and ho identities. Piercings were a major concern within the school. As described earlier, students were not allowed to have body or facial piercings of any kind, with the exception that girls could wear earrings. While some students with prohibited piercings adhered to the rule by placing a bandage over piercings during school hours, other students tested the waters by openly displaying their piercings until school staff members confronted them. More interestingly, many girls wore large hoop earrings that, while permitted by the policy, were part of stereotypes that position Latinas in relation to a range of "sexual-aesthetic excesses" (Hernandez 2009). Hernandez analyzes these stereotypes through the widely circulated stereotypical image of the "chonga," which figures Latinas as "low-class, slutty, tough, and crass young wom[e]n" (Hernandez 2009:64). Engagements with the uniform policy demonstrate the complex symbolic interrelations between figures such as gangbangers, hoes, and Young Latino Professionals. Meanwhile, the antitracking policy called into question the stigmatization of Latinx identity. The negative response to this policy from teachers and students speaks to the deep embeddedness of the educational hierarchies that it challenged.

The difficulties with these policies highlight the problems with the management of multicultural recognition in liberal democratic contexts. Was it just that the students were seen as gangbangers and hoes, or was this who they actually were? Did efforts such as the uniform policy simply seek to change the skewed stereotypes through which people viewed students, or did the students themselves need to become something other than who or what they already were? On a practical level, the uniform policy helped to manage gang signifying and weapons concealment, but as a symbolic project it was limited in its ability to secure unproblematic recognitions of students as Young Latino Professionals. While anchoring ideologies of race, class, gender, and sexuality in some ways recognized even the most dazzling Young Latino Professionals as potential gangbangers and hoes, NNHS was still able to achieve remarkable success in terms of graduation rates. In this sense, the simultaneous interpellation of students as gangbangers, hoes, and Young Latino Professionals did not prevent Dr. Baez from graduating her students. A close ethnographic analysis demonstrates that the uniform policy can by no means be dismissed as a clear-cut example of students' criminalization and domination.

Dr. Baez described to me the way in which far too many urban high schools operate as preparation for prison. From her perspective, the student uniforms and police officers inside NNHS were creating a different environment. Baez chose not to institute a US Army Junior Reserve Officer Training Corps

(JROTC) program in her school, even though this program's emphasis on discipline would seem to coincide with the efforts toward orderliness at NNHS. In fact students who attended nearby ONHS reported that wearing a JROTC uniform was one of the few things in the school that made them feel a sense of pride and importance; similarly, students at the nearby application-based charter school regularly wore their JROTC uniforms while walking along the streets surrounding NNHS. In her analyses of JROTC participation among Latinx youth in Chicago and other Midwestern contexts, Pérez (2006, 2015) points out that Chicago Public Schools "lead the nation with more than 10,000 students participating in a wide range of expanding public school military programs" (2006:57). Pérez also notes that these programs disproportionately target low income youth of color who reside in "neighborhoods regarded in local media as dangerous and are enmeshed in racialized policing practices aimed at containing suspect youth" (2006:58). She argues that for students who are constantly made aware of the presumption that they are criminals, "wearing a military uniform is, perhaps, one way of negotiating the racialized systems of surveillance that not only operate within their neighborhoods, but also within their own schools" (Pérez 2006:58). Baez claimed that JROTC makes empty promises to vulnerable students and overrecruits poor students of color. She took the room that was designed for JROTC during the construction of NNHS and converted it into an Allied Health classroom that would train students to enter a variety of health-related fields upon graduation. In this sense, not just any uniform or mode of discipline would suffice; Baez carefully navigated around JROTC in order to construct alternative possibilities.

The police presence in the school also operated in surprising ways. Students comfortably conversed with the two police officers stationed within the school about whatever legal issues they learned about in the classroom, encountered in popular cultural representations, or experienced in their own lives. One student explained that when he got into an altercation near his home over the summer, the police officer who responded to the situation was Officer López from NNHS. The officer recognized the boy from school and quickly resolved an encounter that might have otherwise resulted in the all too common experience of police brutality and/or unnecessary arrest. This camaraderie also contributed to the fact that during my two years of fieldwork I never heard any students say that they were afraid to attend NNHS. This stands in contrast to the description of the experiences of ONHS students at the beginning of this chapter, for whom fear was a prominent part of everyday school life.

In terms of antitracking and the mainstreaming of students designated as ELLs and LD, 2009 co-valedictorian Carmen Vázquez arrived in Chicago from Cuba just three years before graduating. She self-identified as having known little

English upon arrival but was able to test out of ELL designation within her first two years at NNHS. While this certainly does not mean that mainstreaming is the most beneficial educational approach for most students, it is important to take a closer look at the implementation of these policies in the NNHS context. It is one thing for students designated as ELLs to be mainstreamed in educational contexts in which there are few opportunities to use languages other than English, but at NNHS it was very common for Latinx students and employees to converse in multiple varieties of Spanish and English throughout the day. In this sense, the school adhered to the bureaucratic requirement of English-only while creating its own context of inclusion and validation of Spanish language skills.[51]

Similarly, the emphasis on teacher accountability and student success contributed to the school's remarkable graduation rates of more than 98% for its first two graduating classes. These graduation rates withstood audits that require all Chicago public high schools to demonstrate that they are not simply granting diplomas to students who fail to fulfill the necessary requirements. However, the provision of AVID and honors classes for all students was not enough to provide them with sufficient resources to enter college and remain on track to graduate. While discourses of college preparedness frame movement through institutions of higher education as a matter of acquiring particular academic skills and various forms of so-called cultural capital, the experiences of the aforementioned valedictorian demonstrate the range of structural inequalities that shape one's institutional access and viability. Indeed, as the difficulties of the first NNHS valedictorian demonstrate, even the most straightforward exemplars of Young Latino Professionals face struggles stereotypically associated with gangbangers and hoes. Such experiences reflect the double-bind that constrains efforts to combat the stigmatization of Latinx identities.

Between Stigmatization and Transformation

The joint validation and stigmatization associated with the project of transforming NNHS students into Young Latino Professionals reverberates with a number of historical and contemporary analytical approaches to the study of "problem" identities. Collectively, these approaches point to the benefit of conceptualizing the management of Latinx identity at NNHS as a project of *commensuration*; that is, the careful calibration and reconciliation of modes of institutional and broader social difference. In concrete terms, the question is: What are some of the ways that Latinx students might become "successful" within (i.e., commensurate with) a Chicago public high school? What institutional practices would make this possible? What behaviors would be demanded of students? My analysis of these questions will demonstrate how the management of Latinx identities within NNHS is linked to a long line of ethnoracial paradoxes.

More than a century ago, Du Bois posited a profound incommensurability between Blackness and Americanness. This incommensurability was at the heart of his formulation of double-consciousness, the "sense of always looking at one's self through the eyes of others" (Du Bois 1903:5). For Du Bois, to be Black in America was to develop a felt "two-ness . . . two unreconciled strivings" (1903:5). The desired resolution for Du Bois was a different sort of doubleness, one that would "make it possible for a man to be both a Negro and an American . . . without having the doors of opportunity closed roughly in his face" (1903:5). How could one be Black and "successful" in America? Du Bois' engagement with this question was a precursor to the NNHS-based concept of Young Latino Professional that emerged more than a century later.

What Du Bois described as the "veil" that barred African Americans from the White American world can be productively understood in relation to Latinx subjectivities by drawing on Anzaldúa's theorization of exclusion in *Borderlands/ La Frontera* (1987). For Anzaldúa, borders are recursive structures that can be reproduced on a number of scales, such that the "color line" (in Du Bois' terms) is just one of many possible sites for the production of exclusion and double-consciousness. In her formulation of a New Mestiza Consciousness, the racial and economic exclusion caused by colonialism must always be understood in relation to the sexual and gender domination of patriarchy. Anzaldúa's Chicana feminism involves the experience of multiple forms of double-consciousness in response to the multiplicity of power. In some places, Anzaldúa characterizes her lesbian Chicana feminist consciousness as a "Shadow-Beast . . . that refuses to take orders from outside authorities . . . that hates constraints of any kind, even those self-imposed" (1987:38). Anzaldúa's description of the Shadow-Beast resonated with contradictory discourses surrounding young women at NNHS. At times, young women within NNHS were figured as transcendent vehicles of social mobility. In one teacher's words, "all the smart girls at [NNHS] want to transfer to a better school."[52] In this sense, there were anxieties about high-achieving young women resisting the academic and social "constraints" (in Anzaldúa's words) of NNHS and attempting to escape to a "better" (i.e., selective enrollment/application-based) school. Contrasting discourses positioned girls as the school's biggest behavioral problem. A school administrator reported that violent fights kept breaking out between different girls. She lamented, "The girls are worse than the boys!" In this discourse, girls not only fail to display the proper behavior that is expected of them; their refusal "to take orders from outside authorities" (again, invoking Anzaldúa) makes them more of a problem than the boys. These inverse anxieties—girls as the highest achievers attempting to transfer versus girls as the school's biggest behavioral problems—are linked in that they stipulate normative feminine gender roles in which girls should neither overachieve nor underachieve. The capacity of feminine deviance (whether in the direction of being too good or too bad) to spark popular anxiety is central to Anzaldúa's formulation of the gendered Shadow-Beast.

It is from within forms of consciousness such as the Shadow-Beast that Anzaldúa works toward the commensuration of Indigeneity and Chicanidad, as well as the reconciliation of Chicano cultural nationalism and Chicana feminist insurgency.[53] What Du Bois' navigates as transcendence around and above the exclusionary veil, allowing him to access both the Black and White worlds, Anzaldúa approaches with a hopeful ambivalence: she is without country as a Mestiza, yet possesses all countries through the potential for feminine kinship; she is without race as a lesbian, yet identifies with all races as part of a queer diaspora; and she is without culture as a staunch critic of patriarchal beliefs and practices, yet fully cultural as a creative participant in the production of an emergent reality (1987:102–103).[54] Yesi (PR, Gen. 1.5, Gr. first year college), the aforementioned student who questioned antitracking at NNHS also grappled with the constraints and possibilities that Anzaldúa theorizes. Yesi explicitly rejected normative gender binaries, heternormative sexuality, and ethnoracial stereotypes about Puerto Ricans, Mexicans, and Latinxs in general. She also pursued institutional mobility in ways that both excited and concerned her family. While Yesi experienced alienation and institutional barriers in particular moments, which I describe in the subsequent chapters, she also continually imagined and enacted alternative racial, ethnic, class, gender, and sexual possibilities throughout her educational and broader life trajectory.

Whereas Du Bois and Anzaldúa imagine paradoxical exclusions as sites of social possibility, many theorizations of "problem" identities present perspectives that are decidedly less hopeful. Goffman explains that "the stigmatized individual . . . is told he is like anyone else and that he isn't" (Goffman 1963:124). For Goffman, stigma becomes an unresolved paradox that forces "those who represent the stigmatized . . . to present a coherent politics of identity, allowing them to be quick to see the 'inauthentic' aspects of other recommended programs but slow indeed to see that there may be no 'authentic' solution at all" (Goffman 1963:124).

Goffman distinguishes between two strategies that stigmatized individuals might employ in negotiating what he calls "spoiled identities." On the one hand, there is *passing*, a situation in which a stigmatized identity, whether "in effect or by intent," is rendered invisible. This involves a range of cases, from more or less "temporary" to "permanent" passing. On the other hand, there is *covering*, which involves efforts on the part of the stigmatized "to reduce tension, that is, to make it easier for himself and the others to withdraw covert attention from the stigma, and to sustain spontaneous involvement in the official content of the interaction" (Goffman 1963:102). In describing examples of covering, Goffman points to "'assimilative' techniques employed by members of minority ethnic groups; the intent behind devices such as a change in name and change in nose shape is not solely to pass, but also to restrict the way in which a known-about attribute obtrudes itself into the center of attention, for obtrusiveness increases the difficulty of maintaining easeful inattention regarding the stigma" (103). As Goffman suggests, each of these management techniques runs up against the irreconcilable fact of difference. From what perspectives can NNHS students "pass" as Young Latino Professionals? From what other vantage points are they merely covering a "known-about attribute" that "obtrudes itself into the center of attention" and "increases the difficulty of maintaining easeful inattention regarding the stigma"? Should recognitions of Young Latino Professionals be reanalyzed as modes of "passing" or "covering" Latinx identity?

These questions, as well as the modes of stigmatization with which they are associated, can be productively examined in relation to Bateson's theorization of the double-bind, which involves the presence of a set of competing demands on different logical planes and the inability on the part of the victim to "escape the field" in which these demands are imposed (Bateson 1972:207). The double-bind at NNHS is similar to that experienced by students of color in urban high schools throughout the nation. On one level, these young people are met with the explicit institutional demand that they become successful students. On another level, this demand is contradicted by (1) the refusal to provide comprehensive access to resources that would contribute to educational achievement and (2) the positioning of African American and Latinx ethnoracial identities as inherent barriers to school achievement. What is most interesting about the negotiation of this double-bind at NNHS is that the principal seeks to resolve it not only by providing access to resources but also by projecting the figure of the Young Latino Professional as an alternative possibility for ethnoracial, class, gender, and sexual identities.

While Goffman's and Bateson's analyses powerfully frame paradoxes of identity management on the intersubjective level, these local negotiations must be linked to a consideration of the broader political anxieties that shape them. In this vein, the everyday institutional management of Latinx identity can be contextualized as part of a larger national project of multiculturalism in which specific forms of diversity are positioned as constitutive of or incompatible with constructions of Americanness. As subjects within a governmental institution charged with participating in the (re)production of the nation, NNHS administrators are required to calibrate their understandings of problems and solutions within the school so as to reflect their alignment with this effort. Dr. Baez's project of transforming students into Young Latino Professionals is a complex example of this calibration and alignment. Students are encouraged to be Latinx, but in a careful way such that this identity does not impede them as they continue their education and seek employment. Is this a strategic effort that carefully eradicates negative stereotypes surrounding Latinxs without assimilating them, or is it an attempt to make an unassimilable people more tolerable for particular audiences? The deceptive form of inclusion mobilized by tolerance "crucially sustains a status of outsiderness for those it manages [through incorporation]; it even sustains them as a potential danger to the civic or political body" (Brown 2006:28). To the extent that the transformation from gangbanger or ho into Young Latino Professional is a tolerance project, the problem that necessitates this transformation is depoliticized and framed in terms of individual performances of identity.[55]

Tolerance is also linked to modes of multicultural recognition that are characteristic of liberal democratic societies such as the United States. Part of the difficulty with Dr. Baez's project is that it involves changing the ways in which people "see" her students—this becomes a problem of recognition. Because this recognition requires the channeling of diasporic identities such as "Mexican" and "Puerto Rican" toward an idealized version of a Latinx ethnoracial category, it involves much of the "cunning" that Povinelli (2002) attributes to such negotiations. In distinguishing between postcolonial and multicultural (liberal democratic) political contexts, Povinelli explains that whereas ". . . colonial domination worked by inspiring in colonized subjects a desire to identify with their colonizers . . . multicultural domination seems to work . . . by inspiring subaltern and minority subjects to identify with the impossible object of an authentic self-identity" (Povinelli 2002:6). Fanon's analysis of language and subaltern mimicry in the colonial Antilles theorizes issues related to Povinelli's claims regarding colonial domination: "[t]he negro of the Antilles will be proportionately whiter—that is, he will come closer to being a real human being—in direct ratio to his mastery of the French Language" (Fanon 1967:18).[56] In contrast, the multicultural contradictions of authenticity that Povinelli describes correspond to institutional pressures that require students to find ways to present complex images of their difference rather than mimicking Whiteness. They have to remain unassimilated without signaling national otherness too strongly; similarly, gangbangers and hoes are imagined as authentically Latinx from many in-group and out-group perspectives, but they are also criminalized, hypersexualized, and marginalized. Performances of Latinx identity that escape these modes of stigmatization might raise questions about whether one is betraying one's true self (i.e., selling out). Dr. Baez's category of Young Latino Professional seeks to resolve this double-bind by reframing the relationship between one's ethnoracial, class, gender, and sexual identities. In as much as the creation of this category reflects in-group anxieties about redefining difference, it is the semiotic complement to what some hoped would be the "Obama effect"—a single figure that is symbolically powerful enough to change the way in which an entire category (of African American personhood, particularly African American masculine personhood) is understood and experienced.[57] Dr. Baez attempts to achieve a similar goal via contrasting means: she aspires to create not a single transformative figure, but a critical mass of young professionals that might be symbolically potent enough to redefine Latinx as a social category.

There is a slippery negotiation here that speaks to the challenge of locating the problem that the extreme institutional makeover from gangbanger and ho to Young Latino Professional seeks to address. Does the problem live within the students or within the outside world's recognitions of them? This ambivalence is linked to the emergence of a politics of multiculturalism that includes the shift from biological racism to cultural racism and colorblind/postracial ideologies (Michaels 1992, di Leonardo 1994, Urciuoli 1994, Bonilla-Silva 2014[2003]). Whereas biological racism is rooted in claims about biological inferiority (e.g., the notion that particular groups are evolutionarily inferior), cultural racism redirects notions of inferiority to cultural practices (e.g., the notion that particular groups are characterized by a culture of poverty). This means that the seeming rejection of racism is actually a remapping of presumptions of inferiority. In fact, in the multicultural mode, ethnoracial difference appears to be acknowledged and embraced at the same time that it continues to be stigmatized. Thus, Latinx identity must always be recognized as part of the embrace of "diversity," but it is often figured as a cultural problem that still invokes the long-standing model of biological inferiority. Alternatively, colorblind/postracial ideologies purport to reflect and contribute to the eradication of inequality by disavowing racial difference altogether, effectively denying the existence of structural racial inequality. These shifting racial ideologies demonstrate an insidious range of ways in which the recognition of Latinx identity and the refusal to recognize Latinx identity both participate in the reproduction of disparity.

The simultaneous embrace and stigmatization of Latinx identity is no coincidence. It involves a negotiation with respect to the aforementioned relationship between what Chavez and Dávila call the "Latino threat narrative" (Chavez 2008) and "Latino spin" (Dávila 2008), respectively. These joint discourses allow seemingly opposing characterizations of Latinxs, such as "illegal, tax burden, overly sexual, patriotic, family-oriented, hard-working, and model consumer. . . . [to] circulate in concert" (Dávila 2008:1). On the one hand, Latinx youth are often stereotyped as *gangbangers* and *hoes*—this is the *threat*; on the other, there is some hope that they could become *young professionals* and join the rest of America in the largely imaginary middle class—this is the *spin*. NNHS tries to challenge the inverse ideological relationship between class status and marked ethnoraciality. While prevailing ideologies in the United States position upward socioeconomic mobility in opposition to ethnoracial difference, the category of Young Latino Professional attempts to allow students to escape socioeconomic marginalization without losing their Latinx identities.

Dr. Baez's philosophy, when considered in light of these various theorizations of identity, can be understood in relation to: (1) the different forms of double-consciousness and incommensurability experienced in relation to "problem" identities; (2) the competing societal demands that produce such identities; (3) the liberal democratic political impulses that structure problematic forms of multicultural recognition; and (4) the ways in which these complexities are manifested in relation to Latinx identities. These points suggest that the institutional project of creating Young Latino Professionals is fraught with the potential of contributing to the reproduction of stigmatization, but Du Bois and Anzaldúa remind us that alternative social categories present the possibility for transcendence; incommensurability should be viewed not only as a mode of domination but also as an incitement to imagine alternate worlds, the potential for radical transformation, and the contemporary existence of otherwise realities (Povinelli 2001, 2012).

While graduation ceremonies at NNHS presented a contemporary otherwise in that NNHS's Latinx students graduated at stunningly high rates in the context of CPS, the tedious orchestration of these public events felt like anything but radical transformation. In preparation for the 2009 commencement, graduating seniors spent more than six hours over the course of two school days rehearsing for the ceremony. They had to practice how to enter and exit, when to stand up and sit down, and the order in which they would receive their diplomas. Several teachers and administrators helped to oversee these rehearsals. At one point, Dr. Baez entered and chided the students for not paying attention. She reminded them, "We're NNHS, we're professional, we're perfect!" When the students finally sat down in the correct order, Ms. Jackson, the teacher overseeing the rehearsal, clapped proudly and congratulated them for their effort.

From many perspectives, the strict focus on behavior in this graduation rehearsal and in other examples throughout this chapter might be interpreted as part of the "new paternalism" that is widely heralded in urban school reform efforts across the nation (Whitman 2008). These highly prescriptive efforts seek to teach "students not just how to think but how to act according to what are commonly termed traditional, middle-class values" (Whitman 2008:3). Advocates of this "no excuses" approach suggest that it is "the single most effective way of closing the achievement gap" (Whitman 2008:5).[58] In practice, however, schools that allegedly demonstrate the benefits of this approach often have an application-based system of enrollment. This means that students must have the resources to successfully work through an application process before they can enter these schools. Such application processes favor a self-selecting group of students whose academic achievement cannot simply be attributed to a behavior-focused educational approach. Moreover, the charter schools that practice this approach often have high attrition rates. By pushing out students who are not performing as well as their peers academically (although they are often asked to leave under the guise of behavioral concerns), schools can increase their overall student achievement statistics. As a result, practices characterized by "new paternalism" have become powerful criteria by which to judge contemporary urban schools' merits.

Neighborhood schools such as NNHS cannot simply drop low-performing students. In fact, many students enroll in neighborhood schools after being dropped from "new paternalism"–style charter schools. Dr. Baez frequently lamented the pattern in which many of the community's highest achieving students attended the city's selective enrollment schools; she also pointed out that NNHS willingly enrolls students who were pushed out of other schools. Although NNHS is an open enrollment school, it is held to the same standards as schools populated by many high-achieving students who either met a set of admissions requirements or had the resources to complete an application process. As such, NNHS administrators must find ways to signal alignment with the educational project of "new paternalism" and the broader embrace of neoliberal educational concepts such as "accountability" and "school choice." The category of Young Latino Professional sought to explore the potential for low income, racially minoritized students to signal this alignment. More important, however, is the way in which the projection of this category contributed to NNHS's ability to accomplish the radical task of graduating nearly 100% of its students. Despite the normative signaling in which it engaged, the category of Young Latino Professional served transformative ends within NNHS. This is a school whose students were slated to be classified as underachievers and dropouts after having been placed at the bottom of the hierarchy of Chicago Public Schools. Thus, Dr. Baez's deployment of the complex category of Young Latino Professional was part of a counter-hegemonic effort to challenge an educational structure that systematically failed her students.

Contradictory ideas surrounding Latinx identities were reflected in the delicate bureaucratic path that Dr. Baez carved out at NNHS. Seemingly superficial issues such as uniforms played crucial roles in ensuring students' safety. Seemingly problematic figures such as police officers became supportive community members. Seemingly conservative discourses of teacher accountability contributed to unprecedented graduation rates. Seemingly damaging mainstreaming practices provided students with access to high-level courses from which they would typically be excluded. These are the contradictions that must be negotiated in order navigate the myriad challenges to urban educational achievement in the United States. It is within this context that the notion of a Young Latino Professional could emerge as a complex symbolic vehicle with the potential to contribute to striking degrees of student achievement. Of course the category of Young Latino Professional should not be understood as a magic bullet in itself. Instead, the positioning of this category in relation to a unique local set of pressures, limitations, and possibilities raises questions about other such effective strategies for the management of stigmatized identities and the creation of institutional commensurability across contexts. The following chapters show how students engaged with Dr. Baez's constructions of gangbanger, ho, and Young Latino Professional in order to conceptualize and enact forms of ethnoracial difference that were central to their everyday experiences.

2 "I HEARD THAT MEXICANS ARE HISPANIC AND PUERTO RICANS ARE LATINO"

ETHNORACIAL CONTORTIONS, DIASPORIC IMAGINARIES, AND INSTITUTIONAL TRAJECTORIES

In this chapter I transition from a focus on Dr. Baez's categories of "gangbanger," "ho," and "Young Latino Professional" to what *students* understood to be a primary axis of differentiation within the school: "Mexican" and "Puerto Rican." Students constructed and experienced these categories through diasporic imaginaries that remapped the boundaries of Puerto Rico and Mexico within Chicago. However, Mexican and Puerto Rican were not merely straightforward diasporic or ethnoracial identities that students brought with them to New Northwest High School (NNHS); instead, I demonstrate how the erasure of Mexican-Puerto Rican difference within the school's project of creating Young Latino Professionals paradoxically (re)produced rigid discourses of distinction between self-identified Puerto Rican and Mexican students. Ninth-grade students who had recently entered the school characteristically identified as Puerto Rican or Mexican, but they did not position these identities in rigid opposition to one another. Yet, over the course of students' educational trajectories at NNHS, stereotypes of Mexican-Puerto Rican difference became increasingly important and rigidly defined. Rigid discourses of Mexican-Puerto Rican difference must be analyzed in relation to these institutional trajectories and the broader political-economic dynamics that shape the construction and management of ethnoracial identities within NNHS. This semiotic approach to the analysis of differentiation avoids reifying categories such as Puerto Rican and Mexican as discrete or naturally occurring and links everyday invocations of such categories to specific institutional and interactional contexts.

Whereas previous research has emphasized differences between Puerto Ricans and Mexicans in Chicago and attributed these differences to the unequal politics of race and citizenship (De Genova and Ramos-Zayas 2003), I describe how students twisted and turned their modes of self-identification with respect to constructed tensions between ethnoracial authenticity and assimilation. Students' constructions of Puerto Rican and Mexican identities responded to the institutional management of difference within NNHS. I use the term "ethnoracial" to highlight the co-constitutive relationship between race and ethnicity, which simultaneously produces modes of sociopolitical inclusion and exclusion. I also introduce the notion of *ethnoracial contortions* to characterize the shifting ways in which students discursively constructed, identified with, and became oriented in relation to ethnoracial categories.[1] My use of *ethnoracial contortions* is intended to bring attention not only to how students "alternately challeng[ed] the very notion of simple racial difference and strategically utiliz[ed] race categories . . . in their discourse" (Pollock 2004b:48), but more so to the way in which external definitions and impositions of ethnoracial categories limited Latinx students' ability to engage in "race bending" (Pollock 2004b).[2] Drawing on this framework, I argue that becoming and unbecoming "Mexican," "Puerto Rican," "Hispanic," and "Latinx" must be reframed as multidimensional processes that demonstrate the linkages between diaspora, national (be)longing, and institutional experiences of difference.

Many scholars have productively called into question the presumptions that are frequently associated with the notion of Latinx panethnicity by highlighting the different ways in which Mexicans and Puerto Ricans in Chicago understand and inhabit social categories (Padilla 1985; Rúa 2001; De Genova and Ramos-Zayas 2003; Pérez 2003). In particular, these authors effectively demonstrate how analysts often presume on Latinx identity as a straightforward link between Latinx subgroups, such as Mexicans and Puerto Ricans. However, the conceptualization of intra-Latinx "difference" in some of these studies (namely Padilla 1985 and De Genova and Ramos-Zayas 2003) is characterized by two significant shortcomings (cf. Rodríguez-Muñiz 2010): (1) the positioning of race and citizenship as straightforward possessions through which some Latinx subgroups exercise privilege and power over others and (2) the framing of intimate engagement between Latinx subgroups primarily as short-term, strategic affiliations. This chapter provides an alternative to these approaches not only by analyzing the creation of Latinx panethnicity through institutional and ideological mechanisms that simultaneously erase and reinforce Puerto Rican–Mexican difference but also by demonstrating that such forces are met with competing constructions of Latinx panethnicity rooted in experiences such as long-standing local histories. Analyses that reduce Puerto Rican–Mexican relations to the unequal politics of race and citizenship (De Genova and Ramos-Zayas 2003) or to "manipulative device[s] for the pursuit of . . . interests in society" (Padilla 1985:165) do little justice to the lived experience of Latinidad throughout Chicago. In contrast, Aparicio approaches "interlatino sites" as "sites where two or more Latinas/os from various national origins encounter, construct, and transculturate each other" (2003:94). This chapter analyzes relationships between Mexicans and Puerto Ricans in Chicago as one such interlatino site. It turns out that, much like many close-knit families, Puerto Ricans and Mexicans in Chicago frequently understand, embrace, and even deride their perceived differences all the while making their lives in intimate interrelation with one another. Thus, discourses of Puerto Rican–Mexican difference must be analyzed in relation to the histories, institutions, and shared experiences through which they are produced.

A Linked Contortion, Imaginary, and Trajectory

Yesi (PR, Gen. 1.5, Gr. 12/first year college), a member of the first graduating class of NNHS in 2008, sat down with me during the summers before and after her first year at a highly selective liberal arts college.[3] I met Yesi in the summer of 2007 (following her junior year at NNHS), when she took a class that I taught at a local university in an academic enrichment and college preparation program for high-achieving CPS students. When I asked the students in this class to introduce themselves and to share the names of the high schools they attended, I was surprised and excited to discover that I would be teaching a student from NNHS, where I was planning to begin my fieldwork just a few months later. Many of the activities in this class required students to reflect on their high school experiences, so this would be a preliminary opportunity for me to learn about NNHS from a student's perspective. In one of our first class discussions, which focused on stereotypes, Yesi explained that Mexican and Puerto Rican students in her school constantly stereotype one another, invoking ideas about one another's bodies, music, dance, food, speech, moral character, and citizenship status. She said that these stereotypes are "huge" at NNHS and that they are a constant focus of attention among students.

Yesi's academic performance in my class that summer was outstanding. She took a lead role in class discussions and wrote exceptional papers. At the end of the summer, we held a "culminating event" that allowed students to showcase what they learned in the program to an audience of their families, program staff, fellow students, and friends. Before the event started, Yesi introduced me to her mother and two of her younger siblings. I ended up sitting next to her family during the event and discussing Yesi's success with her mother. As her 12-year-old

brother played with my new iPhone and taught me how to use several of its features, Yesi's mother explained how grateful she and her husband were for their
daughter's opportunity to participate in the program and how proud they were
of the example that Yesi—their oldest child—was setting for her younger siblings. As Yesi slowly but surely became one of the stars of the show, her mother—
certainly not a stage mom—displayed a quiet pride and asked me to save her a
copy of the pictures I was taking throughout the event.

Yesi graduated third in her class at NNHS. In one of my interviews with her,
I asked why she ended up at NNHS, a neighborhood high school with open enrollment, instead of one of Chicago's selective enrollment high schools; I assumed
that she had a choice among many options. She explained to me that she experienced some confusion when, in the eighth grade, the time came to fill out her
applications for selective enrollment schools. A few days before Yesi completed
the application, her mother initiated a conversation about self-presentation. She
asked Yesi a series of questions about her name, address, gender, race/ethnicity,
interests, and goals, simulating applications and interviews she might encounter
in school or when searching for a job. In response to the question about race and
ethnicity, Yesi wondered aloud about the extent to which she should foreground
her Puerto Ricanness when identifying herself. Instead of "Puerto Rican," she suggested "Hispanic" as a possible identifier. Her mother told her that she should
never identify herself as Hispanic, since Hispanic references "Spic," a derogatory
term for Latinxs. She told Yesi that she should identify strongly as a "Latina,"
"Puerto Rican," and as "someone from a Caribbean island"; Yesi came to Chicago
from Puerto Rico when she was 4. She took her mother's words to heart and decided that she would embrace "Latina," "Puerto Rican," and "island" racial and
ethnic identities. When it came time for Yesi to fill out the application for selective enrollment high schools, she was unsure of how to answer the question about
"Ethnic Background." Like many such instruments, the only options it provided
were: "White, Non-Hispanic," "African American," "Native American/Alaskan,"
"Asian/Pacific Islander," and "Hispanic." While "Hispanic" might have seemed
like the obvious choice for Yesi, her mother made it clear that she should not
identify with this category. Neither "Latina" nor "Puerto Rican" was provided as
an option, but Yesi remembered her mother's statement about the importance of
her "island" identity, so she decided to identify as "Asian/Pacific Islander." She was
not admitted to any of the selective enrollment schools, all of which were (and
are) in desperate need of more Latinx students to reflect the district's overall demographics.[4] This is just one—albeit very peculiar—example of a linkage between
an ethnoracial contortion (from Puerto Rican to Hispanic to Latina to Asian/
Pacific Islander, based on a conflict between home and school-based definitions
of these categories), a diasporic imaginary (as a Puerto Rican "islander"), and an

institutional trajectory (that excluded Yesi from selective enrollment schools). Each of these concepts is central to understanding the construction and experience of Puerto Rican, Mexican, and Latinx identities within NNHS.

Constructing Mexican and Puerto Rican Difference

Each school year at NNHS was bookended by parades and carnivals that celebrated Mexican and Puerto Rican identities. September 16 officially marked Mexican independence, and young people in many Northwest and South Side Chicago neighborhoods could be seen waving Mexican flags on street corners and seeking supportive "honks" from passing cars throughout the month. The Puerto Rican complement to these practices began in early May, when vendors lined the edges of Humboldt Park with Puerto Rican paraphernalia of all kinds in preparation for the annual Puerto Rican festival and parade in June. A second annual Puerto Rican festival, "Bandera a Bandera" (flag to flag), was held during the first weekend of September just a few blocks from the school. The name of this festival referred to the massive steel Puerto Rican flags that flanked Division Street between Western and California Avenues (Figure 2.1).

By no means were students' celebrations of Mexican and Puerto Rican identity limited to these scheduled ritual events. Inside NNHS, the respective flags could be seen on headbands, necklaces, bracelets, notebooks, gym towels, book bags, and artwork that hung on classroom walls (Figure 2.2); outside of school, where an entirely different uniform policy took hold, flags adorned sneakers ("gym shoes" in the Chicago idiom), jerseys, t-shirts, shorts, jeans, dresses, cars (e.g., bumpers, rear windows, rearview mirrors, seat covers), houses, apartment windows, storefronts, bicycles, hats, beach towels, key chains, and even haircuts (the flag can be shaved into the back or sides of one's head; this could be seen most frequently around the time of the Puerto Rican parade) (Figure 2.3).

The knowledge of one another's Puerto Rican and/or Mexican identities was often a requirement for everyday interactions. Students either presupposed one another's ethnoracial identities or explicitly inquired about them at the outset of interactions. When I asked students and teachers for a description of the different social groups or cliques within the school, almost all respondents reported that the school was heavily segregated between Mexicans and Puerto Ricans. They claimed that Puerto Rican and Mexican students separated themselves from one another in countless ways: in the lunchroom, in classrooms, in the sports they played, in the food they ate, in the music they liked, etc. Many non-Latinx teachers reported that this situation was completely unanticipated; they assumed that everyone was simply Hispanic. Ms. Ginsberg, a popular young

FIGURE 2.1: Monument to the Puerto Rican flag. The flag in this picture is located on Division Street near California Avenue in Chicago's Humboldt Park community. An identical flag is located a few blocks away, near Western Avenue. The two steel flag monuments flank a strip of Division Street called "Paseo Boricua" (Puerto Rican promenade), which is filled with predominantly Puerto Rican community organizations, businesses, and residences. These flags are the subject of a documentary film, *Flags of Steel*, that tracks the process by which they were created, erected, and dedicated on January 8, 1995 (Three Kings Day). The City of Chicago approved the construction of the flags following controversy surrounding the creation of a statue of Puerto Rican nationalist Pedro Albizu Campos in the early 1990s. Community activists initiated a campaign to place the "larger-than-life" statue in Humboldt Park, but the Chicago Park District rejected the proposal because the statue was allegedly unsuitable for withstanding winter weather (Ramos-Zayas 2003). After activists raised $35,000 and created a new, bronzed statue that would meet the Chicago Park District's weather requirements, it was announced that the statue could not be placed in the park because Albizu Campos was an "anti-American terrorist" (Ramos-Zayas 2003). As a consolation, community activists were invited to pursue alternate sculptural projects, which resulted in the creation to the giant steel Puerto Rican flags. Members of the Puerto Rican Cultural Center and other community organizers who participated in the construction of the flags intended to make a statement about the displacement of Puerto Ricans through processes of gentrification since their initial migration to Chicago. NNHS students made frequent reference to the flags. In particular, they circulated the rumor started by progentrification condominium developers that the flags were going to be taken down and moved to New York City. In fact, there are no such plans to move the flags. They serve as striking anchors that contribute to the nationalist pride of Puerto Ricans born in Chicago and elsewhere. They also buttress claims that the area between the flags is "un pedacito de patria" (a little piece of the homeland), which I will describe in detail later in this chapter. Photo by David Flores.

FIGURE 2.2: Student artwork juxtaposing Puerto Rican and Mexican flags. This artwork was displayed in a freshman classroom at NNHS. On the *left*, the Puerto Rican flag consists of a five-pointed white star contained within a blue triangle that points toward five alternating red and white stripes. Puerto Rican members of the Cuban Revolutionary Party created this flag, which inverts the red and blue colors of the Cuban national flag after which it was modeled. The flag became a symbol of Puerto Rican independence and was outlawed from the beginning of US colonial rule in 1898 until the United States officially designated Puerto Rico's commonwealth status in 1952. Between 1898 and 1952, people were arrested for displaying the flag on the island because of its association with anti-American sentiment. To this day there are ongoing debates surrounding regulations for the public display of the US and Puerto Rican flags in Puerto Rico. Meanwhile, in Chicago, the display of the Puerto Rican flag was once associated with Puerto Rican "terrorist" acts against the United States. The blue in the flag in this drawing is darker than the blue in the steel flag displayed in Figure 2.1. The 1895 Puerto Rican flag used a light blue color that symbolized the sky over the island of Puerto Rico. In 1952, the color was changed to match the blue of the US flag. For this reason, flags with the light blue color are often seen as symbols of proindependence sentiment. On the *right*, the Mexican flag consists of green, white, and red vertical stripes. Inside the white stripe there is an image of an eagle sitting atop a cactus with a rattlesnake in its mouth and talons. This image comes from an Aztec legend in which the god of war, Huitzilopochtli, said that the capital city of Tenochtitlan would be built where an eagle on a prickly pear cactus holding a serpent was found. The flag has been in use since Mexico gained independence from Spain in 1821, but the current version was adopted in 1968. The green, white, and red colors have been valorized in various ways throughout the flag's history. Initially, these colors represented independence (green), Catholicism (white), and the union of Americans and Europeans (red). During the presidency of Benito Juárez (1858–1872), a Zapotec indigenous man from Oaxaca who sought to secularize the Mexican state, the colors came to stand for hope (green), unity (white), and the blood of nation's heroes (red). Photo by author.

FIGURE 2.3: Puerto Rican and Mexican flags juxtaposed in public displays. Photo by author.

White teacher, explained that she found the distinction between the school's Puerto Rican and Mexican students to be one of the most striking things about the school. Mr. Thomas, another popular young White teacher, claimed that the difference between Puerto Ricans and Mexicans is negligible and that he could not distinguish between them. He said that he tries not to think or see in terms of race and that he just wants "to get over the whole race thing."[5] Meanwhile, Ms. Jackson, the school's widely embraced librarian and one of the few African American employees, said that she never would have thought that there was a "big difference" between Mexicans and Puerto Ricans before she started working at NNHS. Ms. Jackson likened the tensions surrounding Puerto Ricans and Mexicans to those between "house slaves" and "field slaves." In this sense, as citizens by birth, Puerto Ricans possess some privileges (akin to house slaves) that non–US born Mexicans (akin to field slaves) do not. But ultimately, in Jackson's view, Puerto Ricans and Mexicans occupied a shared position as marginalized groups. These teachers were surprised to learn not only that the categories of Puerto Rican and Mexican are sometimes distinct from one another but also that there is a seemingly infinite world of cultural knowledge associated with these distinctions. Similarly, the small percentage of

African American students at NNHS often talked about the difficulty of learning to distinguish between Puerto Ricans and Mexicans, but certainly felt compelled to do so. When I asked an African American senior, Tasha, to name the different groups of students in the school, she explained:

> Hispanics rule out everything, it's not even 10% of others. I could probably count about 35 Black people on my hand that make up all the Black people in the school and what's that, like 10%? That's not a lot. And everyone else is Hispanic, I mean Mexican and Puerto Rican. . . . I would never say that they're the same because they would give me a third degree burn for saying that. If I call you Puerto Rican and you Mexican or if I call you Mexican and you Guatemalan . . . I ain't got time, I just think they all the same. Maybe not Puerto Ricans and Mexicans, I guess, but Guatemalans and all them itty bitty countries, they're like, "But I'm Guatemalan!" and I'm like, "Ok, well you still from Mexico, you still Hispanic!" . . . But anyway these Mexicans and Puerto Ricans been teaching me how to tell them apart.

Tasha initially uses the panethnic category "Hispanic" to designate the school's majority population, but then she begins to describe the politics of recognizing subgroups contained within this umbrella category. She alternates between acknowledging differences among Hispanic subgroups and saying that they are the same. As a graduating senior who attended high school in a predominantly panethnic Latinx setting for four years, Tasha was confident that she had learned how to distinguish between Puerto Ricans and Mexicans. As for Central Americans and other Latinxs, Tasha suggested that people from these countries are basically just Mexican. Another African American student, Sierra, graduated in 2008, attended the University of Illinois at Chicago, and returned to NNHS to work in the library with Ms. Jackson. Like Tasha, she alternated between grouping Mexicans and Puerto Ricans together as Hispanics and drawing clear lines of distinction between them:

> The best part about this school would be the population because it's a Hispanic school and they're really funny, but it's also lonely because I was the only Black person in a lot of my classes. I felt like sometimes they was being bogus because they would sit in their own little groups and be talking Spanish and don't nobody know what they're talking about . . . but the main groups of students in this school is the Mexicans and the Puerto Ricans. That's one big divide. Like I used to mistakenly call a Mexican a Puerto Rican and they would get mad like I'm supposed to know the

difference. I thought they was just all Hispanic, but they got on me the whole time I was going here about mistaking the two. And they all look the same to me! That's just like a Chinese person coming up to you and you call them Chinese, and they Vietnamese and they get mad, like how am I supposed to know what's the difference between ya'll? Ya'll all look alike, but they, they be tripping [getting mad for no reason] . . . ya'll all do like alike, I'm sorry. I don't know the difference between Mexicans and Puerto Ricans, other than what they told me.

Sierra said she enjoyed attending a "Hispanic" school because Hispanics—as a group—are "really funny." She also felt alienated at times because she was often the only African American student in her classes. Attending a panethnic Latinx school meant learning the distinctions between Mexicans and Puerto Ricans, which she said was a "big divide." For Sierra, "Hispanic" is a racialized panethnic category that is similar to "Asian." From her perspective, the difference between Mexicans and Puerto Ricans is analogous to the difference between Chinese and Vietnamese; essentially, Hispanics, like Asians, are stereotyped as looking alike. Still, Sierra learned that for Mexican and Puerto Rican students, it was crucial to be able to recognize their differences. Importantly, Sierra alternates between using the umbrella category "Hispanic" and emphasizing differences between Latinx subgroups. While Sierra claimed to be unable to distinguish between Mexicans and Puerto Ricans, on several occasions I observed her playfully misidentifying her Mexican friends as Puerto Rican, and vice versa, which highlights the performative nature of distinctions between Mexicans and Puerto Ricans. Importantly, Sierra's perspective is not simply that of a generic non-Latinx person; instead, the stereotypes she invokes are characteristic of many West Side Chicago African Americans' intimate encounters with intra-Latinx similarities and differences.

Two lines of questioning arise from this discussion of recognitions of Mexican-Puerto Rican difference. First, what does it mean to be Mexican, Puerto Rican, Hispanic, and Latinx in the context of Chicago? How could students identify so strongly with these identities if they were born and raised primarily within the US mainland, or if they had never even visited Mexico or Puerto Rico? And second, what is the nature of Mexican-Puerto Rican difference in Chicago? If Mexican-Puerto Rican rifts are so strongly pronounced, then how useful is "Latinx" as an ethnoracial umbrella category? I will demonstrate that these questions must be engaged by situating individually voiced discourses surrounding Mexican-Puerto Rican difference within everyday interactions among Mexicans and Puerto Ricans. I will also show how contemporary slippages between race and ethnicity in ideas about Latinx identity stem not simply from the recent emergence of this category but also from long-standing negotiations involving the institutionalization of a panethnic Hispanic category. Finally, my analysis will make it clear that race and ethnicity can be productively understood not simply as related but also as co-constitutive categories. The saturation of NNHS with signs of Puerto Rican–Mexican difference reflects the complex way in which the slippery distinction between race and ethnicity "can be used to characterize, categorize, organize, and contrast virtually any kind of social fact: spaces, institutions, bodies, groups, activities, interactions, relations" (Gal 2002:81). In this sense, the recursive quality of Puerto Rican–Mexican difference—the nested relations that make Puerto Ricans more and less Mexican, and vice versa—is characteristic of the process of social category-making more broadly.

¿De qué parte? (From what part?)

Students' constructions of Mexicanness and Puerto Ricanness were not limited to ideas about Chicago or the United States more broadly. While most students were born and/or raised in Chicago, many of them had either lived in Puerto Rico or Mexico or had visited several times throughout their lives. However, Mexican and Puerto Rican identities were not necessarily restricted to students who had immediate ties to these nations, such as family members residing in Mexico or Puerto Rico or family-owned property there. In fact, many Mexican and Puerto Rican students who had either never been to Mexico or Puerto Rico or who had not visited in many years were not recognized as less Mexican or Puerto Rican than anyone else. After learning of one's Mexican or Puerto Rican identity, students would often ask, "¿De qué parte?" (From what part?). One's response to this question was not interpreted literally as a statement of birthplace, but rather of ancestry. Students who were born and raised in Chicago, including those who had never been to Mexico or Puerto Rico, responded to this question by identifying particular Mexican or Puerto Rican locales. The most common Mexican states students identified were Michoacán, Jalisco, Guerrero, and Guanajuato; Puerto Ricans named cities such as Ponce, Bayamon, and San Sebastian.[6]

It is not by chance that students could be born in Chicago and still be "from" Mexico or Puerto Rico. Various parts of Chicago, including areas around NNHS, are formally and informally identified as "Little Puerto Rico" or "Little Mexico." "Paseo Boricua," the stretch of city blocks between the steel Puerto Rican flags described and pictured in Figure 2.1, is popularly referred to as "un pedacito de patria," or "a little piece of the homeland."[7] For many residents and visitors, including visitors from Puerto Rico, Paseo Boricua *is part of Puerto Rico*. From these perspectives, Puerto Rican restaurants, bakeries, music shops, hardware stores, schools, architecture, murals, parades, music, folklore, and festivals resituate

Humboldt Park within the boundaries of Puerto Rico.[8] Similar sorts of formal designations exist in Mexican neighborhoods such as La Villita/Little Village, which has its own monument (Figure 2.4), a gateway arch that states "Bienvenidos a Little Village" ("Welcome to Little Village"), on the South Side of Chicago.[9] Puerto Rican and Mexican activists who participated in the naming of these community areas sought to counter negative images of and ideas about Puerto Ricans and Mexicans that circulated in popular cultural representations, news media, and the everyday conversations of city residents.[10] These activists also attempted to encourage young Puerto Ricans and Mexicans, who might otherwise be ashamed of their identities, to take pride in their respective histories. While diaspora is often analyzed as a phenomenon that is chiefly characterized by territorial displacement, I seek to highlight here the ways that displacement is called into question when social actors such as NNHS students reconstruct Chicago as *part of* Puerto Rico and Mexico, respectively. The previously described ritual events and symbols, in conjunction with extreme forms of neighborhood segregation, inform Chicago Puerto Ricans' and Mexicans' remapping of national borders. In many ways, by reframing spatial segregation, these forms of reterritorialization counteract forces of internal colonialism.[11] That is, decades of community

FIGURE 2.4: Little Village gateway arch on 26th Street in Chicago during Mexican Independence Day Celebration on September 15. Photo by David Flores.

struggle have led to the emergence of diasporic imaginaries through which Chicago-based Puerto Ricans and Mexicans respond to spatial, racial, and class exclusion.[12] By laying claim to parts of the city in which they dwell en masse, generations of Puerto Ricans and Mexicans valorize their national identities and the Chicago-based territories to which they are understood to correspond (Figures 2.5 and 2.6). Such subaltern diasporic imaginaries, which Flores (2009) formulates as "diaspora from below," demonstrate Latinxs' engagement with competing ideas about their identities and unsettle straightforward narratives of assimilation and transnationalism that presume upon discrete borders between nations and national identities.

This diasporic redefinition, or reterritorialization (Appadurai 1996), in which parts of Chicago become linked to Mexico and Puerto Rico, should not overshadow students' affiliation with Mexico and Puerto Rico "proper." Many students (again, even those who had never been to Mexico or Puerto Rico) understood themselves to be displaced from part of their "homeland." They discussed their plans to return to Mexico or Puerto Rico, with Puerto Rican students in particular describing their desire to live on the island in the future. For an assignment that required ninth-grade students to create "mandalas," which were essentially identity collages that characterized the things they valued most, a third-generation Puerto Rican student who was born in Chicago wrote, "My goal is to bring honor to my family and fight for my country." These words appeared next to the image of a large Puerto Rican flag. Puerto Rican and Mexican flags were also prominent in many other students' mandalas. While Mexican students were less likely to romanticize the idea of "Mexico" (based on personal and familial experiences, as well as popular representations of Mexico as underdeveloped and dangerous), they were just as likely to identify Mexico as their homeland. Such diasporic imaginaries demonstrate students' engagement with competing ideas about their identities. In a complex way, their shared experiences of exclusion in the US context, in conjunction with representations of Latinx panethnicity, informed their identification not only with Mexico or Puerto Rico, respectively, but also with one another.

In other instances, when Mexican students were absent from school and teachers inquired as to their whereabouts, friends joked that they had been deported back to Mexico. While making light of deportation might seem cruel, in many ways it reflects these teenagers' efforts to grapple with everyday forms of marginalization that characterize their communities. There were even situations in which particular areas of the classroom became playfully figured as transnational spaces. In one ninth-grade classroom, a group of Mexican students sat together each day. One day in this classroom a Puerto Rican student (Gen. 2, Gr. 9) who was not part of this group announced that he needed to borrow a pencil from someone; when

FIGURE 2.5: Paseo Boricua flag. In 2009, John Vergara, a Puerto Rican artist born and raised in Humboldt Park, created a mural titled "79th" on the corner of Division Street and Campbell Avenue. The title references the 78 municipalities of the island of Puerto Rico and claims Paseo Boricua/Humboldt Park as the 79th. In 2011, the Coat of Arms mural was turned into an official Municipal Flag of Puerto Rico. Paseo Boricua/ Humboldt Park is the only location outside the Commonwealth of Puerto Rico that has been granted permission to display such a flag. Vergara explains the symbolism of the different components of the flag in the following way: "The blue color background represents the efforts of the community to build tolerance and understanding between people of all socio-economic and cultural backgrounds so that together we may develop a truly enriched and prosperous community. The white color represents our desire that peace and unity reign among all the members of this dynamic community regardless of gender, ethnicity, class, sexuality and religion. The palm trees represent the contribution people of the Caribbean have made and continue to make to the rich diversity in our community. The Puerto Rican flag that drapes the City of Chicago marks a geographic and symbolic space as the heart of the city's Puerto Rican community. The shield represents the Spanish Fort in Viejo San Juan, El Morro, and the Spanish legacy, which together with the West African and Taino cultures from the roots of modern day Puerto Rican identity and culture. The Taino Indians and African woman point toward their mutual destination and migration towards the Chicago skyline back-dropped against the historic Humboldt Park boathouse, a familiar landmark in our community" (http://ourhumboldtpark.com/ 2011/03/01/paseo-boricua/ [accessed June 18, 2014]). This description demonstrates how a Chicago-based diasporic imaginary of Puerto Ricanness serves as a platform from which to contest experiences of racial, spatial, and class marginalization. Photo by author.

FIGURE 2.6: Representations of diasporic imaginaries that reterritorialize Chicago as part of Mexico and Puerto Rico, and vice versa. The *top left* image is a Nike Air Force One sneaker with the Mexican flag and the Chicago skyline. The *top right* image is a tattoo featuring the Paseo Boricua steel flag, the Chicago skyline, the phrase "City of Wind" (the tattoo artist used Spanish syntax to remix Chicago's well-known nickname, "The Windy City"), and in smaller print beneath the skyline the phrase, "Yo soy de aquí" (I am from here). The *bottom left* image is an advertisement created by the Little Village Chamber of Commerce and displayed on a Chicago Transportation Authority train. The advertisement contains pictures of several Mexican restaurants in Little Village, as well as the phrases "THE HOME OF AUTHENTIC MEXICAN CUISINE," "Dine in Little Village," and "Tú México, Tú Chicago" ("Your Mexico, Your Chicago," with a nonstandardized use of accent marks on the possessive "Tú"). The *bottom right* image is a tattoo in the shape of the State of Illinois, with the Mexican flag, and the phrase "Lil Village," a vernacular reference to the Little Village neighborhood. These images demonstrate diasporic imaginaries through which the boundaries of Chicago, Mexico, and Puerto Rico are reimagined and imbricated. Photos by David Flores.

a Mexican student (Gen. 2, Gr. 9) in the aforementioned group offered to let him borrow one, he joked with her that he would have to cross the border to get to her. The Mexican student playfully turned the table by demanding that the Puerto Rican student show his green card in order to approach his desk.[13] Similarly, a group of 12th-grade Puerto Rican students who ate lunch together referred to their table as "Division and Cali." This phrase is a reference to the Humboldt Park intersection between Division Street and California Avenue where one of the steel Puerto Rican flags pictured in Figure 2.1 can be found. In many ways, the phrase "Division and Cali" is emblematic of Puerto Rican identity. Talk of national borders, papers, and green cards was common in classroom interactions and showed how students, the majority of whom were born in Chicago, understood one another in relation to broader conceptions of Mexicanness and Puerto Ricanness (I will explicitly outline models of Mexican and Puerto Rican personhood in Chapter 3). Thus, reterritorialization takes place on multiple scales.

Importantly, these diasporic imaginaries collapse the heterogeneity internal to the categories of Mexican and Puerto Rican. In contexts that are either predominantly Mexican or Puerto Rican, labels that distinguish between types of Mexicans or types of Puerto Ricans are much more prevalent. In predominantly Puerto Rican contexts, this conventionally takes the form of distinctions between US mainland–based Puerto Ricanness and island-based Puerto Ricanness. In the mainland context, Puerto Ricans who are associated with the island are often referred to as "jíbaros." The folkloric image of the jíbaro is most often figured as a creolized Spanish-dominant male with light skin from the Puerto Rican countryside.[14] In predominantly Puerto Rican mainland contexts, however, jíbaro/a/x can be used to characterize any Puerto Rican (regardless of gender or skin tone) whose language use and other cultural practices (e.g., food, clothing) are stereotypically associated with the island more so than the US mainland.

Similar distinctions between individuals are often made in predominantly Mexican contexts. In segregated Mexican communities on the South Side of Chicago, categories such as "brazer" and "paisa" are used to measure one's position with respect to the distinction between authentic Mexicanness and assimilated Americanness. Brazer was stereotypically associated with a recently arrived Mexican who unsuccessfully attempted to be "cool" by participating in US-based Mexican practices. They might do so by wearing the wrong brand of clothes (e.g., "uncool" brands such as South Pole and Paco, which were sold in discount stores vs. "cool" brands such as "Ecko" and "Sean John," which were sold in more expensive stores). A brazer might also wear the right clothes in the wrong way. Rubber bands worn around the bottom of one's jeans could be "cool" if worn properly, but a brazer might pull the rubber band up too high or leave too much slack in the jeans under the rubber band. "Paisa" was stereotypically associated with Mexicans who were socialized within the United States or Mexico and strongly displayed affiliation with Mexico through styles of dress (such as "Western wear," consisting of cowboy boots and Wrangler jeans) and musical tastes (i.e., traditional Mexican music, such as rancheras, norteñas, and banda). Brazers and paisas were both "uncool" from the perspective of young people who asserted "cool" US-based Mexican identities on the South Side of Chicago. Mendoza-Denton analyzes similar intra-Mexican and intra-Latina youth distinctions between Americanized Norteña (northern) girls and Mexican or Latin American–oriented Sureña (southern) girls in Northern California, which she terms "hemispheric localism" (2008:87). Categorical distinctions such as norte/sur and brazer/paisa/Mexican American are certainly important in other parts of the United States and even in other parts of Chicago, but they were not prevalent in the Mexican-Puerto Rican context of NNHS.

Racialization, Ethnicization, and Competing Projections of Latinidad

While students frequently highlighted their Mexican and Puerto Rican particularity, NNHS administrators simultaneously sought to validate *and* transform students' Latinx identities through the aforementioned intraracial and intersectional project of socioeconomic uplift. To make sense of the ethnoracial contortions surrounding Latinx identity in NNHS, this section presents an overview of processes of racialization and ethnicization in the United States. The goal is to understand the categorical creation of a racialized, panethnic Latinx category with respect to historical shifts involving ethnic assimilation and racial exclusion. How were students' conceptions of Puerto Ricanness and Mexicanness, and Dr. Baez's notion of Young Latino Professionals, linked to the relationship between racial and ethnic categories more broadly?

Many of the problems associated with the ethnographic documentation of racialization involve difficulty with the articulation of identity in the face of its theorization as a social construct. That is, if identity is socially constructed, then are we unable to locate and engage it analytically without merely reifying it? In fact, a consideration of ethnicity as a closely linked social category is a crucial way to think through the production of racial difference.[15] Urciuoli explains that, "race and ethnicity are both about belonging to the nation, but belonging in different ways" (Urciuoli 1996:15). Ethnicity emerges as a category of difference that, while marked and susceptible to stigmatization, involves a comparatively legitimate position in relation to the nation-state.[16] Ethnicization thus describes a process in which groups are portrayed as contributors to the nation. Racialization, on the other hand, is a problematic process in which groups are figured as *impossibly* different and unassimilable.[17] It is important to note here that each of these processes plays closely on ideas about the potential for class mobility and the imagination of the conventional American. Thus, the effort to unpack the relationship between ethnicization and racialization becomes a key way to understand the management of political and economic power within the nation-state. In Urciuoli's account, race and ethnicity are linked to each other in the way they differentially cast images of alterity either as inherently problematic or as a welcomed contribution. This said, she also claims that they work in concert with one another, insofar as "ethnicizing and racializing are both about markedness in ways that reaffirm the terms that define the unmarked American" (Urciuoli 1996:38). NNHS students discussed Americanness in their everyday interactions. For example, Mr. Ford, a popular White teacher beloved by students, faculty, and administration, made a jocular reference to the title of a popular television show when he told a classroom full of seniors who had not completed an assignment that they "should be called America's biggest losers!"[18] A Mexican girl (Gen. 3, Gr. 12) retorted, "But we're not even American!" This kind of comment reflects Latinx students' awareness that they were positioned as somehow un-American.[19] In a playful classroom exchange between two boys, an African American senior told a Mexican junior (Mex, Gen. 2, Gr. 11), "Shut up, nigga!" When the Mexican boy replied, "I'm not Black," the African American boy reframed his command, "Well, Mexican, Puerto Rican, whatever you are."[20] These interactions succinctly demonstrate conceptions of Latinx students' racialized panethnic status within NNHS.[21]

Urciuoli's analysis provides a useful framework for considering the contemporary creation of Latinx identity in relation to processes of ethnicization and racialization. In particular, it is important to examine how competing forces position Latinx identities in different racialized and ethnicized ways. As students oriented themselves to the school's project of transforming (recognitions of) them into Young Latino Professionals, they negotiated the production of Latinx identities in relation to disparate institutional frameworks, including public schools and other such governmental institutions, as well as community-oriented social networks. To be sure, the school is a prime site for a governmental project of population management and subject-making. From this perspective, Latinx identity is generally equated with "Hispanic," a category that is alternately represented as ethnic or racial in official demographic terms, yet is certainly racially marked. The separate 2010 US Census questions regarding race and "Hispanic, Latino, and Spanish" origin (Figure 2.7) reflect the bureau's strategic effort to make "the notion of Hispanic panethnicity commensurate with, though not officially equal to, race" (Mora 2014:118).[22] In contrast to Yesi's curious ethnoracial identification as described at the beginning of this chapter, a governmental notion of Hispanic identity emerged in my interviews and interactions with NNHS students. Almost all students claimed that Mexicans and Puerto Ricans are different races.

> → **NOTE: Please answer BOTH Question 8 about Hispanic origin and Question 9 about race. For this census, Hispanic origins are not races.**
>
> **8. Is Person 1 of Hispanic, Latino, or Spanish origin?**
> ☐ No, not of Hispanic, Latino, or Spanish origin
> ☐ Yes, Mexican, Mexican Am., Chicano
> ☐ Yes, Puerto Rican
> ☐ Yes, Cuban
> ☐ Yes, another Hispanic, Latino, or Spanish origin — *Print origin, for example, Argentinean, Colombian, Dominican, Nicaraguan, Salvadoran, Spaniard, and so on.* ↗
>
> [ ]
>
> **9. What is Person 1's race?** *Mark* ☒ *one or more boxes.*
> ☐ White
> ☐ Black, African Am., or Negro
> ☐ American Indian or Alaska Native — *Print name of enrolled or principal tribe.* ↗
>
> [ ]
>
> ☐ Asian Indian ☐ Japanese ☐ Native Hawaiian
> ☐ Chinese ☐ Korean ☐ Guamanian or Chamorro
> ☐ Filipino ☐ Vietnamese ☐ Samoan
> ☐ Other Asian — *Print race, for example, Hmong, Laotian, Thai, Pakistani, Cambodian, and so on.* ↗   ☐ Other Pacific Islander — *Print race, for example, Fijian, Tongan, and so on.* ↗
>
> [ ]
>
> ☐ Some other race — *Print race.* ↗
>
> [ ]

FIGURE 2.7: 2010 US Census questions on race and Hispanic, Latino, or Spanish origin. The differences from the year 2000 in the "Hispanic, Latino, Spanish origin" question are the word order and use of commas instead of forward slashes in the question (in 2000 it was "Spanish/Hispanic/Latino" and in 2010 it was "Hispanic, Latino, or Spanish"), the listing of additional examples of "Hispanic, Latino, or Spanish origin" (i.e., "Argentinean, Colombian, Dominican, Nicaraguan, Salvadoran, Spaniard, and so on."), and, most importantly, the following instruction: "NOTE: Please answer BOTH Question 8 about Hispanic origin and Question 9 about race. For this census, Hispanic origins are not races." This note was intended to clear up previous confusion about whether answering one question exempted one from answering the other. However, this distinction between "Hispanic origins" and "races" in the Census form is belied by reporting of Census statistics using categories such as "White, non-Hispanic," which essentially positions Hispanic as a racial category. Of the approximately 50.5 million 2010 Census respondents who identified as people "of Hispanic, Latino, or Spanish origin," more than one-third identified as "Some other race" (https://www.census.gov/content/dam/Census/library/working-papers/2014/demo/shedding-light-on-race-reporting-among-hispanics/POP-twps0102.pdf [accessed March 23, 2016]). These sorts of demographic questions, which treat race and Hispanic/Latino/Spanish origin as separate issues caused great confusion for NNHS students and Latinxs throughout the United States who find the current official Census categories for race incapable of representing their identities. There are ongoing debates about whether to include "Hispanic, Latino, or Spanish origin" as a race category in future versions of the Census.

When I asked students if they could think of any situations in which Mexicans and Puerto Ricans share an identity as Hispanics or Latinxs, one girl (Mex, Gen. 2, Gr. 12) responded, "yeah, I can think of one time . . when I'm filling out a survey and I mark Hispanic." This suggests that governmental gazes, materialized through surveys and other practices, erase Mexican and Puerto Rican difference and consolidate Hispanic and Latinx as umbrella categories.

Alternate pronouncements of Hispanic panethnicity and Mexican-Puerto Rican racial difference could easily overshadow the close relationships that Mexican and Puerto Rican students built in their everyday interactions with one another. Despite the ubiquitous claim that Puerto Ricans and Mexicans are separate races, when I asked students whether they consider romantic relationships between Puerto Ricans and Mexicans to be interracial, they were usually stumped for a moment but almost always ended up deciding that such relationships are definitely not interracial. In their responses to these questions, not only did students grapple with Hispanic and Latinx as governmental concepts, but they also understood these categories in terms of their long-standing local historical relationships.[23] Mexicans and Puerto Ricans constitute the two largest US Latinx subgroups. Chicago is the only city in which Mexicans and Puerto Ricans have been building their lives alongside one another in large numbers since the mid-20th century.[24] Students made sense of Mexicanness and Puerto Ricanness not simply in terms of governmental categories but also through these long-standing histories of face-to-face, frequently intimate interactions that made their differences all the more tangible and, often, negligible. They were classmates, boyfriends, girlfriends, teammates, neighbors, and family members. There were many students with one Puerto Rican and one Mexican parent, a situation that has led to the creation of "MexiRican" and "PortoMex" as identifiable categories (Rúa 2001; Potowski and Matts 2008).[25] Thus, for some students, intra-Latinx relations were definitional of their identities (Figure 2.8). One such student, Victor (Mex[m]/PR[f], Gen. 3, Gr. 11), identified primarily as Latino because he did not want to "leave anyone out." Rivera-Servera (2012) uses the notion of "friction" to characterize intimate intra-Latinx relations that involve the creation of shared relationships through the emphasis on differences between Latinx subgroups.[26]

In addition to these mundane interrelations, Mexican-Puerto Rican intimacy in Chicago has also emerged in the context of political organizing. Many "Latino rehearsals" (DeGenova and Ramos-Zayas 2003) in Chicago are regularly staged in the Humboldt Park community area. Since its inception more than 35 years ago, the creators of the Puerto Rican Cultural Center (PRCC)—located in Humboldt Park—have identified solidarity with Chicago's Mexican community as a key component of their efforts. Although Puerto Ricans are US citizens by birth, the PRCC has continually advocated

FIGURE 2.8: "MexiRican" representations that students displayed and circulated, often via social media.

for immigrants' rights.[27] On many occasions, Mexicans marching from the city's South Side have joined with Puerto Ricans marching from Humboldt Park to proceed together to downtown immigration rallies, often chanting "¡Boricua y Mexicano, luchando mano a mano!" (Puerto Rican and Mexican, fighting hand in hand!). These efforts toward solidarity have garnered national attention. In the summer of 2006, the Adalberto United Methodist Church (Figure 2.9), which is located on Division Street in the heart of Chicago's Puerto Rican community and closely affiliated with the PRCC, provided sanctuary for Elvira Arellano, an undocumented Mexican woman facing deportation.[28] In fact, Arellano was named the honorary marshal of the 2007 Chicago Puerto Rican People's Day Parade. Following Arellano's departure from the church, another undocumented Mexican woman facing deportation, Flor Crisóstomo, took sanctuary in the same church in 2007 and remained there until October 2009. She was also named an honorary marshal in the 2008 Puerto Rican People's Day Parade.

Some analysts of panethnicity (Lopez and Espiritu 1990), particularly Latinx panethnicity in Chicago (Padilla 1985), have claimed that these sorts of collaborations take shape only to meet temporary political needs and are unlikely to contribute to the creation of enduring shared identities. In contrast, scholars such as Fernández (2012) and Rodríguez-Muñiz (2010) have shown how Puerto Rican and Mexican social movements in Chicago, far from fleeting initiatives, are built on a long-standing historical foundation of shared experiences and recognition of what African American studies scholars have called "linked fate" (Harris-Lacewell 2004). Rodríguez-Muñiz (2010), in particular, argues that these understandings constitute a form of historical and contemporary Latinidad that is rooted neither in fleeting political efforts nor homogenized governmental notions.

Perspectival Recognitions and Trajectories of Latinx Difference

Recall Dr. Baez's efforts toward challenging the stereotypes in relation to which NNHS students were commonly recognized by fashioning the category of Young Latino Professional. For Dr. Baez, Mexican and Puerto Rican students were

FIGURE 2.9: Puerto Rican and Mexican flags juxtaposed at Adalberto United Methodist Church, a Mexican-Puerto Rican church in Humboldt Park where Elvira Arellano, an undocumented Mexican woman, took sanctuary in 2006 to avoid deportation. Photo by author.

stereotyped similarly, which meant that Mexican-Puerto Rican difference was not a central concern for her project of creating Young Latino Professionals. Still, Dr. Baez occasionally identified differences between Mexican and Puerto Rican students. I asked her whether she thought that Mexican and Puerto Rican students face separate challenges:

Yes, for example, some of these students who are Mexican are here illegally and they are always afraid that they will be taken or that their parents will be taken. For example, sometimes when they go [to Mexico] and they have trouble getting back. It's not that they don't want to be in school, but that they couldn't get back in [the country]. And then probably they are much poorer than our Puerto Rican group, because they are busy taking terrible jobs that don't pay, and that's why they probably have two jobs. Their parents are not there. They are emotionally drained and are young adults. A lot of these kids have to work. I have students here who work from 11 [pm] until 7 in the morning. I had a student the other day who came in very tired on Wednesday and you could see it in his face. He said, "I just finished working until 3 o'clock this morning." And it was 8 o'clock [in the morning] and all I did was praise him. I said, "I want to thank you. I commend you for coming to school." He wouldn't be doing that unless they needed it, probably because they're here illegally, they're afraid, so the little bit of work helps. With our seniors, if our numbers are not here in terms of being on time for graduating, it's because a lot of them are working. And I see that more with Mexicans than Puerto Ricans. . . . In this country we have this thing about being nationalized, like we should all identify just with the United States, but I think that everyone should take pride in everything they are. The bottom line is that we should all be proud that we are human beings. I take pride in who I am, but I am also proud of being part of the United States. But I am proud, I love my food, I love my culture, and I've been here all my life in the United States, but why should I put that aside? Why can't we be diverse enough that I could appreciate the Black culture, the Hispanic culture? We should all be taught to be the best human beings possible. I should strip away my title of having a doctorate. The bottom line is we're all equal, especially in the eyes of God. I don't see myself as better than anybody else. I see you as my equal. And that's the kind of things that we should teach, and that's what we work on with our students. So students always say, "What are you?" and I tell them, "I'm Puerto Rican, but my children are Mexican and Puerto Rican, hey!" And they say, "Oh!" and they connect. And my grandchildren are Puerto Rican, Mexican, and Polish, you see?

In her response to my question, Dr. Baez initially presents a nuanced characterization of Mexican-Puerto Rican difference that invokes broader stereotypes about citizenship status and labor participation.[29] She transitions to a discourse of "Hispanic culture" alongside "Black culture" and eventually voices a multicultural, humanitarian perspective (i.e., "The bottom line is that we should all be proud that we are human beings.").

While many non-Latinx NNHS employees were not even aware of Mexican-Puerto Rican difference before they started working at the school, Latinx teachers voiced varying perspectives on Puerto Rican–Mexican difference. Two young, well-liked Puerto Rican teachers are a good example of this. Ms. Rivera said that she felt as though it was important to show the students that Mexican-Puerto Rican difference does not really matter. She highlighted the fact that her boyfriend was Mexican and that she had been the only Puerto Rican on her high school soccer team. For Ms. Rivera, a romantic relationship with a Mexican was not "going outside of [her] culture too much." In contrast, Ms. Arroyo said that she prefers to be called Puerto Rican before anything else, such as Hispanic or Latina. She claimed that the school was divided along racial lines: "Puerto Ricans stay with Puerto Ricans, Mexicans stay with Mexicans, and Blacks stay with Blacks." She described her own life in similar terms. Upon further questioning, however, I learned that Ms. Arroyo had dated many Mexicans and that she had several Mexican cousins. There was a marked disconnect between her way of talking about difference and her actual lived experience of intimate relationships across lines of Puerto Rican–Mexican difference. This disconnect was also characteristic of the discourses and experiences of NNHS students, some examples of which I analyze later in this chapter. I attribute this shared perspective between Ms. Arroyo and many NNHS students to the fact that she grew up near the school and had lived in its surrounding community for her entire life.

Still, students' worlds were saturated with stereotypes about and signs of Mexican-Puerto Rican difference. From Puerto Rican perspectives, Mexicanness was stereotypically associated with passivity, illegality (in terms of citizenship status), and industriousness (in terms of wage earning jobs, not schoolwork); from Mexican perspectives, Puerto Ricanness was stereotypically linked to rudeness, laziness, and attractiveness.[30] Whereas the principal's project of transforming recognitions of students into Young Latino Professionals elided Mexican-Puerto Rican difference, students' reception of this project served to reproduce these very differences. How could Mexicans become Young Latino Professionals if they were imagined as unsavvy national outsiders? How could Puerto Ricans become Young Latino Professionals if they were understood as lazy and rude? Thus, orienting oneself to the school's project of socialization necessitated students' engagement with—and reproduction of—stereotypes about Puerto Rican–Mexican difference.

My initial observations at NNHS seemed to confirm the findings of previous research on Puerto Rican–Mexican relations in Chicago (De Genova and Ramos-Zayas 2003), which suggests that Puerto Ricans and Mexicans oppose one another in relation to their disparate, pejorative positioning as a racialized underclass (Puerto Ricans) and as illegal aliens (Mexicans), respectively. Over the course of my fieldwork, however, it became increasingly clear that distinctions between Puerto Ricans and Mexicans in terms of race and citizenship status are misleading for several reasons: (1) Mexican and Puerto Rican students stereotyped one another's differences while building close relationships with one another inside and outside of school; (2) students' in-depth knowledge about and engagement with Puerto Rican and Mexican practices suggested long-standing histories of shared experiences with one another; and (3) the intensity and rigidity of the discourses surrounding Mexican-Puerto Rican difference varied directly with students' class years (i.e., length of time attending the school). That is, not only did students' relationships with and intimate knowledge of one another contradict discourses surrounding Mexican-Puerto Rican difference, but the nature of these discourses also shifted over the trajectory of students' school careers.

In my second year of fieldwork, I frequently tutored in freshman classrooms during first period (8:29–9:15 a.m.) and in senior classrooms during second period (9:15–10:47 a.m.). This juxtaposition threw into relief something that I previously intuited but had not documented directly. Whereas freshmen and seniors alike distinguished between Puerto Ricans and Mexicans and were familiar with the aforementioned stereotypes, freshmen disputed the rigidity of these categories and openly acknowledged their contradictions. In fact, Mexican and Puerto Rican freshmen were much more comfortable joking with one another about stereotypes than seniors, and freshmen were more forthright about challenging one another when they agreed that someone had taken a joke too far. In one scenario, Leti (Mex, Gen. 2, Gr. 9) joined with several Puerto Rican students in her class to let a Puerto Rican boy (PR, Gen. 2, Gr. 9) know that he should not make fun of Mexican students' celebration of Mexican independence each September. She told me that to confront him, she wore a headband with a Mexican flag to that class for an entire month. Puerto Rican friends of hers in this class showed their support by putting Mexican stickers on their notebooks. This is just one example of how freshmen entered into dialogue with one another about the meaning of Mexican and Puerto Rican difference. For these ninth-grade students, Puerto Ricanness and Mexicanness were not necessarily rigidly distinct or opposing categories.

Seniors explained to me that one clear difference between Puerto Ricans and Mexicans was baseball and soccer, yet freshmen pointed out that Mexicans and Puerto Ricans all played soccer together in the field next to the school and that there were Mexicans on the school's baseball team. While seniors disparaged one another's stereotypical Mexican and Puerto Rican language practices, freshmen recognized these differences but were far less likely to rank one another's practices as more or less "cool" or "correct." Seniors reported that Mexicans and Puerto Ricans were different races. Meanwhile, freshmen claimed interchangeably that Puerto Ricans and Mexicans were racially "Latino" or "Hispanic." Although seniors claimed that they were only friends with fellow Mexicans or Puerto Ricans, freshmen reported that they had both Mexican *and* Puerto Rican friends.

Discursive articulations of Mexican-Puerto Rican difference are highly deceptive. Without situating these discourses of difference within students' broader social lives, one might conclude that Mexicans and Puerto Ricans in Chicago simply end up hating each other by the end of high school. Upon closer analysis, however, it became clear that the discursive shifts from freshman to senior year did not correspond to substantive shifts in Mexican-Puerto Rican relations. That is, Mexican and Puerto Rican seniors were just as intimate (if not more intimate) with one another as Mexican and Puerto Rican freshmen. Progressions in grade year heightened ideas about Mexican-Puerto Rican categorical differences and erased contradictions that first- and second-year students recognized comfortably. These shifts reflected students' ongoing engagement with the principal's project of transforming them into Young Latino Professionals. Recruitment to this category shaped Mexican and Puerto Rican students' engagement in ethnoracial contortions and articulation of rigid distinctions between one another in a number of ways.

In an interview with David [PR, Gen. 3, Gr. 12] and Jimmy [PR, Gen. 3, Gr. 12], I asked whether Mexicans and Puerto Ricans are separate races:

```
 1  JR:     And Puerto Ricans and Mexicans are separate races?
    Jimmy:  Yes.
    JR:     What's that mean?
    Jimmy:  They're different.
 5  David:  They're different?=
    Jimmy:                    Well, they're Hispanic, both of them are
            Hispanic, they're just different=
    David:                                   No, they're Hispanic, we're Latino.
    JR:     How's that work?
10  Jimmy:  What the fu(ck)?
    David:  They're Hispanic, I'm, I'm Latino.
    JR:     What's that mean?
```

Jimmy: ¡Papichulo!=
             [Sexy guy!]
15 David: We're Latin.
   JR: What's that mean?
   Jimmy: We're fr=
   David: [We're from Puerto Rico.
   Jimmy: [That's him talking.
20 David: We're from an island. I, I think I'm from an island=
   Jimmy: And they're,
             from a=
   David: they're from=
   Jimmy: a fake state=
25 David: whatever we, whatever we
   Jimmy: [that we took over.
   David: [let them have.

David and Jimmy show how stereotypes about Mexicans and Puerto Ricans can be used to accomplish interactional tasks while charting a curious path toward defining Puerto Rican–Mexican difference. While Jimmy takes the lead in responding to the question and establishing difference in panethnic sameness—"both of them are Hispanic . . . they're just different"—David initially questions this difference. He then disagrees with Jimmy by categorizing Mexicans as "Hispanic" and Puerto Ricans as "Latino." Jimmy is confused by this distinction, but he clarifies that categorizing Puerto Ricans as Latino means that Puerto Ricans are papichulos, or sexy guys. Jimmy and David then collaborate to draw a geopolitical distinction between Mexico and Puerto Rico. That is, Puerto Rico is an island and Mexico is a "fake state" that "we let them have." While they never mention the United States explicitly, the notion that Mexico is a "fake state" suggests that it is not a sovereign nation, but an illegitimate attachment to the United States. This stands in contrast to Puerto Rico, which is folded into the US-oriented "we" that Jimmy and David both claim.

These two boys drew on stereotypes about Puerto Ricans and Mexicans to engage in a struggle of one-upmanship in an interview context in which they presupposed general solidarity with me as Puerto Ricans but also creatively entailed the specific nature of this solidarity through their responses. David was known as a humorous student who had romantic troubles with girls. In my previous interactions with him, I found that he was constantly calculating comedic punch lines and pickup lines. During one of our tutoring sessions we began to study two-party political systems. Before we could get started, David said that he already knew these systems well and that he used them in his own life: the regular party and the after party. In this instance, David made a humorous reference to a lyric commonly heard in hip-hop songs, "after the party, there's the after party." His comedic timing did not translate to romantic success. In fact, he was best known in the school as the boy whose ex-girlfriend broke up with him by hitting him in the head with a combination lock in front a crowd of students. On the other hand, Jimmy was a baseball player who also liked to make jokes, but his coolness did not depend on it. In line 8, David presents a seemingly contradictory articulation of Mexican-Puerto Rican difference: "they're Hispanic, we're Latino." Based on Jimmy's response in line 10 ("What the fuck?), it is apparent that he either disagrees with or does not understand what David is saying. In line 11, David reframes the initial distinction: "They're Hispanic, I'm Latino." This reframing signals to Jimmy the components of Mexican and Puerto Rican stereotypes that are in play—personality and relationship with respect to the United States—which prompts him to enter into the game of one-upmanship with David. Jimmy draws on David's classification of Mexicans as Hispanic (out-group, "they're") and Puerto Ricans as Latino (in-group, "I'm") to suggest in line 13 that this means Puerto Ricans are papichulos (sexy guys). In response to my request for clarification in line 12 ("What's that mean?"), David replies "We're Latin" (line 15). This builds from Jimmy's suggestion that they are papichulos to invoke sexiness by way of the stereotypical figure of the "Latin lover." In response to my additional request for clarification in line 16 ("What's that mean?"), David states, "We're from Puerto Rico" (line 18), while Jimmy simultaneously steps out of the game for a moment by attributing its development to David, "That's him talking" (line 19). Unfazed, David ups the ante in line 20 with his claim that "We're from an island. I, I think I'm from an island. . . ." Jimmy rejoins the game and ups the ante by interrupting David to finish his sentence: "And they're (21), they're from a (22), a fake state (24)." In a flash finish, David and Jimmy simultaneously position Mexicans as being from "whatever we let them have" (David, lines 25, 27) and "a fake state that we took over" (Jimmy, lines 24, 26). Here, David and Jimmy attempt to one-up each other by identifying elements of Puerto Rican stereotypes, namely the island as a geographical space and a more legitimate claim to Americanness as compared with Mexicans. Thus, they are able to simultaneously valorize the island by suggesting that it is somehow a more politically legitimate and sovereign space, *and* claim Americanness by suggesting that Mexico either wants to be part of the United States (i.e., is a "fake state") or was given away by the United States (i.e., "whatever we let them have"). In that Mexico is formally recognized as a sovereign nation-state and Puerto Rico, a US commonwealth that is subject to US federal law but has no congressional or presidential voting power, is widely recognized as one of the world's most glaring examples of the continued existence of direct colonialism in the 21st century, Jimmy and David construct a remarkable narrative. They pull from different parts of Mexican and Puerto Rican stereotypes to contribute to their efforts to one-up each other.

Jimmy and David draw on stereotypes about Mexicans and Puerto Ricans to engage in an interactional game of one-upmanship. Their comments could be easily misinterpreted as evidence of deep-seated Puerto Rican–Mexican animosity. In particular, they succinctly contrast Mexicans/Mexico and Puerto Ricans/Puerto Rico in terms of physical attractiveness, geographical value, and political power. While these ideas are certainly worrisome in their invocation of xenophobic discourses that are also present in problematic anti-immigrant policies, they must not overshadow the fact that David and Jimmy shared close relationships with countless Mexican friends, neighbors, teammates, and even family members. The nature of these relationships is misrepresented by the origins that Jimmy and David claim for themselves ("I'm from Puerto Rico/an island") and attribute to Mexicans ("they're from a fake state [that we took over/ let them have]"). They engage in an ethnoracial contortion and construct a complex diasporic imaginary; Jimmy and David were born in Chicago and had never visited the island of Puerto Rico, but they claim to be "from Puerto Rico." These claims suggest that Puerto Rican–Mexican difference is discursively produced in relation to ideas about belonging to the United States, Puerto Rico, and Mexico. Jimmy's and David's ideas demonstrate their socialization to a US institutional setting that inadvertently reinforced students' stereotypes about Mexican-Puerto Rican difference. These experiences of socialization shaped the engagement with Mexican and Puerto Rican stereotypes and the potential uses of such stereotypes in everyday interactions such as Jimmy's and David's struggle of one-upmanship. The ideological twists and turns that enabled them to validate their Puerto Rican identities reified ideas about Mexican-Puerto Rican difference. Yet, these articulations of difference must be understood in relation to the complexity of shared experiences between Mexicans and Puerto Ricans in the Chicago context.

Shared Identifications and Experiences of Exclusion

Returning to the issues that opened this chapter, it should now be clear that Puerto Rican, Mexican, and Latinx categories, stereotypes, and identities were created in a number of alternately competing and collaborating ways within NNHS. These cultural categories were reconfigured as students navigated different institutional frameworks. De Genova and Ramos-Zayas claim that Mexicans' and Puerto Ricans' "contrasting sociopolitical locations within the field of citizenship inequalities have contributed to the production of distinct and competing racial formations of 'Mexican'-ness and 'Puerto Rican'-ness that frequently came to be juxtaposed as mutually exclusive" (2003:213). In contrast, I have emphasized that these "sociopolitical locations" are far more complex than explicit articulations of Mexican-Puerto Rican difference suggest.

In fact, these political and economic forces play important roles in creating forms of frictive intimacy that allow Mexicans and Puerto Ricans in Chicago to experience difference *and* solidarity in relation to one another. Whereas De Genova and Ramos-Zayas highlight the different positionalities produced by the criminalization of "undocumented Mexican migrants' 'illegality'" and the demonization of "endemic Puerto Rican poverty" (2003:213), I argue that discursive differences in Puerto Ricans' and Mexicans' articulations of their respective political and economic positionalities must always be considered in relation to linked subjectivities and forms of frictive intimacy that emerge from shared experiences of exclusion. These experiences place Chicago Mexicans and Puerto Ricans alongside one another in marginalized residential, employment, and educational spaces. Neither Puerto Rican citizenship nor Mexican labor participation provides full access to US economic and political inclusion.[31]

Many scholars have noted the different ways in which Mexican and Puerto Rican youth in Chicago inhabit social categories, but there are characteristic shortcomings in these studies. In particular, Latinx identity either is taken for granted as an inherent link between Mexicans and Puerto Ricans or is positioned as a straightforward object of contention in relation to which Mexicans' and Puerto Ricans' distinctive citizenship statuses and modes of labor participation present irreconcilable divides. By introducing the notion of "ethnoracial contortions" and situating it in relation to diasporic imaginaries and institutional trajectories, this chapter has sought to highlight the complex ways that racialized constructions of Latinx panethnicity engage with prevailing paradigms of US racial difference (Torres-Saillant 2003; Bonilla-Silva 2004; Fergus, Noguera, and Martin 2010). It also questions the conceptualization of citizenship as a concrete object that one either does or does not possess. Students' engagements with institutional and societal constraints show how citizenship is in fact a social potential and not simply a set of rights that one possesses or lacks in straightforward, continuous ways (Fikes 2009). Indeed, this is Rosaldo's (1994) key point in his theorization of "cultural citizenship" as a way in which Latinxs stake claims to belonging in the face of the denial of access either to formal or substantive citizenship (Holston 1998).

Analysis of the alternate ethnicization and racialization of Latinx identities, and the corresponding embrace and erasure of Mexican-Puerto Rican difference, must always draw connections not only between broad political and economic forces but also between local histories of shared experience. Interrelations among these realms demonstrate the potential for social domination to limit

Latinx students' access to resources in a number of institutional contexts; in contrast, a careful consideration of these linkages can also highlight the surprising categorical coalitions that emerge as possibilities for challenging and transforming Mexican, Puerto Rican, and Latinx marginalization. In the next chapter, I explore particular affective dimensions of these categories and show how they become linked to emblems, embodiments, and enactments of Latinidad.

3

"LATINO FLAVORS"

EMBLEMATIZING, EMBODYING, AND
ENACTING LATINIDAD

This chapter analyzes the ways that emblems of Latinx identity are made recognizable in everyday life. In particular, I focus on the processes through which qualia (Chumley and Harkness 2013)—culturally mediated sensations that structure embodiment and experience—associated with objects, practices, and bodies become linked in the contemporary fashioning of Latinx identities. By analyzing qualia related to a range of cultural sites, from hairstyles, clothing, and language, to food, dance, and music, I track the semiotic operations that connect the circulation of Latinx things to the embodiment of Latinx people. These processes of embodiment, or the historical, political, and economic "mattering" of Latinx bodies (Butler 1993), structure experiences and enactments of Latinx identities. My crucial point here is that the construction of perceived differences between Latinx subgroups on the one hand, and between Latinxs and non-Latinxs on the other, is central to the production of emblems, embodiments, and experiences that constitute the fact of Latinidad.[1] Building from the previous chapter's analysis of discourses of Mexican-Puerto Rican difference, this chapter shows how the construction of and familiarity with Mexican and Puerto Rican models of personhood emerge as *repertoires of Latinidad*. Latinx New Northwest High School (NNHS) students' constructions and experiences of Latinidad enter into critical dialogue with broader discourses of "Latino threat" (Chavez 2008) and "Latino spin" (Dávila 2008). In the context of NNHS, "Latino threat" discourses correspond to the figures of "gangbanger" and "ho," while "Latino spin" narratives align with the figure of "Young Latino Professional." Although NNHS students creatively contest the boundaries that render these figures recognizable, they are limited in their ability to escape stigmatizing gazes that view them as unfit for legitimate political subjectivity. Students alternately reproduce, refract, reclaim, and reject this stigmatization. By forging racialized panethnic identities that neither embrace nor eschew these hegemonic discourses of Latinidad in straightforward ways, Latinx NNHS students demonstrate how "Latinidad as a practice of identity or affect maintains and exploits the friction between the hegemonic and the radical" (Rivera-Servera 2012:196).

The interplay between Dr. Baez's strategy for transforming students from gang-bangers and hoes into Young Latino Professionals on the one hand, and students' investment in their Puerto Rican and Mexican identities on the other, involved qualia of "ghettoness" and "lameness" that anchored presentations of self and perceptions thereof within NNHS.[2] As a result, there was ongoing debate among students about how the categories of Puerto Rican and Mexican were positioned with respect to the opposition between being "ghetto" (i.e., gangbangers/hoes) and "lame" (i.e., Young Latino Professionals), each of which was stigmatized in relation to stereotypes about deviance ("ghettoness") and uncoolness or by extension disability ("lameness"). Figures 3.1 and 3.2 provide an emic snapshot of these categorical interrelations. These figures show maps that a freshman, Lynette (Mex, Gen. 2, Gr. 9), and a senior, Jimmy (PR, Gen. 3, Gr. 12), drew of groups of students in different lunch periods. Whereas Lynette's only explicit reference to Puerto Ricanness or Mexicanness is her identification of two tables as Mexican, Jimmy explicitly distinguishes between tables that are Mexican and Puerto Rican.[3] As described in the previous chapter, this reflects the increased recognition of Mexican-Puerto Rican difference from the perspective of a senior compared with that of a freshman. Despite these disparate recognitions

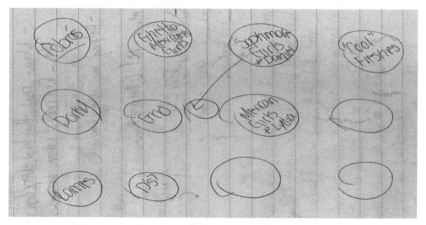

FIGURE 3.1: Map of the lunchroom drawn by Lynette. Lynette (Mex, Gen. 2, Gr. 9) refers to categories such as "Cobras" (a gang), " Dorky," "Lames," "Ghetto Mexican Girls," "Emo" (brooding fans of English-language alternative rock music), "D's" (a gang), "Sophomore Girls + Daniel," "Mexican Girls + Lydia," and " 'Cool' Freshies" (i.e., cool freshmen). This map indexes a freshman student perspective because sophomores, juniors, and seniors typically would not say that freshmen could be cool. Photo by author.

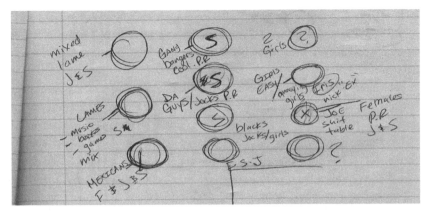

FIGURE 3.2: Map of the lunchroom drawn by Jimmy. Jimmy (PR, Gen. 3, Gr. 12) references students' class years (F = freshmen, S = sophomore, J = junior, "S" inside of a circle means senior) along with a range of social categories, including "lames" (i.e., uncool), "Da Guys/jocks," "Gangbanger," and "Easy Girls/Annoying Girls." In three places he writes "P.R." for Puerto Rican; he writes "Mexican" once; but anywhere he writes "mixed," he is saying that Mexicans and Puerto Ricans sit together. These categories invoke stereotypes surrounding race, ethnicity, class, gender, and sexuality, among other local dynamics. Photo by author.

of Mexican-Puerto Rican difference and invocations of social categories in their diagrams, a shared feature is their identification of "ghetto" students (i.e., using categories such as "ghetto," "easy girls," "gangbangers," and references to specific gangs) and "lame" students (i.e., using categories such as "dorky" and "lames"). Throughout this chapter, I demonstrate the ways that the dichotomies of Mexican-Puerto Rican and gangbanger/ho–Young Latino Professional became associated with qualia of "ghettoness" and "lameness," and I show how perceptions of these qualities constitute emblems, embodiments, and enactments of Latinidad.

Scales of Latinidad, Ethnoracial Emblems, and Latinx Embodiment

The shared local histories among Puerto Ricans and Mexicans in Chicago described in the previous chapter reverberate with respect to relatively emergent national and increasingly global popular cultural representations of Latinidad. Scholars such as Dávila (2012) and Zentella (2003) have pointed to the worrisome material, political, and cultural implications of the booming Hispanic marketing industry and the "chiquita-fication," or homogenization and exoticization, of Latinxs. NNHS students recognized one another in new ways based on these representations, which strip practices associated with specific Latinx subgroups of their particularity and project them as quintessential emblems of Latinidad—think tacos stripped of their Mexican particularity and consumed as "the" Latinx food (Figure 3.3) and salsa music stripped of its Puerto Rican/Cuban particularity and consumed as "the" Latinx music. In this context, Mexican and Puerto Rican students, many of whom experienced tacos and salsa music in terms of their national particularity throughout their lives, felt themselves being recognized in new ways. For example, Jimmy (PR, Gen 3, Gr. 12) noted the "Hispanic Foods"[4] aisle at the local "Jewels"[5] grocery store. He wondered aloud whether this was the only aisle in which we were permitted to shop and joked that the Latinx-oriented grocery store, Cermak Produce,[6] should have an aisle called "White Foods." Jimmy's juxtaposition of "Hispanic" and "White" demonstrates his racialized conception of Latinx identity, on the one hand, and his way of grappling with its commercial de-racialization, on the other. The humor of suggesting that a Latinx-oriented grocery store should have an aisle called "White Foods" derives from the unthinkability of actually seeing such a representation of race in a mainstream public setting. This speaks to the unmarked status of Whiteness, the ideological capacity for Whiteness to serve as a stand-in for Americanness, and the logics of political correctness that shape public representations of race and ethnicity.[7]

Governmental, local, and popular cultural notions of Latinidad alternately collaborated and competed with one another to define this ethnoracial category in NNHS. In some moments Mexican and Puerto Rican students drew on definitions of Latinidad that pointed to their intimate knowledge of one another and long-standing shared histories, while in other moments they understood themselves as occupying different positions with respect to the relatively

FIGURE 3.3: A mural that reads "latino flavors with the spice of life." This mural adorned the side of a Latinx fusion restaurant, "Carnivale," located in Downtown Chicago. It succinctly signals the coherence of Latinx panethnicity, its sensory existence in experienceable "flavors," and its stereotypical association with a "spicy" way of life. Photo by David Flores.

recent emergence of Latinidad as stereotypically displayed in music, movies, and television. And still yet in other situations they maneuvered with respect to governmental categories that positioned them as an undifferentiated and often problematic mass.

These varying constructions of Latinidad point to some of the ways that cultural conceptions associated with material objects, practices, and bodies are mapped onto one another in the context of the contemporary fashioning of Latinx panethnicity. By considering these conceptions in relation to the suggestion in previous scholarship on racial embodiment that "Latino identity is, with few exceptions, a visible identity, for all its variability" (Alcoff 2006:227), it becomes possible to reframe both Latinx "visibility" and "variability." Latinx "visibility" should be understood as a semiotic phenomenon that is structured by the creation and circulation of emblems of ethnoracial difference that render Latinidad perceivable and recognizable. Additionally, Latinx "variability" (or heterogeneity) should be understood neither as a distinguishing feature of nor a barrier to the emergence of Latinx visibility. Instead, variability is a characteristic feature of *all* ethnoracial categories, which are produced through systematic processes of differentiation and homogenization. Alcoff (2006) grapples with the heterogeneity of embodiment on the one hand, and the powerful consequences of visible identities on the other. Her description of Latinx identity as a visible identity *despite* its variability suggests that this variability is somehow exceptional or particular to Latinxs. In fact, perceived variability is indicative not of the particularity of Latinxs, but rather of its contemporary construction in ongoing processes of naturalization; Latinx identity is a visible identity because of (not despite) its variability.

Gilroy explicates what he characterizes as a "novel problem" (Gilroy 2000:106) with racial identity and heterogeneity, namely that "the desire to fix identity in the body is inevitably frustrated by the body's refusal to disclose the required signs of absolute incompatibility people imagine to be located there" (2000:104). Locating this heterogeneity and bodily refusal in relation to Latinxs, Alcoff explains, "we simply don't fit . . . [w]e have no homogeneous culture, we come in every conceivable color, and identities such as 'mestizo' signify the very absence of boundaries" (Alcoff 2006:229). This account seems to imply the homogeneity of other ethnoracial groups. However, the presumed homogeneity of other racialized populations compared with Latinx heterogeneity should not be approached primarily as a matter of groups whose bodies are more or less physically similar. The self-evidence of visible similarity must be understood not as an objective phenotypic phenomenon, but instead as the product of historically mediated perceptions and processes of racial naturalization (Carbado 2005; Shankar 2013). Thus, it is important to build from Gilroy's and Alcoff's accounts of visible, embodied identities to shed light on the cultural processes that make perceptions of visibility and embodiment possible. The negotiation of visible ambiguity and heterogeneity is neither a phenomenon that is particular to Latinxs nor a specifically contemporary emergence. In fact, the production of every ethnoracial identity has always required the joint creation and erasure of difference.

A consideration of emblems of ethnoracial identity can illuminate aspects of category-making and embodiment that Alcoff and Gilroy theorize in their work. In the context of NNHS and its surrounding communities, Latino hairstyles were one such set of emblems I encountered that demonstrate the aforementioned points about the relationship between visibility and variability.[8] During the period of my fieldwork I lived a few blocks away from NNHS, on the third floor of an apartment building that had a combination beauty salon/barbershop on the first floor. I alternated between getting my hair cut in the barbershop in my building and getting it cut by a student from NNHS in my apartment. The large beauty salon/barbershop in my building was set up with female stylists along one wall and male barbers along the opposite wall. Most of the female stylists were Mexican, and most of the male barbers were Puerto Rican. The female stylists cut hair for men, women, and children, while the male barbers cut hair mostly for school-aged boys and young men. On the walls of the shop were several style charts designed to help barbers and customers agree on a particular style (Figure 3.4). The charts displayed a range of hairstyles on a multiaged group of males who were all presumably Latino. At first I did not make much of these charts, which were familiar elements of barbershops I had visited throughout Chicago, New York, and other US cities. In the summer of 2009, shortly after I finished conducting fieldwork in NNHS, I began a fellowship residency in Washington, DC. During the term of this residency, I got my hair cut in a barbershop in a predominantly Latinx neighborhood. When I discovered that this barbershop displayed the same style charts that I had seen in Chicago, I took a closer look at them to find out where they were made. The charts were created by a Chicago barbershop and sold by a Chicago poster company. This prompted me to look into how many different "Latino" style charts exist. I learned that the Chicago charts are standard Latino style charts, and I have since encountered pictures of them hanging in barbershops in multiple US cities with large Latinx populations, including New York, Los Angeles, San Francisco, and Miami. While one might expect cities with larger Latinx populations to serve as more likely sites in which emblems of Latinidad are produced, the wide usage of these charts suggests something about Chicago's unique position vis-à-vis Latinx embodied emblematicity. Recall that Chicago is the only major US city that contains large, long-standing populations of the nation's two largest Latinx subgroups, Mexicans and Puerto Ricans. This demographic, geographic, and cultural history uniquely shapes Chicago's capacity to produce emblems of Latinidad. The charts also derive their powerful emblematicity from the ethnoracial portrayal of Latinxs as a people who are stereotypically

FIGURE 3.4: The Barber Hairstyle Guides. These charts and similar versions were displayed in multiple barbershops near NNHS. The charts, which were created by a Chicago barbershop, have become the standard Latino hairstyle charts and can be found in barbershops throughout the nation. Photos by author.

located between Whiteness and Blackness in a spectrum-based racial logic of skin color. This echoes the previous chapter's analysis of Hispanic and Latinx as categories that are commensurate with, but not equal to, existing categories of race and ethnicity.

I showed pictures of the charts to Mexican and Puerto Rican NNHS students and asked them to classify the images by Latinx national subgroups. While there were debates about the national subgroups that correspond to some of the images, primarily focused on distinguishing between Mexicanness and Puerto Ricanness, all of the students agreed that the charts are panethnic. That is, they said that the images constituted a variety of Latinx national subgroups. Students classified the images not only in terms of national subgroups but also in relation to many of the salient social categories in the school and surrounding community, including descriptors such as "lame," "cool," and "ghetto." Other such qualia played a key role in differentiating Puerto Rican and Mexican hairstyles. On the morning of the 2009 NNHS prom, I accompanied Jimmy (PR, Gen. 3, Gr. 12) as he went to give his best friend, Michael (PR, Gen. 3, Gr. 12), a haircut. The haircut took place in a garage behind Michael's house. Unlike in a typical barbershop setting, Jimmy did not cover Michael with a barber's cape to keep hair from falling directly onto him. Michael got a "low fade"[9] from Jimmy almost weekly. Shortly after Jimmy initiated this particular haircut, Michael began frantically sweeping his hands across his forearms to brush off the hair that fell from the clippers. He exclaimed, "I hate that feeling of hair on me, I feel like a Mexican." For Michael, hair and embodiment were central to differentiating Mexicanness and Puerto Ricanness, which in this case involved the stereotype that Mexicans have more body hair than Puerto Ricans. Crucially, this axis of differentiation created a situation in which Michael could alternately *feel* Puerto Rican and Mexican. What on the surface appears to be a straightforward expression of Puerto Rican disdain toward Mexicans, in fact expresses an anxiety about Mexican-Puerto Rican intimacy in relation to hairstyles and modes of embodiment.

NNHS students often suggested that hair textures and styles are straightforward ways to distinguish between Mexicans and Puerto Ricans. These stereotypes were particularly pronounced among male research participants. Two students, Julio (Mex, Gen. 2, Gr. 9) and Carlos (Mex, Gen. 2, Gr. 9), said that whereas Puerto Ricans have short hair, Mexicans "slick it back, spike it, or wear a mohawk." Similarly, Ashley (PR[m]/Polish[f], Gen. 2, Gr. 11) suggested that "Mexicans have longer hair or they spike it up," while Puerto Ricans have fades (short, stylized haircuts described earlier) or braids (also know as "cornrows"). Francisco (Mex, Gen. 1.5, Gr. 11) explained to me that Mexicans wear gel in their hair, whereas Puerto Ricans have "fades."[10] Two Puerto Rican seniors, David (PR, Gen. 3, Gr. 12) and Jimmy (PR, Gen. 3, Gr. 12), whose interview I described in the previous chapter, questioned why "Mexicans wear all that gel in their hair." Of course countless students' hairstyles contradicted these claims. Rigo (Mex, Gen. 2, Gr. 11), a proudly baldheaded boy, had no interest in wearing gel in his hair. While working with him on a project that asked students to imagine that they were the President of the United States, Rigo told me that if he were president he would make everyone be bald on Fridays! After Rigo was arrested with his "tagging crew" (this incident and the definition of a tagging crew are analyzed in detail in Chapter 6), he felt that he had no choice but to grow his hair out in order to look less "ghetto" when he went before the judge. Rigo said that he almost never left his house in between the arrest and the court date, for fear of being seen looking "bogus" (i.e., uncool) with a little bit of hair on his head. Meanwhile,

David (PR, Gen. 3, Gr. 12), the student quoted earlier, had no interest in getting a fade or braids. He wore his hair long and created the slogan "curls for the girls" to symbolize his efforts toward increasing his attractiveness. David noted that some people might think his long hair looked "ghetto," but he said he wanted to try something different. After a disciplinary infraction at school, his mother punished him by making him trade his cherished curls for an extremely short cut with his hair at an equal length all over his head (i.e., because his hair was all the same length, it was not a fade and thus uncool). Crucially, this short haircut came with no "lining," which describes a barber's use of a straight razor to clean up the edges of the haircut all around the head. David's friend Jimmy (PR, Gen. 3, Gr. 12) recounted how "bogus" (i.e., uncool) David looked when he came into school with no lining. In these two cases, students who were recognized by their peers as being stereotypically Mexican and Puerto Rican, respectively, only adopted hairstyles with qualities that corresponded to these categories (i.e., long hair for Mexicans and short hair for Puerto Ricans) as forms of punishment.

Rigo and David were both concerned with looking stereotypically "ghetto" (i.e., deviant from the perspective of school authorities and associated with gang-banging) or "lame" (i.e., uncool from students' perspectives, but positively valued by the school's administration). Each boy negotiated these concerns in relation to a range of hairstyles associated with Mexicans and Puerto Ricans, respectively. Rigo's bald head could be seen as ghetto and gang-related from many perspectives, but there were still other hairstyles that indexed gang participation much more directly. For example, Rigo could have worn his hair in a "shag," which is widely recognizable as a sign of gang participation. This hairstyle consists of an entirely bald head with a patch of hair on the back. This is considered a "haircut design," which is a prohibited haircut as stated in the NNHS student code of conduct. Still, a bald head in this context contributes to potential misrecognition as a gang member by police and neighborhood residents. Rigo self-identified as a cholo, which he defined as a Mexican "who is tough but who doesn't have to be in a gang." He said that being "pelon" [bald] was part of what it meant to look like a cholo. Like David's curls, Rigo also understood his bald head as a potential way to attract girls. While anyone could clearly be bald, other signs of identity had to be co-present in order for baldness to make one recognizable as a cholo. Rigo's stereotypical Mexican physical appearance, confident demeanor, well-known participation in a tagging crew, and regular public displays of affection with his girlfriend, Karina (Mex, Gen. 2, Gr. 9), contextualized his bald head as a sign of a cholo identity. While this identity made Rigo cool and intimidating in school, on the street and in the courtroom it could be interpreted as a sign of criminality. Growing out his hair for the court case was incredibly bothersome for Rigo. He preferred to stay inside his house and wait until the court date rather than find a way to recontextualize a cholo identity in relation to his new hair. Rigo shaved his head bald immediately after the court case.

David's curls were roughly four to six inches in length. For someone like David who typically got a fade, this was extremely long. He would push his curls through a hair band, pulling them back in a circle from the top and front of his head to the top of his neck. David said that this hairstyle made him look like a "G," which generally means extremely cool but can also signify "gangster." For many Puerto Rican male students, growing one's hair out to this length often suggested that one planned to get braids (also known as "cornrows").[11] David said that braids would make people think he was ghetto and that he had no desire to get them. In fact, to offset the potential ghettoness associated with his curls, he would regularly wear his prescription eyeglasses. He said that the glasses made him a "sensitive G." It is unclear whether this overconfident "G" persona led David to get into an altercation with Ms. Arroyo, the much-feared NNHS Dean of Discipline, but this incident was the beginning of the end for his curls. For David's mother, the hairstyle was clearly a part of the problem. Following a three-day suspension, David returned to school with a shaved head. When his friends saw him, they speculated that he got a $5 haircut from "Betty & Nick's," a low-cost barbershop/hair salon that they associated with unskilled barbers. One friend, Jimmy (PR, Gen. 3, Gr. 12), suggested that it looked like Betty (the presumed owner of Betty & Nick's) cut David's hair all by herself. Jimmy referenced the misogynistic stereotype that women are unable to cut hair as well as male barbers.[12] Needless to say, David's new, low-maintenance look, which his friends called "bogus" and "lame," prevented him from continuing to self-identify as a "G." David no longer wore his glasses, which suggested that they meant something very different in the context of his "bogus" buzz cut compared with their previous role in making him a "sensitive G."

In fact, Rigo's and David's efforts to strike a balance between looking stereotypically ghetto and lame invoke the dichotomy between gangbanger and Young Latino Professional. Both of these boys worked within sets of hairstyles stereotyped as Mexican and Puerto Rican in order to contextualize their identities in relation to the attractiveness of gangbanger/ghetto aesthetics and the institutional legitimacy of Young Latino Professional/lame aesthetics. The categories of Puerto Rican and Mexican became infused with the distinction between gangbangers and Young Latino Professionals. Thus, enactments of Puerto Ricanness and Mexicanness were linked to the embodiment and experience of Latinidad.

In broader terms, the cultural notions associated with these hairstyles demonstrate the ways that Latinx visibility is made possible through the creation and

FIGURE 3.5: Latino Express. This Latinx emblem corresponds to the creation of a Chicago bus company named "Latino Express." Busses with the company's name prominently displayed on them can be seen throughout the city. The ability of this company to present itself in ways that would potentially be received as offensive if "Latino" were replaced with the name of another ethnoracial group underscores the way in which "Latino" operates as a category that is commensurate with but not equal to existing racial categories. Whereas paradigmatic US racial categories such as White and Black are associated with histories of struggle over bussing, "Latino" is often positioned both as a racial and a cultural concept that shapes its circulation in commercial contexts such as the bus company displayed in this image. Photo by David Flores.

circulation of emblems of identity that are commensurate with a broader assemblage of ethnoracial categories. The varied, panethnic images in the hairstyle charts and the distinctive stereotypes surrounding these styles contribute to the visibility of Latinx identity. Regardless of the Mexican-Puerto Rican distinctions that Rigo and Jimmy drew between the hairstyles that they saw as options for themselves, all of their potential styles had a place on the Latino barber hairstyle guide. They became part of a set of racialized panethnic emblems. Chicago's unique Latinx population and its social history position the city as a ritual center for the in-group production of emblems of Latinx panethnicity (Figure 3.5). In-group and out-group engagements with these emblems link local calibrations of identity, such as those of Rigo and David, to broader processes of social category-making.

Metapragmatic Models of Latinidad

It should now be clear that for NNHS students, Mexican and Puerto Rican were prominent overarching categories in the school. As described earlier, signs of Mexicanness and Puerto Ricanness were ubiquitous. Yet, the relationship between signs of identity and enactments of identity is by no means straightforward. Wortham, building on Agha (2004, 2007), Silverstein (1976, 2004), and Urban (2001), suggests that:

[A] sign—any utterance or object that people find culturally meaningful—has meaning only with respect to a "metapragmatic" or "metacultural" model of it. A metapragmatic model is a model of recognizable kinds of people . . . participating in a recognizable kind of interaction. These models are "meta"-pragmatic because they frame the "pragmatic" or indexical signs of identity. That is, participants and analysts understand the meaning of a sign only as a relevant model constrains the possible meanings. . . . Such models make available the types of people that can be enacted in a given social context. Without them, we could not identify who people are or what they are signaling about themselves and others. (2006:32–33)

In NNHS, Mexican and Puerto Rican became metapragmatic models that organized students' identifications of themselves and others. While metapragmatic models such as Mexican and Puerto Rican are associated with broad ethnoracial categories, I will show how these models took a particular shape in the domain (Agha 2007; Wortham 2008) of NNHS.[13]

Tables 3.1 and 3.2 highlight practices, objects, and cultural knowledge that were central components of "Mexican" and "Puerto Rican" metapragmatic models within NNHS. On the one hand, these tables list fascinating sets of stereotypes that are linked to one another as part of larger metapragmatic models. The stereotypes range from ideas about conventional Puerto Rican and Mexican names (first and last, male and female) to geographical spaces associated with each category. Thinking back to Rigo's and David's respective hairstyle crises, there is a familiar recurring theme in these metapragmatic models. Mexicans and Puerto Ricans alike alternately characterize themselves and each other as "ghetto" and "lame." This pattern sheds light on the nature of Mexican-Puerto Rican difference and shows how this distinction became structured in relation to conceptions of gangbangers and Young Latino Professionals. Regardless of their potentially disparate experiences of racialization and positioning with respect to citizenship, Mexican and Puerto Rican students alike were specifically concerned with gauging their own "ghettoness" and "lameness" vis-à-vis one another.

While "Mexican" and "Puerto Rican" took shape as metapragmatic models associated with distinct objects, practices, and characteristics, each of these concepts became an indexical measure by which to locate a given person's proximity to the categories of gangbanger, ho, and Young Latino Professional. The distinction between gangbangers/hoes and Young Latino Professionals regimented the indexical "ghettoness" and "lameness" of Puerto Rican and Mexican signs. In the tables of metapragmatic stereotypes/models of personhood, I have placed

Table 3.1 "Puerto Rican" Metapragmatic Stereotypes/Model of Personhood

	From Mexican Students' Perspectives (m = male, f = female)	From Puerto Rican Students' Perspectives (m = male, f = female)
Food	lechon (roasted pork), pork chops, tostones (fried green plantains), anything with coconut	arroz con habichuelas (white rice with red kidney beans), pork chops, arroz con gandules (yellow rice with pigeon peas), lechón (roasted pork), greasy, fried, flavorful, large portions
Bodies	light skin, long heads, big butts (f), big chest (f), curvy (f), sexy, dirty	attractive, big butts (f), flat chests (f), razor-arched eyebrows (m)/shaved bodies (m), curvy, bottom heavy, lanky (m)
Hair	curly hair, "fade" (short) haircuts (m), kinky hair, not straight	"fade" (short, stylized) haircuts (m), cornrows/braids (m), long curly hair (f), textured kinky hair (f), straight blow-dried hair (f)
Clothes	too baggy (m), big earrings (f), short shorts (f), ghetto, big shirts (m)	in style/name brands/trendy, "hood"/ghetto, wear pajamas outside, rubber bands at the bottom of jeans, fitted hats, guayaberas
Language	loud, don't get words right/cannot understand what they say in Spanish (can't pronounce the letter "r"), have accents in Spanish	big mouths/loud/ghetto/slang Spanish/Spanglish, fast Spanish, smooth Spanish and English, don't say the "s" in Spanish/don't enunciate in Spanish, accents in Spanish
Names (FN = First Name; S = Surname)	Zoraida (f, FN), Stephanie (f, FN), Jasmine (f, FN), Alex (m, FN), Damien (m, FN), Jonathan (m, FN), David (m, FN), Xavier (m, FN), Ortiz (SN), Martínez (SN), Bautista (SN), Sotomayor (SN), Rivera (SN), Burgos (SN)	Angel (m, FN), José (m, FN), Miguel (m, FN), Jonathan/Jonnie (m, FN)/Jonnie, Jimmy (m, FN), Yadixtza (f, FN), Yahaira/Jahaira (f, FN), Magdalia (f, FN), Destiny (f, FN), Lisandra (f, FN), Zoraida (f, FN)

Table 3.1 continued

	From Mexican Students' Perspectives (m = male, f = female)	From Puerto Rican Students' Perspectives (m = male, f = female)
Personality	ghetto, lazy, funny, loud, attract too much attention, obnoxious	ghetto, lazy, always late, spicy, partiers, jíbaro (old school, closer to island culture)
Sports/Hobbies/ Music	baseball reggaeton, bachata, hip-hop	baseball, boxing, dominoes salsa, reggaeton, bachata, hip-hop
Relationship to Government/ Americanness	more Americanized, undeserving of citizenship	more Americanized, have citizenship, might as well be working here on a Visa, not seen as American, not seen as contributing to America
Socioeconomic Position/ Qualities	beggars, on welfare, homeless, dirty, ghetto	ghetto, on "Link" (welfare)
Geography	Puerto Rico/wanna-be 51st state, New York, Humboldt Park	come from a little island, Humboldt Park, Brickyard (NW Chicago), Logan Square (NW Chicago), New York City, New Jersey

constitutive elements of Mexican and Puerto Rican metapragmatic models into the following categories: food, bodies, hair, clothes, language,[14] names, personality, sports/hobbies, music, relationship to government/Americanness, socioeconomic qualities, and geography. This is by no means an exhaustive list. Countless other aspects of social life in and around NNHS were perceived as Mexican and Puerto Rican.[15] Within NNHS, these categories measured the relative "ghettoness" and "lameness" of Puerto Rican and Mexican students, which in turn located them in relation to the school's project of socialization. In fact, the focus on ghettoness that emerged from students' reception of the distinction between gangbangers/hoes and Young Latino Professionals heightened ingroup anxieties about the meanings of particular practices and characteristics. For example, Mexican students spoke affectionately about Puerto Rican food, yet Puerto Rican students expressed anxieties about whether their food had too much flavor, was too fried, and was served in portions that are too large. These excesses were potentially ghetto. Similarly, Mexican students suggested that

Table 3.2 "Mexican" Metapragmatic Stereotypes/Model of Personhood

	From Mexican Students' Perspectives (m = male, f = female)	From Puerto Rican Students' Perspectives (m = male, f = female)
Food	tacos, tortas (sandwiches), horchata (rice water), pozole (stew), pico de gallo (vegetable-based salsa), guacamole (avocado-based dip), enchiladas, quesadillas, jalapeños, burritos	chorizo con huevos (sausage with eggs), frijoles (beans), tortillas, quesadillas, fresh fruit, chile/spicy, healthy food, will eat every plant, cactus, elotes (corn-based snack food generally sold from outdoor food carts), candy with chile
Bodies	short, brown skin, flat butts, too much makeup, have lots of babies (f)	round heads, small/no butts/culo plancha'o (ironed butt) (f), dark skin, short, a lot of makeup/drawn-on eyebrows (f), fertile/have lots of children (f), top heavy
Hair	spiky hair (m), mohawk hair cuts (m), slicked-back hair (m), straight hair	spiky hair (m), too much gel in their hair (m), slicked-back hair (m), glued down hair to their face (f), straight, black, thick, a lot of body hair
Clothes	cowboy boots (m), Wrangler jeans (m), sombrero (m), high heels (f), short mini-skirts (f), tank tops that reveal too much cleavage (f)	out of style, not matching, overly formal, flannel shirts (m), pointy white shoes (m), rubber bands too high at the bottom of pants (in a way that is out of style)
Language	best/proper Spanish, phrases such as "no mames, güey" (don't fuck around), all Mexicans speak Spanish	thick accents, correct Spanish, words such as "güey" and "paisa," have the "Mexican scream," do not speak English, canta'o (songlike speech), soft spoken
Names (FN = First Name; S = Surname)	José (m, FN), Arturo (m, FN), Jesús (m, FN), Vanessa (f, FN), Mayra (f, FN), Yesenia (f, FN), Guadalupe (f, FN), Sánchez (S), Salazar (S)	Juan (m, FN), José (m, FN), Jesús (m, FN), a lot of names that end in –ito, Guadalupe, Gomez (S), Garcia (S), Mendoza (S)

Table 3.2 continued

	From Mexican Students' Perspectives (m = male, f = female)	From Puerto Rican Students' Perspectives (m = male, f = female)
Personality	cholos (gangsters) (m), ghetto, quiet/shy, polite/proper	nice, emotional, uncool/lame, boys and girls stay separate, passive, immature
Sports/Hobbies/Music	soccer, drinking beer cumbia, durangüense, quebradita, banda, corridos, ranchera, norteña, Spanish rock	soccer, banda (traditional Mexican music), corridos, ballads
Relationship to Government/Americanness	immigrants, sin papeles (without papers)/wetbacks/illegals, paisas (love Mexico)	illegal
Socioeconomic Position/Qualities	hard working, ghetto	hard working, take any job, work many jobs
Geography	Mexico, Little Village, Pilsen, entire South Side of Chicago, California, Southwest, all Mexicans were born in Mexico	Mexico/big country, "fake state," Pilsen, Back of the Yards (South Side), Cermak Road, entire South Side of Chicago

Mexican girls wore excessively revealing clothing that made them ghetto. From Puerto Rican students' perspectives, however, Mexicans were overly formal in their attire. In other situations, Mexican and Puerto Rican conceptions of ghettoness aligned. Puerto Ricans' stereotypically nonstandardized language use, baggy styles of dress (for boys), and bold personalities made them ghetto from both Puerto Rican and Mexican students' perspectives. Meanwhile, Mexican girls' stereotypically excessive use of makeup and Mexican boys' stereotypical insubordination made them ghetto from both Mexican and Puerto Rican students' perspectives. Each of these examples shows how NNHS students' recognitions of Puerto Rican–Mexican difference became infused with indexical signs of ghettoness. Insofar as ghettoness was associated with gangbangers/hoes and defined in opposition to Young Latino Professionals, measuring ghettoness was an indirect way for students to negotiate their recruitment to the role of Young Latino Professional.

Puerto Rican and Mexican students enacted identities by drawing on practices associated with one another's metapragmatic models. After speaking with Jimmy (PR, Gen. 3, Gr. 12) on the telephone several times to schedule tutoring sessions, I discovered that his standard phone greeting was "¿Bueno?" In the Chicago context this is stereotyped as the conventional telephone greeting for Spanish-speaking Mexicans.[16] Here, Jimmy appropriates what is understood as an unmarked Mexican telephone greeting and revalorizes it as cool and funny by contextualizing it in relation his self-described monolingual English speech. Alternative, English-language phone greetings were: "Hello?," "What's up?," "What up?," "What's good?," and "Yo!" Whereas "Hello?" might be considered lame, "What's up?" was too conventional. "What up?," "What's good?," and "Yo!" could all be associated with ghettoness. When voiced by a young, English-dominant Puerto Rican male from Humboldt Park, "¿Bueno?" allowed Jimmy to enact coolness by striking a balance between stereotypical Puerto Rican linguistic ghettoness and stereotypical Mexican linguistic politeness. In fact, when juxtaposed with Jimmy's perceived English dominance, his use of this Mexican Spanish greeting is just the mix of assimilation and authenticity implied by the category of Young Latino Professional.

Rigo (Mex, Gen. 2, Gr. 11), the Mexican student whose hairstyles I described earlier, attempted to appropriate stereotypically ghetto Puerto Rican language practices to impress Puerto Rican girls, but this was only outside of school. He explained to me that he was at a friend's party when he saw a girl he found attractive. Based on her physical features—namely, her "big butt"—he was sure that she was Puerto Rican. Rigo, who was regularly identified as a stereotypical Mexican cholo, approached this young woman and told her, "¡Coño, mami, te ves buena!" (Damn, girl, you look good!). Locally, both "coño" and "mami" are conventionally associated with Puerto Rican speech. He said that she looked at him like he was stupid and ignored him for the rest of the night. Rigo later learned that she is Mexican. For Rigo, addressing a presumed Puerto Rican using Puerto Rican Spanish might allow him to enact coolness and smoothness with this young woman.

Students policed the boundaries of Puerto Rican and Mexican authenticity in complex ways. The presumption of students' Puerto Ricanness and/or Mexicanness in the highly segregated context of NNHS allowed them to engage in practices that might call their authenticity into question in settings that are not so clearly defined as Mexican, Puerto Rican, and/or Hispanic/Latinx. For example, while students could be identified as "skaters" (i.e., skateboarders), "rockers" (i.e., listen to Spanish-language rock music), "emos" (i.e., listen to English-language alternative rock music), "Christians" (i.e., practice evangelical Protestantism), "gamers" (i.e., video game enthusiasts), and "athletes" (i.e., participate in NNHS sports teams), these categories were constructed on top of an assumed backdrop of Mexicanness and Puerto Ricanness.

Some students' practices and enactments of identity juxtaposed characteristics associated with Mexicanness and Puerto Ricanness in ways that became marked and problematic. Yesi (PR, Gen. 1.5, Gr. 12/first year of college), the student whose ethnoracial contortion I detailed at the beginning of the previous chapter, was told by her Puerto Rican friends that her Spanish was slow and that she had a Mexican accent. They questioned whether Yesi was trying to sound "smart" in Spanish, invoking the idea that Mexican Spanish is more proper. In the opposite direction, Jimmy (PR., Gen. 3, Gr. 12) told me that he did not appreciate the fact that a Mexican student, Jorge (Mex, Gen. 2, Gr. 12), tried to act like he was not Mexican by only hanging out with Puerto Rican and African American students. Jorge played for the school's basketball team, thereby deviating from stereotypes that positioned soccer as the sport for Mexicans. Jimmy said he thought that Jorge was Puerto Rican when they first met because he talked "like us." Jorge was one of three boys in the running for the title of 2009 Prom King. Jimmy was glad that Jorge lost to another Mexican student, Raúl (Mex, Gen. 2, Gr. 12). Raúl was a reserved and slightly awkward boy who wore thick glasses, yet Jimmy said that he was "the shit" (i.e., cool). From Jimmy's perspective, Raúl's enactment of Mexicanness made him cool, whereas Jorge's perceived enactment of Puerto Ricanness was interpreted as an unlicensed appropriation, thus making him "an asshole." At the prom, most students cheered excitedly as Raúl and Leti (Mex, Gr. 12, Gen. 1.5) were crowned King and Queen. Both Leti, an undocumented Mexican student,[17] and Raúl enacted unproblematic Mexican identities that allowed Puerto Rican and Mexican students to embrace them. In contrast, Jorge's and Yesi's experiences show how particular enactments of Puerto Ricanness and Mexicanness were viewed as problematic. Not coincidentally, Jorge and Yesi became marked in part because of their Spanish and English language practices, respectively; Chapters 4 and 5 present a detailed analysis of the ideas about language that brought attention to the linguistic practices of students such as Yesi and Jorge.

These examples point to some of the ways that Mexican and Puerto Rican metapragmatic models could be enacted to achieve different social effects inside and outside of school. Importantly, students sought to balance "ghettonness" and "lameness" stereotypically associated with each of these models. The infusion of qualia of ghettoness and lameness into the categories of Mexican and Puerto Rican reflected students' uptake of the distinction between gangbangers/hoes and Young Latino Professionals. Rigo and Jimmy provide just two examples of the ways that these distinctions shaped students' presentations of self and experiences of embodiment inside and outside of NNHS.

Repertoires of Latinidad

Linked colonial histories and experiences of racialization vis-à-vis the United States create a context in which Puerto Ricans and Mexicans in Chicago interact with homogenizing political and popular cultural representations in powerful ways. These interactions contribute to the creation of emblems Latinidad that draw on what are perceived as one another's distinctive cultural practices. This is why working-class Puerto Ricans in Chicago, following Mexicans, now celebrate quinceañeras (15th birthday parties for young women), although not without some controversy in discerning which practices involved in this tradition are more "Mexican" or "Puerto Rican"; in Puerto Rico, these are almost exclusively middle-class celebrations. Likewise, many Northwest Side Chicago Mexicans have shifted their culinary practices so that the rice they cook most often is arroz con gandules (a traditional Puerto Rican rice cooked with pigeon peas); this would be virtually unthinkable in other diasporic Mexican contexts. One Mexican student was a member of a "Banda crew" (a traditional Mexican music and dance group) led by a Chicago Puerto Rican; meanwhile, many Chicago Mexicans participate in Bomba y Plena groups (folkloric Puerto Rican music and dance organizations). These shared practices are unique not simply to the United States but more specifically to the history of shared Latinx experiences in the City of Chicago. Discourses of Mexican-Puerto Rican difference must be analyzed not as direct reflections of lived experiences, but instead as distinctions that reflect intra-Latinx intimacy and repertoires of Latinidad. In fact, in-group knowledge of Mexican-Puerto Rican difference became central to the embodiment and enactment of Latinidad.

Out-group perspectives also play a crucial role in producing emblems of identity. Mexican and Puerto Rican students alike shared humorous stories about African American students and White teachers who thought that everything "Hispanics" did was "just Spanish." These ideas about "Spanishness" became a point of contention at the NNHS prom, which took place in May 2009. In the weeks leading up to this event, one of the most crucial concerns for the school's prom committee was the music playlist. The teacher who worked with the prom committee to organize the event shared the students' music requests with me. In their requests, students specified genres of music, styles of dance, names of artists, and song titles. The list that they created contained a wide variety of genres and dance styles, such as hip-hop, R&B, merengüe, bachata, salsa, reggaeton, cumbia, durangüense, and juke. This includes genres and dance styles associated specifically with the United States broadly (hip-hop, R&B), Chicago (juke),[18] Central America/South America/Mexico (cumbia), Mexico/Chicago (durangüense),[19] the Spanish Caribbean (reggaeton, merengüe, salsa), and the Spanish Caribbean/Mexico (bachata).[20]

On prom night, there were two problems concerning the music. The first was that Dr. Baez did not appreciate the sexually suggestive manner in which students were dancing with one another to hip-hop and juke songs. She clearly viewed such styles of dance as much more closely aligned with the behavior of "gang-bangers" and "hoes" than "Young Latino Professionals." Dr. Baez marched up to the DJ, reminded him that she was writing his check, and told him that if he wanted to get paid at the end of the night he had better answer her requests before those of the students. The DJ promptly switched genres and began playing merengüe, salsa, bachata, reggaeton, cumbia, and durangüense. Tasha, an African American student and one of three girls in the running for prom queen, was visibly upset by the abrupt musical transition. She complained to the DJ and then sat down at a table near the dance floor with a small group of African American students. Tasha pointed out that "they" (the Latinx students) were dancing just as suggestively to the "Spanish music" as everyone had been dancing to hip-hop and juke music.[21] In particular, Tasha referred to the way that students were dancing to reggaeton, a style of music often associated with island-based Puerto Rican artists, predominantly Spanish-language lyrics, a distinctive syncopated beat, and Latin American/Caribbean/hip-hop roots. Indeed, reggaeton music is known for its highly sexualized lyrics and corresponding modes of dance.[22] Puerto Rican and Mexican students said that reggaeton was "ghetto." In recent years, this genre has become extremely popular among youth throughout Latin America and among US Latinxs from various national subgroups, as well as among non-Latinxs worldwide. To the extent that Tasha was talking about reggaeton in particular when she complained about the Latinx students dancing suggestively to "Spanish music," she was not at all mistaken. There was as much suggestive dancing to this music as there was to the hip-hop and juke songs that the DJ had just played. Yet, the "ghettoness" of reggaeton was muted by its contextualization as "Spanish" music alongside genres with dance styles that involved intricate partnering perceived as more respectable, such as salsa (which was stereotyped as smooth), bachata (which was stereotyped as romantic), and merengüe (which was stereotyped as celebratory). Thus, Dr. Baez did not have a problem with reggaeton music, despite the vulgar lyrics and sexually suggestive ways in which Mexican and Puerto Rican students danced to it.

As the DJ shifted between genres, however, Mexican and Puerto Rican students went back and forth between their tables and the dance floor after almost every song. From Tasha's perspective, cumbia, reggaeton, salsa, merengüe, bachata, and durangüense were all part of a single genre: "Spanish music." Meanwhile, Mexican students complained that the DJ was playing too much salsa, and Puerto Rican students complained that he was playing too much cumbia. Tasha's out-group perspective, which channeled broader cultural presumptions about Latinx homogeneity, rested on interrelated ideas about concepts such as "Spanish music,"

"Spanish food," and the "Spanish language," none of which existed to Latinx students as homogeneous categories in the ways that that these labels might suggest.

"Spanishness" is a particularly powerful emblem of Latinx identity.[23] Whereas Part I of this book has focused primarily on how Latinidad comes to be institutionally constructed, contorted, and embodied in relation to intersectional experiences of race, ethnicity, class, gender, and sexuality, the final three chapters pick up on this theme of "Spanishness" in order to explore the powerful role that language ideologies and linguistic practices play in the creation of Latinx identities. Whether in terms of the framing of "Hispanic, Latino, and Spanish origin" as a separate category on the US Census, or perspectives such as Tasha's wherein "Spanish music" sounds like a homogeneous genre associated with all Latinxs (as described earlier), ideas about language shape perceptions of Latinxs as a racially recognizable population. While Chapters 4 and 5 approach these issues in relation to the multiple forms of stigmatization that map onto students' English and Spanish language practices in NNHS, Chapter 6 explores how students' literacy practices reflect their complex engagement with efforts toward transforming their identities. Similar to the various practices described in these opening chapters, language use was infused with ideas about ghettoness and lameness and came to signal one's position with respect to the figures of gangbanger, ho, and Young Latino Professional.

At the end of her ninth-grade year, Leida (Mex, Gen. 2, Gr. 9), earnestly asked the group of students with whom she was sitting, "Do I sound ghetto? Do I look like I sound ghetto? I think I sound ghetto." The remaining chapters of this book explore the nature of these anxieties by showing how, in situations where Latinx bodies refuse to produce straightforward signs of their always already constituted racial subjectivity, language and related signs of identity serve as semiotic stand-ins through which race is rendered perceivable. This co-naturalization of linguistic and racial categories results in the profound social fact that populations come to look like a language and sound like a race across cultural contexts.

II SOUNDING LIKE A RACE

LATINX RACIOLINGUISTIC ENREGISTERMENT

4 "THEY'RE BILINGUAL . . . THAT MEANS THEY DON'T KNOW THE LANGUAGE"

THE IDEOLOGY OF LANGUAGELESSNESS IN PRACTICE, POLICY, AND THEORY

In June 2008 New Northwest High School (NNHS) held its first graduation ceremony. At the beginning of the event, Dr. Baez welcomed the audience with an English-language greeting. She stood alongside Ms. Díaz, a well-respected Dominican staff member who was designated as the Spanish language translator for the event.[1] After Díaz offered a translation of the greeting, Baez intervened momentarily to account for her use of a translator:

BAEZ: Good morning, and welcome.
DIAZ: Buenos días, y bienvenidos a todos.
BAEZ: Ustedes saben que yo hablo Español, pero a veces no recuerdo todas las palabras. (You all know that I speak Spanish, but sometimes I don't remember all of the words.)

Dr. Baez's comments, which were *not* translated into English, elicited a small, warm, and knowing chuckle from the audience.

This was my first encounter with Dr. Baez's linguistic insecurity, which can be analyzed in relation to particular teachers' ideas about her intellectual and interlingual shortcomings.[2] Earlier that year, a self-identified White, monolingual English-speaking teacher explained to me that, among other signs of her stupidity, Dr. Baez's English language skills are "horrible, and from what I hear, her Spanish isn't that good either." The fact that Dr. Baez effectively conducted full meetings with teachers, staff, parents, and students in English and/or Spanish, depending on the context, suggests that criticisms of her language practices were channeling ideas about some deeper inferiority. These ideas surrounding Dr. Baez's language and intelligence demonstrate how Latinxs can be doubly stigmatized through their presumed lack of English *and*

Spanish proficiency. If Dr. Baez, the bilingual school principal with multiple university degrees, including a doctorate in education, was subjected to such discriminatory thinking, then what could this mean for students, who were positioned in highly subordinate institutional positions?

These forms of stigmatization are part of a political economy of raciolinguistic identity (Rosa 2016) and of code choice (Gal 1988), in which language communities become internally and externally stratified. Silverstein suggests that this stratification can be understood as a conical phenomenon, in which "[t]op-and-center folks can look downward-and-outward, as it were, toward peripheries at various degrees of negatively valued deviation from their imagined full-time, default, or unmarked identity" (2003b:535). Within any culture of language standardization, these top/bottom and center/periphery hierarchies organize the construction of models linking language, personhood, and place.[3] Through standardizing institutions such as NNHS, people are socialized to ideologies about ideal and less ideal language practices, the people who use them, and the places where they are used.[4] Silverstein's conical model of language standardization captures the ways that these ideological bundles linking language, person, and place are hierarchically positioned in relation to one another. Throughout this chapter, I seek to highlight an additional characteristic of this conical model of language standardization. Specifically, I am interested in the slippery nature of this cone and the ways that the racialization of language can push minoritized populations to the lowest and most peripheral points. The aforementioned statements about Dr. Baez's illegitimate English and Spanish exemplify this slipperiness. In this case, a high school principal who holds a doctorate in education is pushed to the stigmatized downward and outward peripheries of English and Spanish cultures of standardization. Thus, for US Latinxs, it is crucial to note that perceived deviations from the unmarked "top-and-center" are measured in relation to English *and* Spanish language usage.[5]

I show how national discourses surrounding language and Latinx identity, now framed in terms of a political economy of raciolinguistic identity and of code choice, are linked to linguistic ideology, policy, and practice in NNHS. I also point to some of the implications of these interrelations for scholarly analysis of the creation of ethnolinguistic and raciolinguistic identities. I theorize an ideology of "languagelessness" that delegitimizes Latinxs' English *and* Spanish use within NNHS. As people expected to produce two languages legitimately but understood to use neither correctly, US Latinxs' linguistic practices come to be framed as "supposed 'non-languages'" (Gal 2006:171) in relation to a racialized ideology of languagelessness. I develop the notion of a racialized ideology of languagelessness to characterize the simultaneous stigmatization of US Latinxs' English and Spanish linguistic practices. This raciolinguistic ideology (Flores and Rosa 2015), which frames the linguistic practices of racialized populations as deficient regardless of the extent to which they might be perceived as corresponding to standardized norms, creates an inverted conceptualization of bilingualism. Whereas bilingualism is generally associated with abilities in two languages (e.g., English and Spanish), it becomes redefined as linguistic deficiency altogether. The notion that US Latinxs produce neither "correct" English nor Spanish invokes the idea that they utilize *no* language properly, which simultaneously constructs them as raciolinguistic. Others and legitimates their broader societal marginalization. I argue that this reflects the racializing nature of ideologies of standardization and languagelessness.

"They're bilingual . . . that means they don't know the language"

When I began working as a classroom tutor at NNHS in the AVID (Advancement Via Individual Determination) program, I was troubled by a noticeable pattern.[6] In one classroom after another, students who were officially designated as English Language Learners (ELLs) sat in the corners of the classroom, usually closest to or farthest from the door.[7] All of the students sat in individual desks that were clustered together in groups of four or five. They were allowed to choose their own groups so long as they did not become a disruption, in which case the teacher would intervene and rearrange the groups. Whereas mainstreamed students (i.e., students not designated as ELLs) interacted freely among groups, students designated as ELLs seemed to be cut off from general classroom affairs. The tutors, some of whom were bilingual in English and Spanish, quickly discovered that some students designated as ELLs were unable to understand many of the teachers' instructions in these English-dominant classrooms. Teachers who were bilingual in English and Spanish—approximately one-fourth of the teachers with whom I interacted—occasionally provided instructions in Spanish to students privately if they noticed that students designated as ELLs did not understand a given task. In most cases, however, students designated as ELLs were isolated from general classroom interactions and activities.

Based on my observations and interactions, the majority of students in any classroom engaged in English and Spanish linguistic practices regularly, but there was little interaction between students designated as ELLs and mainstreamed students.[8] Despite fraught relations between bilingual adolescents who were born and/or raised in the US and their ethnoracial counterparts who had more recently arrived to the US and/or were viewed as possessing limited English language skills, I still wondered how teachers and administrators could work to foster mutually beneficial educational relationships among these students.⁹ In the fall of 2008, the beginning of my second year of fieldwork, I had the opportunity to sit down with Dr. Baez to discuss this topic. The following exchange reveals our disparate language ideologies:

  1 JR: A lot of the Spanish-dominant kids who are immersed into
        English-dominant classrooms, a lot of times when I'm in the
        classrooms, they sit in the corners of the room, in the front corner
        or the back corner=
  5 DB: But that's up to the teacher because that wouldn't
        happen with me. I would make sure I paired them off
        (with kids who speak Spanish and English)=
    JR: Well that's, this is the
        point, there are so many kids in the classroom who are
10   fully bilingual, so I wonder=
    DB: We only have eighty-nine students
        who are bilingual here. It's very deceiving.
    JR: What do you mean?
    DB: We have nine hundred and something (total students), but only
15   eighty-nine are bilingual.
    JR: <u>Come on.</u>
    DB: Yes.
    JR: What does that mean?
    DB: They're bilingual. That means they don't know the language. The
20   other ones just don't want to speak it.
    JR: No, when I say bilingual, oh, so you're saying that there are only
        eighty-nine who speak English and Spanish?
    DB: No, there are eighty-nine who need help=
    JR: Who are English
25   Language Learners.
    DB: Right.
    JR: Ok, ok, we're talking about two different things.
    DB: Right.
    JR: So eighty-nine English Language Learners, right?
30 DB: Uh-huh.
    JR: I'm saying that when those kids are in classrooms, a lot of
        times=
    DB: The English Language Learners?
    JR: Yeah.
35 DB: The eighty-nine of them?
    JR: The eighty-nine of them, a lot of times they'll sit in the corners

together, and, and, they're sort of, it's almost like they're separate, and my concern is that=

DB: But those, those eighty-nine are in 40 sheltered classes, which means those are all . . . bilingual.

My well-meaning, yet naïve effort to probe this issue resulted in the principal's explicit articulation of language ideologies surrounding bilingualism in a form that I had not previously encountered. She defined "bilingual" in relation to the transitional bilingual education program, such that bilingualism was equated with Limited English Proficiency (LEP).[10] When I claimed that there are "so many kids in the classroom who are fully bilingual" (lines 9–10),[11] Dr. Baez was quick to disagree and to remind me that the school had only 89 bilingual students. She was emphatic about this number because Illinois state laws require schools to hire additional staff depending on the number of students they serve who are designated as ELLs. If more than 89 students were designated as ELLs, NNHS would have been out of compliance with state laws. This is why Dr. Baez made sure to restate the exact number of students designated as ELLs in lines 35 and 39.

In one sense, Dr. Baez was merely using "bilingual" as an abbreviation for the transitional bilingual education program.[12] Her statement that there were 89 bilingual students meant that there were 89 students officially designated as ELLs and participating in the transitional bilingual education program. In another sense, the normative practice among students and school employees of referring to students designated as ELLs as "the bilingual kids" suggests that the hundreds of students who regularly engaged in both English and Spanish linguistic practices in the school were not defined as bilingual.[13] This corresponds to Fishman's long-standing insight that since the Bilingual Education Act of 1968, which "was primarily an act for the Anglification of non-English speakers and not an act for bilingualism" (1981:519), the notion of " 'bilingualism' has become a newspeak euphemism for 'non-English mother tongue' " (519).[14] As a result, " 'bilinguals' are . . . non-English mother-tongue speakers; 'bilingual teachers' are those who teach them; 'bilingual programs' are those that Anglify them" (519). Thus, the definition of students designated as ELLs as "bilingual" within NNHS was the product of decades of educational language policy and ideology.

This problematic redefinition of bilingualism is tied to what many analysts have critiqued as "subtractive" bilingual education programs, in which English language skills are gained alongside the loss of Spanish language skills (Valenzuela 1999; Valdés 2000). However, I want to argue here that bilingualism was ideologically positioned in relation to another mathematical operation. Bilingualism was not merely devalued or subtractive in this context; it was completely inverted. "Bilingual" students' language skills were measured only in relation to their imputed limited English proficiency; there was no formal way in which their Spanish language abilities were recognized as academically useful.[15] To be bilingual was not to use more than one language; it was to use less than one language in particular. Bilingualism was figured as what I term here *language-lessness*, which slips from standardized assessments of proficiency in particular languages to views that some people are unable to use any language legitimately.[16] I will demonstrate how this racialized ideology of languagelessness informs the creation and implementation of language policy in several interrelated contexts.

When I asked Dr. Baez about her philosophy regarding bilingual education, she described her concerns with the assessment of students' language abilities and the level of curricula designed to meet their educational needs:

1 DB: I think sometimes even bilingual education, it, it, keeps people back. For example, I'm looking at those ACCESS tests now, our students, they're made to, set up to fail.[17] I mean those tests are not even made up for them to move on to the next level.

5 I believe after three years, whether they succeed on those tests or not, three years is sufficient time. Sometimes students abuse it, they, they want to be in bilingual because they find it easier. I do believe more in an immersion program.

JR: But I mean a demanding bilingual program. Do you think that
10 there could be a bilingual program that had high, high standards?

DB: Right now, I believe in bilingual education just for transitioning, because what happens is, they become crutches, it becomes a crutch. When you're in for five years and all that and you still don't learn, kids will take advantage. Whereas
15 when I came here there was no bilingual. I didn't know the language, but when I'm immersed in it, I do not believe though that they should dumb you down and say okay you don't know the language and they put you in fourth grade when you should be in sixth grade. That's, that's wrong.

20 JR: So if the kids are going to be immersed, then, my only concern=

DB: I mean,
let's put it this way: Do you dumb down the Polish kids? Do you put them down in a less grade? You put them in an immersion program, they all learn. Everybody that comes to this country, you know?

In Dr. Baez's view, language proficiency assessments underestimate students' language abilities; similarly, prolonged stays in bilingual education programs prevent students from learning at grade level. In line 3, Dr. Baez refers to the ACCESS language proficiency assessment used in the State of Illinois and 27 other states. This assessment, created by WIDA (World-Class Instructional Design and Assessment), measures language proficiency in reading, writing, speaking, and listening. There is an initial assessment to determine placement for new students and an annual assessment that determines students' progress and readiness to exit the program. In my interviews with testing consultants who helped to design this assessment program, I discovered that policy implications are not generally a part of the discussion as the assessment is being designed. The trouble is that policy implications shape the ways schools administer the assessment. Dr. Baez viewed this test as an inherently flawed instrument that was incapable of gauging students' full English language abilities. Because of this perspective, she wanted as many students as possible to avoid being labeled by the test as Limited English Proficient.

Furthermore, Dr. Baez was concerned that Latinx students were more likely than students from other ethnoracial groups (e.g., Polish students) to fall behind grade level because of their participation in bilingual education. Her Chicago-based perspective reflects her experiences living and working in predominantly Latinx, African American, and Polish neighborhoods since she migrated to the city from Puerto Rico as a toddler. She evaluated bilingual education not only in terms of her more than 30 years of employment in Chicago Public Schools (CPS) but also in relation to her experience of entering CPS as a monolingual Spanish speaker and learning English in an immersion context. Like Dr. Baez, many Latinx parents in Chicago and elsewhere have strong opinions about the negative impact of bilingual education programs and seek to prevent their children from being placed in such programs (Baltodano 2004). Recalling their own educational experiences, particularly the stigma attached to students designated as ELLs, they fear that participation in such programming will cause their children to become objects of scorn and fall behind grade level. The interesting irony is that these perspectives are often held by bilingual Latinxs who raise their children speaking Spanish and English. By ensuring that their children are placed into "mainstream" (i.e., English-dominant) classrooms, they inadvertently contribute to the stigmatization of the Spanish language practices to and through which they socialized their children. Yet, these parents' views reflect their critical awareness of the lack of enriching bilingual education programming in public schools, such as two-way bilingual and biliteracy programs that are advocated by many bilingual education scholars and practitioners (García 2009).

Dr. Baez's ideas about bilingual education were in many ways similar to her broader educational approach. She wanted her students to be seen as "Young Latino Professionals," which meant that they needed to learn English as quickly as possible. Silverstein (2003b) frames these negotiations as matters of ethnolinguistic assimilationism and ethnolinguistic multiculturalism. While the former involves decreasing space for legitimate displays of ethnolinguistic difference (in relation to the unmarked linguistic "top-and-center"), the latter seeks to increase these spaces and to place different languages on equal footing. Like Dr. Baez's broader project of transforming students, the surface assimilationism of the English-only language policy that she embraced was counterbalanced not only by the ubiquity of her Spanish language use but also by other employees' and students' regular displays of bilingualism. In fact, NNHS's limited authorization of Spanish language use for official educational purposes was not so much a sign of the school's allegiance to assimilationism, but rather an entailed outcome of broader district-wide, state, and national language policies. These policies promote the creation of English-only schools in which languages other than English are used only in "foreign language classrooms"[18] or transitional bilingual education classrooms.[19]

The administratively sanctioned use of Spanish throughout NNHS resisted these directives. As discussed in Chapter 1, NNHS alumni created a group Facebook page titled "You know you went 2 NNHS when. . . ." In one student's contribution to the group, she stated: "You know you went to NNHS when you hear people talking in Spanish through the intercom." This student referenced the use of Spanish in schoolwide announcements, which reflects the expectation that English would be used for these kinds of official purposes. Not only could Spanish be heard regularly over the intercom, it was also a default language for Dr. Baez's communication with students. She regularly addressed students as "mijo/a" (my son, daughter), usually followed by her demand that they tuck in their shirts ("¡Métete la camisa por dentro!"). While strictly adhering to prevailing language policies, Dr. Baez also created an educational context in which both Spanish and English language use was normative for informal communication throughout the school. This Spanish language use defied the English-only sentiments that informed the broad rubric of "transitional bilingual education."

Mandatory language policies create a stratified, class-based distinction between elite and remedial bilingualism (Duchêne and Heller 2012; Heller 2006).[20] That is, while bilingualism is understood as a valuable asset or goal for middle-class and upper-class students, for working-class and poor students it is framed as a disability that must be overcome. The following section explores these inequalities further, drawing connections between manifestations of ideologies of languagelessness within NNHS's approach to bilingual education and those within broader spheres of educational language policy.

Scales of Educational Language Policy

While Dr. Baez occasionally spoke favorably about "immersion programs" (i.e., mainstreaming students designated as ELLs into English-only classroom settings), "transition" was the educational approach that she advocated most frequently. This is no coincidence because "transition" is the policy of both CPS and the State of Illinois. These policies distinguish between two types of transitional programming: "Transitional Bilingual Education" in schools with 20 or more students designated as ELLs who speak the same language and "Transitional Program of Instruction" in schools with 19 or fewer students designated as ELLs who speak the same language. The chief distinction between these programs is that Transitional Bilingual Education requires the use of students' first language to provide core curriculum instruction (i.e., math, science, literature, and social studies). The Transitional Program of Instruction uses an English as a Second Language (ESL) model, which does not necessitate the use of students' "first" language.[21] Note that these programs encourage neither the maintenance nor the development of skills in languages other than English; that is, overcoming English language deficiency is paramount in each approach.

Transitional programming as stipulated by CPS and the State of Illinois corresponds to educational language policy on the federal level. Contrary to popular belief, while the paradigmatic 1974 Lau v. Nichols Supreme Court ruling required the provision of resources for students designated as ELLs, it "did not mandate bilingual education" (Wiley 2007:100). The subsequent 1978 reauthorization of the Bilingual Education Act began to redefine the federal policy definition of bilingualism. Efforts toward broadening legislation that was largely defined in relation to "Spanish speakers" resulted in the use of categories such as "children of limited English-speaking ability" in amendments to this act (2007:102). The emphasis on English language deficiency rather than Spanish language proficiency laid the groundwork for bilingual education programs that would focus on transitioning students from the use of languages other than English to monolingual English use. These programs presupposed assimilation and monolingualism as educational best practices.[22]

National educational language policies, as well as various English-only movements, are linked to language ideologies that frame the United States as a nation in which standardized English is and should be the nation's only official language (Woolard 1989; Santa Ana 2004; Baltodano 2004; Crawford 2003). As a result, "non-English languages are spoken of as foreign, native, or indigenous languages, regardless of where the speakers live" (Santa Ana 2002:212). Santa Ana (2002) analyzes these issues in the context of California's Proposition 227, popularly referred to as "English for the Children." This antibilingual education legislation, which was voted into law in 1998, sought to ensure "that all children in California public schools shall be taught English as rapidly and effectively as possible" (2002:198). Santa Ana shows how metaphors such as "language as water" inform English "immersion" policies in which "language is characterized as a *stream*, shifting between languages is described as occurring *fluidly*, and linguistic competence and communicative competence are *fluency*" (2002:202). Proposition 227's method of Sheltered English classes for students designated as ELLs was similar to the State of Illinois transitional programming; in each of these approaches, "the primary language of children is considered a problem, and treated as inessential to 'real' education" (2002:204).[23] Santa Ana offers a strong critique of these language-learning programs:

> In the case of non-English-speaking public school students, [Sheltered English] is a diversion from real education. Furthermore, the school year spent in Sheltered English, in which language learning is emphasized at the expense of literacy and other educational content, places the child at an unnecessary disadvantage when the child is then placed in English-only classrooms to compete with monolingual English-speaking peers who did not take a similar educational detour. In the hands of Proposition 227 proponents, the Sheltered English method denies the validity of Spanish and other languages in serious education. Most grievous, normal children are treated as if they suffered from an educational liability. Even though they arrive at school possessing a linguistic advantage, bilingual children are viewed as having a limitation which must be corrected. Sheltered English "repairs" an alleged educational deficit with a remedial program. (2002:205)

Like Santa Ana, Dr. Baez and many other Latinxs view transitional/sheltered programming as educational detours. Illinois educational language policies leave no room for two-way bilingual education (that seeks to maintain and build skills in more than one language), which Santa Ana characterizes as "a complete pedagogy based on how learning can best be facilitated" (2002:206). It is not clear, however, that students designated as ELLs, their families, or schools would be interested in pursuing two-way bilingual education. This was certainly not a battle that Dr. Baez was interested in waging. For Santa Ana, an important part of bilingual education is that "the social background of the children is a central issue . . . an issue which is far less likely to be addressed in English-only instruction" (2002:206). Dr. Baez worked to make NNHS an educational setting in which the social background of the children is a central issue while still adhering to the prevailing, English-focused language policies.

NNHS's approach to serving students designated as ELLs reflects the hegemony of deficiency-based approaches to language assessment and anxieties surrounding the high stakes of educational accountability. Dr. Baez embraced transitional programming as a best practice and articulated bilingualism in terms of limited English proficiency. Each of these views coincides with district, state, and federal policy. She vehemently rejected my claim that there were "so many" bilingual students in her school. "Bilingual" students were those designated as ELLs, and only 89 students were officially classified as such. If more students should have been designated as ELLs, then the school would be in violation of district, state, and federal policy.

Several teachers claimed that students in their mainstream classes should have been designated as ELLs and placed into bilingual education programming. These teachers' concerns point to the multiple ways in which students designated as ELLs can be disserved through the hegemonic embrace of transitional bilingual programming. Students officially designated as ELLs are placed into transitional programs that devalue skills in languages other than English and frequently deliver content that is below their grade level. Meanwhile, the rapid mainstreaming of students previously designated as ELLs into classrooms where English is the default language devalues their skills in languages other than English. Administrators and teachers are therefore required to choose between two detrimental options.

The effort to transition students into mainstream English language classrooms as quickly as possible emerges from anxieties about the ways that educational underachievement both stems from and leads to linguistic deficiency. MacSwan, Rolstad, and Glass show how these notions of deficiency have led to the classification of thousands of Latinx students as "non-nons," a category of "Spanish-background school-age children living in the United States who are reported to be non-verbal in both English and Spanish" (2002:395). They show how this classification stems from biased language assessments that define Spanish and English linguistic competence in highly narrow terms that systematically erase students' Spanish and English skills. The notion of "non-non" is an explicit example of a racialized ideology of languagelessness. Again, the striking point is that on a different scale, even a highly credentialed, bilingual school principal such as Dr. Baez can be framed similarly as a "non-non" of sorts. As such, it is important to critically analyze these linguistic classifications in relation to ideas about group inferiority based on axes of difference such as race, class, and gender.

Race and class dynamics are acutely reflected in the contrast between the remedial notion of bilingualism that informs the creation of categories such as "non-non" and the conceptualization of cosmopolitan, elite bilingualism that shapes the approach to language learning in more economically privileged educational settings. The difference here is in the particular kind of deficiency associated with classification as an ELL in the US context, where concepts such as "English Language Learner," "English as a Second Language," and "Limited English Proficient" would make little sense if one were to replace "English" with the name of any other language.[24] The class-based distinction between remedial bilingualism as practiced within open enrollment schools such as NNHS and elite bilingualism as practiced within selective enrollment or application-based schools is structured such that students designated as ELLs are served almost exclusively in open enrollment schools. This creates the ironic situation in which many application-based charter schools in Chicago are called "language academies," despite the fact that they serve few students designated as ELLs, if any at all. This situation is not particular to CPS; in fact, it is a common characteristic of urban districts throughout the nation.

A special education teacher at NNHS suggested to me that students designated as ELLs and special education students occupy a shared position as second-class students in public schools. Selective enrollment schools and application-based charter schools accept almost none of these students. In many of these selective settings, all students can take core courses in languages other than English, and classroom language learning is combined with trips to countries in which languages other than English predominate. One CPS language academy's website states, "Spanish, German, French, Italian or Chinese are as much a part of your day as social studies, mathematics, science, language arts, music, art, and physical education." Its homepage highlights stories such as "April in Paris," "Students leave to Italy," and "Students in Barcelona, Spain." Unlike the overall demographics of CPS, schools designated as language academies often have far fewer low-income students and far more White students. The homepage of the language academy described previously also highlights the school's Parent Teacher Association, which "is dedicated to raising more than $100,000 each year to enhance and advance our children's educational experience." In contrast to NNHS and other open enrollment schools in which bilingualism is typically experienced as a problem to be managed, such language academies draw on parents' resources to create school environments that override the English-only ethos of mainstream educational language policy. Schools such as NNHS are not afforded the same privilege to reframe language policies in these ways, nor do NNHS students' parents have the resources to fund enrichment educational activities. These dynamics highlight the ways that race and class frame some students as legitimate learners of various languages and other students as linguistically deficient or languageless.[25]

Linguistic Stigmatization Across Contexts

In June 2010, Fox News Chicago broadcasted a story about "Chicago's language divide," titled "Inside the 'Spanish Bubble.'"[26] The report opens with the following statement:

> Within the next 20 years, one out of every three people in the Chicago-area will be of Spanish-speaking descent. In fact, there are some long-time residents in the city, at this very moment, who never speak English, because, well, they say there's not really been a need to learn it. Critics say they're living in a "Spanish bubble"—isolating themselves from mainstream American society and creating a cultural divide.

The story goes on to profile Latinxs who claim that they do not need to speak English in "Pilsen, or Little Village, or Humboldt Park, among other areas of Chicago, and many suburbs." It also presents the perspectives of Chicagoans who are "concerned they'll need to learn Spanish long before the growing Latino community learns English." In the end, though, the report assuages viewers' and readers' fears:

> The next generations of Chicago Latinos, including those who just graduated from the predominantly-Hispanic Metropolitan Leadership Institute, are breaking out of the "Spanish Bubble" with encouragement from folks like their commencement speaker, Mayor Richard M. Daley. "In Chicago, all of us respect the past. But we live in the present, and there's always a vision for the future," Daley said. "If you don't have it, that's where your city fails, that's where everybody else fails, where your family fails, where you fail."

This story succinctly presents a striking bundle of language ideologies: (1) it racializes language and Latinxs by referring to people of "Spanish-speaking descent" and implying that language is biologically inherited; (2) it completely obfuscates rapid Spanish language loss among US Latinxs by suggesting that it is normative for US Latinxs to be monolingual Spanish speakers; (3) it suggests that Latinxs strategically create a "bubble" around themselves, which frames segregation and marginalization as the products of individual choices rather than structural phenomena; (4) it naturalizes English monolingualism and hegemony; and (5) it chronotopically positions the Spanish language/Spanish speakers as parts of Chicago's past that should be respected, compared with the English language/English speakers who compose the city's present and future.

Ideas such as the "Spanish bubble," which pertain to language and Latinx identity in Chicago, are linked to ideologies of languagelessness on broader scales. In 1980 the US Census Bureau began posing a two-part language question: (1) Does this person speak a language other than English in the home? and (2) How well does this person speak English? The first question requires respondents to report the language other than English that is spoken at home, and the second question requires respondents to categorize themselves as speaking English "very well, well, not well, or not at all." Between 1990 and 2011, the Census Bureau classified all members of a household in which no one over the age of 14 self-identified as speaking English "very well," as linguistically isolated[27]:

> A linguistically isolated household is one in which no person aged 14 or over speaks English at least "Very well." That is, no person aged 14 or over speaks only English at home, or speaks another language at home and speaks English "Very well." A linguistically isolated person is any person living in a linguistically isolated household. All the members of a linguistically isolated household are tabulated as linguistically isolated, including members under 14 years old who may speak only English.[28]

The classification of "linguistically isolated" completely erases skills in languages other than English for people older than 14; English language skills of children aged 14 and younger in so-called "linguistically isolated" households are similarly erased. As Zentella has pointed out:

> "Linguistically isolated" is an inaccurate and discriminatory label, since it categorizes as "isolated" only the 45 percent of households in the USA where adults who speak another language have some difficulty with English (55 percent speak English very well), not the great majority of the U.S. households (82 percent) in which no one speaks anything but English. (Zentella 2007:34)

The one nation–one language–one people thinking that informs notions such as "linguistic isolation" also plays a structuring role in English-only language legislation and remedial bilingual education policies. The notion of linguistic isolation is an example of a racialized ideology of languagelessness because it slips from an assessment of abilities in English to claims about linguistic deficiency altogether.[29]

The notion of "linguistic isolation" demonstrates that while remedial bilingual education policies detrimentally affect everyday school life for students designated as ELLs, the broader language ideologies that shape these policies have implications for all Latinxs. Recall that from some teachers' perspectives, even Dr. Baez was presumed to speak no language legitimately. The forms of linguistic stigmatization faced by NNHS students frame them as languageless. The racialized nature of the ideology of languagelessness as it applies to US Latinxs suggests that this ideology can be understood as what Skutnabb-Kangas calls *linguicism*, "linguistically argued racism" (Skutnabb-Kangas 1988:13; Phillipson 1992).[30] The notion of linguicism corresponds to the remapping of race "from biology onto language" (Zentella 2007:26; Uricuoli 1996, 2001). Whereas claims about biological inferiority are no longer acceptable in mainstream US public discourse, claims about linguistic inferiority are often perceived as perfectly legitimate. Latinxs' simultaneous positioning in relation to English *and* Spanish is a crucial component of the remapping of race from biology onto language in the context of NNHS. This remapping is articulated through a racialized ideology of languagelessness that subjects Latinxs to the experience of double-stigmatization in relation to their perceived illegitimate use of English and Spanish.[31]

Examples of the racialized ideology of languagelessness and the stigmatization with which it is associated can also be found in scholarly approaches to the analysis of language use. In his well-known article, "Literate and Illiterate Speech," famed linguist Leonard Bloomfield provides one such example:

> White-Thunder, a man round forty, speaks less English than Menomini, and that is a strong indictment, for his Menomini is atrocious. His vocabulary is small; his inflections are often barbarous; he constructs sentences on a few threadbare models. He may be said to speak no language tolerably. His case is not uncommon among younger men, even when they speak but little English. Perhaps it is due, in some indirect way, to the impact of the conquering language. (Bloomfield 1927:437)

In Bloomfield's analysis, White-Thunder speaks neither English nor Menomini legitimately. Bloomfield's expectation that White-Thunder should demonstrate proficiency in both languages contributes to his scathing assessment. As Martin-Jones and Romaine (1986) demonstrated more than 20 years ago, these formulations, like "semilingualism," are half-baked theories of communicative competence. Martin-Jones and Romaine also emphasize that it is not by chance that such assessments of linguistic incompetence characteristically emerge in studies focused on minoritized populations. These assessments are rooted in language ideologies that imagine particular populations as linguistically and culturally inferior, compared with more idealized models of linguistic and cultural personhood.

In addition to being "half-baked theories of communicative competence," such formulations are also constitutive elements of racialized ideologies of languagelessness. These ideologies' effects can be discovered in countless contexts. In educational institutions alone, I have encountered these effects at elementary, secondary, and university levels. Many of the younger siblings of the Latinx students among whom I conducted ethnographic research in Chicago were bilingual English-Spanish users yet learned to deny their Spanish language abilities in school and became ashamed of their perceived accented English as soon as they entered mainstream educational settings. These young people were already facing the racialization and stigmatization of their language use.

Recall the discussion of Yesi (PR, Gen. 1.5, Gr. 12/first year of college) that opened Chapter 2. One of the highest achieving students at NNHS, Yesi was a member of the first graduating class and went on to attend a highly selective liberal arts college.[32] Yesi came to Chicago from Puerto Rico at the age of four. In interactions with family and friends, I regularly observed her drawing on a range of English and Spanish linguistic practices. In her first year of college, Yesi enrolled in an intermediate Spanish composition and conversation course. A stereotypical overachiever, she attended the professor's office hours every week, carefully noted his comments, turned in all assignments on time, completed five extra-credit essays, and did not miss a single class. At the end of the semester Yesi called me in tears and reported that she was only able to achieve a "D" in the course. She attributed the grade to her trouble with the various writing assignments that constituted the primary graded work for the course. Yesi explained that this course made her feel as though she couldn't speak "her language" and that as a result she had failed her family and herself.

Yesi's experiences with stigmatizing ideas about her Spanish language use are similar to those that heritage language users face in a variety of educational contexts (Leeman 2012). As a heritage user of Puerto Rican Spanish, Yesi was not perceived as producing spoken and written Spanish forms that corresponded to the standardized language and literacy practices that her professor required. In a particularly embarrassing incident, her professor excoriated her publicly for saying troque instead of camión (truck). He viewed troque as a problematic calque from English to Spanish, and suggested that Yesi's father would never talk like that. Yesi interpreted this incident as a public shaming. She explained, "it hurt a lot, I felt like he was calling me stupid." As one of only two non-White students and the only Latina in the class, Yesi felt pressured to outperform her classmates. This was unlike her Advanced Placement Spanish class at NNHS, which Yesi described as an "amazing experience." She said that the Advanced Placement course produced far less anxiety than her other courses and that "Spanish was a neutral ground" she shared with her Latinx classmates. Yesi's Cuban Spanish teacher at NNHS made it clear that Puerto Rican and Mexican Spanish are perfectly legitimate varieties and that students should see the class as an opportunity to improve the skills that they already possessed. Yesi said that this class helped her to communicate with her Spanish-dominant father more comfortably than ever before. She also scored a 4 out of 5 on the Advanced Placement exam; this score counts for college credit at many US institutions of higher education.

Yesi's Spanish course in college was another story. The biggest problems were essay assignments, for which Yesi regularly received failing grades. Her professor told her, "Estás haciendo errores básicos." (You are making basic mistakes.) The forms in question included verb conjugations and gender agreement between articles and nouns.[33] Yesi's strong speaking abilities and extensive knowledge of Puerto Rican and Mexican vocabulary did not count toward her grade. Her perceived inability to produce standardized spoken and written forms made her feel as though she did not know Spanish at all. This stigmatization demonstrates the different shape that the projected tension between assimilation and multiculturalism takes depending on the context. In NNHS, it was crucial to be perceived as speaking "unaccented" English so as not to be labeled an ELL. At her elite liberal arts college, however, Yesi's marked linguistic practices—Spanish and English, alike— were part of the "diversity" that she was recruited to contribute to the campus. In these contexts, diversity is a commodity constituted by the presence and practices of students marked as culture-bearers; "culture" operates as a stand-in for race (Urciuoli 2009). Yesi's duty to contribute to campus diversity pulled her in several directions. She felt the need to display both Puerto Rican and pan-Latina diversity. Her Puerto Rican Spanish provided the linguistic means to achieve the former, but she would need to take a college Spanish course to achieve the latter. Yesi struggled to manage the competing authenticities that her particular "diversity" required her to emanate. She was recruited to enact Latina authenticity through her use of the Spanish language at the same time that she nearly failed her Spanish course. While Yesi was met with the stigmatization of her Spanish language skills in her Spanish course, her peers often corrected her English language use, and more than one professor asked whether English was her native language when commenting on the papers she wrote in English. In some instances, Yesi's Spanish was not good enough; in others, her English was perceived as incorrect or contaminated by Spanish. Yesi said that on campus she felt as though she did not know how to use any language legitimately and wondered whether she should say or write anything at all.

This student's experiences reflect the cumulative ways in which stigmatization through ideologies of language standardization can position one as languageless.

In the summer following Yesi's first year at college, she worked with the same college bridge program for CPS students that helped her to gain acceptance to college while she was a student at NNHS. Approximately one-third of the program's 100 participants were Latinx. The program, based in a prominent Chicago university, had no Latinx or English-Spanish bilingual employees other than Yesi. Upon learning about the expected cost of college tuition, many (im) migrant Latinx parents pulled their children out of the program. The program's directors needed someone to help bilingual English-Spanish speaking students explain to their Spanish-dominant parents in a culturally resonant way that they would have a variety of financial aid opportunities. By stepping into this role, Yesi became one of the program's most prized employees. Her cultural and linguistic knowledge of Spanish and English was suddenly made valuable just a few short weeks after she nearly failed an intermediate Spanish language course and faced constant correction of her spoken and written English. This demonstrates the dramatically disparate, contextual ways that one's language use can be framed as an invaluable resource or a sign of deficiency. These shifting valuations are characteristic of the slippery, racialized relationship between ideologies of language standardization and languagelessness.

This mildly redeeming story must not distract from the broader analysis of the multiple ways in which Latinxs' Spanish and English language skills are multiply stigmatized and inverted into languagelessness. Too often we are left with the impression that the English language in itself will provide US Latinxs with access to societal inclusion. For Latinxs who are designated as "English Language Learners" in US schools or as "Limited English Proficient" in other mainstream institutional contexts, the implication is that there is a "language barrier" that must be overcome in order for them to become legitimate participants in and members of the nation. However, millions of US-born and/or raised Latinxs who identify as bilingual, English-dominant, or monolingual English users and yet still experience profound forms of inequality in the realms of education, employment, housing, health care, the criminal justice system, electoral politics, and so on, clearly demonstrate that this is not the case. The same could be said for countless other racialized people in the United States, such as many African Americans and Native Americans, who face profound forms of structural inequality even if they identify as monolingual English users. For various racialized groups, neither the use of a particular "national" language nor the standardized variety of that language alone can ensure societal inclusion. Note that the similar quotations from Bloomfield about White-Thunder and the NNHS teacher about Dr. Baez were articulated more than 80 years apart in relation to completely different ethnoracial groups, languages, and social contexts. The striking similarity between these quotations speaks to the powerfully entrenched nature of the relationship between ideologies of standardization and languagelessness on the one hand, and the anchoring of these ideologies in processes of racialization on the other.

NNHS's localization of transitional bilingual education programming created a context in which Spanish language use was not stigmatized by school administrators as it might be in other contexts. Still, the school was subject to city and state policies that frame bilingualism as an impediment for racially minoritized students, which constrained the potential for these students' bilingual repertoires to contribute to their academic achievement (Cummins 2000). Instead, policy was driven by "*a monoglossic ideology*, which values only monolingualism and ignores bilingualism . . . and sees language as an autonomous skill that functions independently from the context in which it is used" (García and Torres-Guevara 2010:182, authors' italics). Anxieties that the Spanish language—and those who use it—are taking over the United States obscure the fact that US Latinxs "are undergoing language loss similar to, and even exceeding, that of other groups in U.S. history" (Zentella 2003:331–332; Veltman 2000). Despite this fact, 32 US states had passed legislation making English the official language as of 2016. These ideologies, anxieties, policies, and processes of language shift make it difficult to imagine the potential for multilingual education to take "its rightful place as a meaningful way to education *all* children and language learners in the world today" (Gárcia 2009:9, author's italics).

This is an initial account of how Latinx identities are constructed and experienced in relation to racialized language ideologies, policies, and practices. Chapter 5 expands on this analysis of languagelessness to demonstrate how racialized language ideologies shaped linguistic practices within NNHS. These practices responded not only to the multiple forms of linguistic stigmatization created by the educational policies described earlier but also to Dr. Baez's project of transforming (recognitions of) students from gangbangers and hoes into Young Latino Professionals.

5 "PINK CHEESE, GREEN GHOSTS, COOL ARROWS/PINCHES GRINGOS CULEROS"

INVERTED SPANGLISH AND LATINX RACIOLINGUISTIC ENREGISTERMENT

This chapter builds from the preceding analysis of the multiple forms of stigmatization associated with Latinxs' English *and* Spanish language practices, to demonstrate some of the complex ways that Latinx New Northwest High School (NNHS) students attempted to fashion linguistic escape routes from this stigmatization. I present a set of sociolinguistic biographies of Latinx NNHS students that characterizes the range of linguistic repertoires in NNHS and demonstrates how concepts such as monolingualism and bilingualism are limited in their ability to capture the complexity of students' language use. In efforts to situate these linguistic practices in relation to broader scales, I show how linked ideologies and institutional pressures recruit US Latinxs to find ways to produce Spanish *in* English without being perceived as having an accent. I suggest that a process of *raciolinguistic enregisterment* creates a set of language practices that allows them to manage these competing demands. These practices, which I refer to as "Inverted Spanglish," signal intimate familiarity with the English and Spanish languages. I refer to these practices as "Inverted Spanglish" because they flip the script on normative presumptions about patterns associated with linguistic forms, racial categories, and their interrelations. I highlight particular aspects of these practices by rethinking Jane Hill's notion of "Mock Spanish" (Hill 1993, 1998, 2008). Whereas Hill claims that Whites' "Mock Spanish" usages indirectly stigmatize Spanish speakers and "members of historically Spanish-speaking populations" en masse, I suggest that Mock Spanish stigmatizes populations *racialized* as US Latinxs regardless of their linguistic practices. I argue that Latinxs appropriate Mock Spanish and transform it into Inverted Spanglish to enact particular identities that are specific to the US context. Inverted Spanglish also represents NNHS students' satirical response to Dr. Baez's project of transforming them into Young Latino Professionals.

On the morning of Tuesday, May 26, 2009, just as freshman students in a classroom at NNHS were beginning to sit down for first period, Mr. Thomas silenced the lively ninth-grade chatter: "Raise your hand if you are Puerto Rican." Approximately half of the 26 students and four tutors in the classroom raised their hands. Mr. Thomas, a young White teacher known for his energetic and approachable pedagogical style, said that everyone with their hands in the air should be proud to be Puerto Rican that day. He had just read on the news section of the website "Yahoo!" that President Barack Obama was preparing to announce his nomination of Sonia Sotomayor, a Bronx-born Puerto Rican, to the US Supreme Court later that morning. My visible excitement was met with blank stares from the group of four students—two Puerto Rican, two Mexican—with whom I was sitting. I explained the historical significance of the nomination to them, emphasizing aspects of Sotomayor's biography that were similar to several of these students' everyday realities (i.e., she grew up working class and was raised primarily by her mother, who migrated to the United States from Puerto Rico). Mr. Thomas was somewhat annoyed by the students' lack of interest in what he considered to be such an important event; he quickly shifted gears to provide students with instructions for the day's activities.

Within 24 hours of President Obama's announcement of Sotomayor's nomination, commentators of varying political persuasions weighed in on a range of issues regarding her candidacy for the Supreme Court. These commentators voiced opposing viewpoints not only on Sotomayor's legal, ethical, and academic qualifications for the nation's highest court, but also on the syllable stress that should be used in the pronunciation of her surname! On May 26, Mark Krikorian, executive director of the Washington-based Center for Immigration Studies, contributed a posting titled "Assimilated Pronunciation"[1] to "The Corner," the blog portion of the online version of the *National Review,* a popular biweekly conservative newsmagazine. He initially poses this question about the pronunciation of Sotomayor:

> So, are we supposed to use the Spanish pronunciation, so-toe-my-OR, or the natural English pronunciation, SO-tuh-my-er, like Niedermeyer? The president pronounced it both ways, first in Spanish, then after several uses, lapsing into English.

In a follow-up post on May 27 titled "It Sticks in My Craw,"[2] Krikorian presents a more pointed take on the situation:

> Most e-mailers were with me on the post on the pronunciation of Judge Sotomayor's name (and a couple griped about the whole Latina/Latino thing—English dropped gender in nouns, what, 1,000 years ago?). But a couple said we should just pronounce it the way the bearer of the name prefers, including one who pronounces her name "freed" even though it's spelled "fried," like fried rice. . . . Putting the emphasis on the final syllable of Sotomayor is unnatural in English (which is why the president stopped doing it after the first time at his press conference), unlike my correspondent's simple preference for a monophthong over a diphthong, and insisting on an unnatural pronunciation is something we shouldn't be giving in to. . . . And there are basically two options—the newcomer adapts to us, or we adapt to him. And multiculturalism means there's a lot more of the latter going on than there should be. (May 27)

For Krikorian, the assimilation of apparent non-American linguistic practices to American linguistic norms must be strongly encouraged.[3] In this case, pronouncing "Sotomayor" with final-syllable stress signals the problematic assimilation of English to Spanish.[4] For Krikorian, the difference between what he describes as a monophthong and a diphthong is an entirely reasonable alternation, but final-syllable stress crosses the linguistic line.[5] Krikorian is similarly concerned with the apparent backwardness of the gender marking of Spanish nouns, and the way that the use of gendered terms such as "Latina" and "Latino" poses a threat to the advancement of English beyond such primitive tendencies. Above all else, he interprets these language practices as signs of multiculturalism run amuck. Thus, Latinx difference must be managed carefully to prevent it from unraveling the nation's cultural fabric.

Within two hours of Krikorian's May 27 posting, Andrew Leonard, author and contributing editor to *Newsweek*, responded directly to Krikorian on "How the World Works," a blog section of the liberal online magazine, *Salon.com*. Leonard's posting, titled "How to pronounce Sotomayor,"[6] presents the liberal counterpoint to Krikorian:

> Personally, I feel that pronouncing someone's name the way they would like it pronounced is a sign of courtesy and respect. . . . But most ridiculous is the idea that something is not "natural" in *English*. In all of the world, there is no more mongrel or polyglot tongue than English; no language more gleefully willing to taint its purity. English borrows from every other

language with abandon, steals "foreign" vocabulary without remorse, scoffs at any and every linguistic boundary. Such free-and-easy kaleidoscopic adaptability is English's great strength. . . . Multiculturalism is a writer's delight! It gives us more room to play, expands the possibilities built into our minds. Krikorian appears to be suggesting that we emulate the French, who are always striving so hard to keep their language free of foreign contamination. He's either forgotten, or never understood, that what makes the language he speaks so great is that it welcomes all comers and adapts effortlessly to them, without chagrin or fear or hate.

For Leonard, the adaptability of the English language is its very strength. In fact, he ventures so far as to claim that there is no language in the world that contains more "diversity" than English.[7] The English language, in Leonard's view, is uniquely capable of welcoming and incorporating linguistic difference.

At first glance, Krikorian and Leonard appear to present clearly opposing viewpoints in a now familiar debate between multiculturalism and assimilation.[8] "Multiculturalism," in this case signaled primarily by syllable stress in the pronunciation of one's surname, either strengthens or threatens the nation's character. Beneath this surface appearance of opposition, however, Krikorian and Leonard draw on a strikingly similar set of language ideologies:

1. English is a personified object with natural qualities.
2. English is (hyper-)modern, sits atop the linguistic food chain, and should be celebrated for its superiority.
3. English is made "unnatural" or "mongrelized" by its incorporation of linguistic difference.
4. A language corresponds to a people and a nation.
5. The pronunciation of a name is a simultaneous reflection of the character of individuals and the nation.

From each of these perspectives, the English language is uniquely powerful and superior in quality to other languages. The question for Krikorian and Leonard is whether the increasing prominence of Latinx identity, in conjunction with its ideological linkage to the Spanish language, challenges or enhances English language hegemony. While Krikorian and Leonard disagree on whether the assimilation of Latinx difference threatens or strengthens the nation, they both view Latinx difference as something to be managed and changed.[9]

These debates demonstrate how Latinx difference is always created in close ideological proximity to a set of conceptions of the relationship between language and identity. In particular, Latinx identities emerge as complex phenomena that ideologically link a variety of English and Spanish language practices to eth-noracial categories. As is evident in the debate between Krikorian and Leonard described earlier, Latinx language practices can signal dramatically distinct ori-entations to Americanness. These shifting projections of Americanness structure the interrelation between processes of linguistic and ethnoracial enregisterment, on the one hand, and the double-stigmatization of Latinxs' English and Spanish language use, on the other. Enregisterment (Silverstein 2003; Agha 2007) pro-vides a theoretical vantage point from which to track the co-naturalization of social and linguistic categories. That is, rather than seeking to identify a discrete set of Latinx language practices, an enregisterment-based analysis focuses on the ideological production of distinctive sets of linguistic forms and social identities. To situate local negotiations of these processes of language and identity forma-tion in relation to a broader frame, the following section provides an overview of language ideologies and the racialization of US Latinxs.

Raciolinguistic ideologies and US Latinxs

Mexican and Puerto Rican NNHS students' identification and demonstrated fa-cility with varying repertoires of Spanish and English forms can be understood in relation to broader conceptions of Latinx languages and identities. For example, in the book *Living in Spanglish: The Search for Latino Identity in America*, Puerto Rican journalist Ed Morales (2002) asks:

> Why Spanglish? There is no better metaphor for what a mixed-race cul-ture means than a hybrid language, an informal code. . . . Spanglish is what we speak, but it is also who we Latinos are, and how we act, and how we perceive the world. It's also a way to avoid the sectarian nature of other labels that define our condition, terms like Nuyorican, Chicano, Cuban American, Dominicanyork. (Morales 2002:3)

In Morales' take on what many autobiographers have described as a fractured Latinx identity (Rodriguez 1982; Anzaldúa 1987), *Spanglish* is proposed as a unifying force among Latinxs, Morales analogizes Latinos, as members of a "mixed-race culture," with *Spanglish*, "a hybrid language." Note here the fasci-nating play on the Herderian ideology of one language–one nation–one people (Herder 1968; Bauman and Briggs 2003; Irvine 2006), in which the "one lan-guage" of Latinxs is a Spanish-English hybrid. Yet, many analysts have noted that the Spanish language, if even spoken at all, often provides grounds for the recog-nition of intra-Latinx difference, not similarity (De Genova and Ramos Zayas 2003; Ghosh Johnson 2005; Zentella 2007; Mendoza-Denton 2008). That is,

Spanish is by no means an unequivocal unifying force for Latinxs because: (1) many Latinxs do not engage in what are conventionally understood as Spanish language practices often, if at all; (2) some Latinxs disidentify with the Spanish language; and (3) varieties of Spanish are frequently the most straightforward signs of, for example, Mexican-Puerto Rican difference.[10]

Despite Latinxs' heterogeneous linguistic repertoires, the continued presumption of their primordial linkage to Spanish demonstrates the iconic relationship between ethnoracial and linguistic categories. Throughout the United States, Latinxs look like the Spanish language, and Spanish sounds like Latinxs. This means that Latinxs are imaginatively heard to be speaking Spanish regardless of whether they are speaking what from many perspective might be perceived as "unaccented" English or have experienced minimal socialization to or through the Spanish language. The experience of *looking like a language* was particularly bothersome for a Filipino NNHS teacher, Mr. Maldonado, who complained that Dr. Baez continually insisted on speaking to him in Spanish despite the fact that he told her on several occasions that he spoke no Spanish whatsoever. He suggested that the combination of his brown skin and his surname led most people (inside and outside of NNHS) to assume that he was Latino and could speak Spanish.[11] Mr. Maldonado jokingly mentioned that even though he was born and raised in Chicago as a monolingual English user, many people told him he had a Spanish accent and asked him where in Latin America he was from. Another teacher, Mr. Rios, told me that he conducts an "eyeball test" when he walks into a classroom to gauge the number of Spanish speakers. Rios, a dedicated young Puerto Rican teacher, said that he greets his classes by saying, "Hola, familia" ("Hello, family"). He reported that even when every student in the class is Latinx, several of them make it a point to remind him that they do not speak Spanish.

As a counterpart to these instances of looking like a language, NNHS students often encountered the experience of sounding like a race. When I asked David (PR, Gen. 3, Gr. 12) whether he has an accent, he responded, "No! . . . I think I might though."[12] He explained that while playing an Internet-based video game that allows players to hear one another's voices through a microphone, one of his virtual opponents told him to "Shut the fuck up, you Mexican!" David went on to describe the confusion that this attack prompted: "Whoa! He came real hard at me. Why you say I'm Mexican? I was just talking English and they come and say I'm Mexican out of nowhere. . . . So yeah, I think I might [have an accent], but I don't know." To be clear, this student neither wanted to be perceived as possessing an accent nor misidentified as Mexican. From his perspective, it did not make sense that one could "sound Mexican" in English. Yet, from many non-Latinx perspectives, "Mexican" often serves as a stand-in for Latinxs in general and Latinxs' English language practices can be racially perceived as non-White. Thus, David was grappling with what it meant to sound like a race.

A theorization of what it means to look like a language and sound like a race can be found in the opening chapter of Frantz Fanon's *Black Skin, White Masks*, titled "The Negro and Language":

> The problem that we confront in this chapter is this: The Negro of the Antilles will be proportionately Whiter—that is, he will come closer to being a real human being—in direct ratio to his mastery of the French Language. . . . What we are getting at becomes plain: Mastery of language affords remarkable power. . . . The Black man who has lived in France for a length of time returns radically changed. To express it in genetic terms, his phenotype undergoes a definitive, an absolute mutation. (1967:18–19)

Fanon's evocative description of interactions in the French Caribbean context speaks to the powerful ways that categories of language and race become iconic of one another, such that linguistic practices can shape one's racial ontology. The counterpart to this dynamic, in which race shapes linguistic ontologies, was regularly displayed in interactions at NNHS; this is demonstrated by the aforementioned case of Mr. Maldonado, the Filipino teacher perceived as speaking Spanish.

It is crucial to build from Fanon's account to rethink the construction and navigation of boundaries associated with categories of language and identity. The status of French in particular Caribbean contexts in the previous Fanonian example is not entirely unlike English language hegemony in the United States, which relies heavily on schools as flagship institutions for language standardization.[13] This positions standardized English both as an institutional norm and aspiration. While school actors used different varieties of Spanish and English, standardized English was understood as the normative language variety for official business. Most school-wide announcements were made in English, and all formal staff meetings were conducted in English. Meanwhile, the majority of school employees perceived as Spanish-dominant occupied subordinate hierarchical positions as security guards, custodians, and lunchroom workers. This reflects the structural stigmatization of the Spanish language.

Students clearly received and reported these ideas about language and identity. In the example of David sounding like a race, his ideas about Spanish and English reflect not only monolingual ideologies that associate "one people" with "one language," but also monoglot ideologies (Silverstein 1996) that erase differences between varieties of a given language. He was surprised to learn that he might be perceived as possessing an accent because he simply understood himself to be speaking unmarked English. Importantly, his ideas demonstrate how monolingual and monoglot ideologies simultaneously shape perceptions of multiple languages and varieties thereof. The idea that David might "sound like a Mexican" led him to emphasize that he "was just talking English," thus positioning Mexicanness outside of the English language. On other occasions this same student highlighted differences between Mexican and Puerto Rican Spanish, but in this case monoglot ideologies positioned Mexican Spanish as "the" Spanish.[14]

For students designated as English Language Learners (ELLs), differences between varieties of Spanish were crucial. These students occupied distinctive institutional positions based on the varieties of Spanish with which they came to be associated. Whereas those associated with Mexican varieties of Spanish generally sat quietly in the front or back corners of mainstream classrooms, those associated with Puerto Rican Spanish varieties were vocal participants in classroom affairs, often purposefully disrupting the class and bringing active attention to their perceived linguistic distinctiveness. A particularly interesting example of this phenomenon involved a sophomore student designated as an ELL, Jaime (Honduran, Gen. 1, Gr. 10). Based on the stereotypical Caribbean phonological features that inflected both his English and Spanish (e.g., syllable-final /s/ aspiration/deletion, intervocalic/word final /d/ deletion), in conjunction with stereotypical corporeal and sartorial signals (e.g., coarse hair texture and the latest hip-hop fashions), I assumed he was Puerto Rican. In both mainstream (English-dominant) and sheltered (bilingual) classrooms, Jaime positioned himself as the center of attention, proudly speaking Spanish and what mainstreamed students perceived as heavily accented English. He would roam throughout the entire classroom, initiating conversations with students in both languages. Teachers constantly struggled to manage Jaime's rambunctiousness. This stood in stark contrast to the behavior of other students designated as ELLs (the majority of whom were Mexican) in mainstream classrooms. These students rarely spoke English aloud, for fear of bringing attention to their perceived accents, and spoke Spanish only with students sitting nearby. While observing Jaime's confident classroom interactions, I began to work closely with him as a classroom tutor. Several months after we started working with one another, I asked him— in Spanish—what part of Puerto Rico he was from; as described in Chapter 2, this was a common question among students and could be asked in relation to Puerto Rico or Mexico. He shook his head, laughed, and told me that he was from Honduras. Students sitting nearby were shocked to discover that he was not Puerto Rican. We laughed and went on to discuss characteristics of his language use. I knew that Honduran Spanish shared characteristics with other Caribbean Spanish varieties, especially phonological features, but Jaime frequently used emblematic Puerto Rican Spanish lexical items, including interjections such as ¡Diantre! (Wow!), ¡Wepa! (Yay!), and ¡Puñeta! (Fuck!). He explained that he learned Puerto Rican Spanish from his neighbors when he moved to Chicago. When I asked why he did not learn Mexican Spanish, he told me that Mexican Spanish sounded "bogus" (i.e., uncool).

Here, Puerto Rican Spanish becomes linked to integration into and disruption of classroom activities, whereas Mexican Spanish indexes politeness and isolation—a double-bind. On another level, many students recognized Mexican Spanish as correct (yet "lame") and Puerto Rican Spanish as "cool" (yet incorrect); these familiar stereotypes structure debates between Mexicans and Puerto Ricans (and members of other Latinx subgroups) about what practices and characteristics—linguistic and otherwise—constitute an ideal pan-ethnic Latinx identity.[15] Meanwhile, self-identified English-Spanish bilinguals and English-dominant students, many of whom had limited interactions with students designated as ELLs, questioned presumptions about their language proficiencies. On one occasion, a Mexican teacher in a mainstream English classroom addressed a Mexican student in Spanish, telling her "escoge un tema" (choose a theme) for an essay assignment. When the student did not respond, a Puerto Rican friend sitting next to her intervened in her best "Mock White Girl" (Slobe 2018) voice: "Just because she knows Spanish doesn't mean she can't speak English. That's, like, so discriminating!"[16] The teacher and other students laughed, signaling the playfulness of this voicing. Note, however, that the joke did not call into question the student's Spanish language abilities. Instead, it parodically reinforced the notion that she possessed both Spanish *and* English language skills.

Most students suggested that it is important to be able to speak Spanish. Jimmy (PR, Gen. 3, Gr. 12), a self-described monolingual English user, was frustrated by situations in which he felt that his limited Spanish language skills prevented him from communicating effectively. He joked that this was especially frustrating during the summer months at the home improvement and construction store where he worked. He said that as the weather warmed up and he spent more time outside, his skin became darker and that this prompted more customers to speak to him in Spanish (i.e., he looked like a language). Jimmy's White bosses also continually asked him to help customers who presented or were perceived as Spanish-dominant. Latinxs and non-Latinxs alike expected Jimmy to use Spanish.

As much as Jimmy and his fellow NNHS students felt compelled to use Spanish, they also sought to position themselves as unmarked English users and were quick to police what they perceived as accented English. Students regularly performed impressions of school employees whom they understood to speak with thick accents. The perceived accented English of Mr. Burgos, a popular Dominican teacher, was a regular topic of discussion and a model for parodic performances. At times students attempted to carefully mimic him, like when he told them, "you need your book," which the students repeated as /dʒu: ni: dʒu:/ book," pronouncing the "y" in "you" as though it sounded like an English "j" and deleting the "d" sound at the end of "need." In other cases, they repeated his speech with exaggerated Spanish pronunciations. For example, when Mr. Burgos told them that they needed to use the order of operations and work from "left to right always" to evaluate arithmetic expressions, students impersonated him by trilling the "r" in the word "right" even though he pronounced the word with normative American English phonology.[17]

Ms. Lopez, a Puerto Rican support staff member, was another frequent target of students' linguistic derision. The Facebook group that I described in Chapters 1 and 4, titled "YOu know YOu went 2 NNHS When...," included these postings:

"You know you went to NNHS when U cant understand a damn thing Ms. Lopez says!!! Hahahaha."
"when you had 3 yrs of Spanish and you still cant understand Ms. Lopez"

Ms. Lopez generally spoke to students in English, so the joke here is that even though the students know English and Spanish they still cannot understand Ms. Lopez. The same students who valued Spanish language skills disparaged these staff members' perceived Spanish accents. Spanish language skills were valuable only if they did not interfere with one's ability to produce perceived unmarked English.[18] These ideas positioned employees such as Mr. Burgos and Ms. Lopez as objects of students' ridicule. Meanwhile, students designated as ELLs became repositories of authenticity. Their presumed Spanish language knowledge and marginalization in classroom communication (i.e., they generally only communicated with one another and very rarely allowed mainstreamed students to hear their perceived accented English speech) allowed them to avoid ridicule. While many mainstreamed students and those designated as ELLs could be understood to share a great deal in common, few moved across this institutionally created divide. To do so, students designated as ELLs would have to risk bringing attention to their perceived accented English (thereby potentially becoming laughingstocks), and many mainstreamed students would have to risk bringing attention to their lack of confidence using Spanish (thereby calling into question their ethnoracial authenticity). In English-dominant educational settings, however, students designated as ELLs are at a great disadvantage in these negotiations. The following section explores these dynamics further by presenting sociolinguistic sketches of several students.

Linking Language Ideologies to Linguistic Practices

In efforts to provide a clearer picture of Latinx NNHS students' language ideologies and practices, I highlight here five students in particular: one self-identified English monolingual (Jimmy), three self-identified English-Spanish
bilinguals (Victor, Carlos, and Mayra), and one self-identified Spanish monolingual (Lupita). Building from the analysis of ideologies of languagelessness in
Chapter 4, the point that I hope to make with these descriptions is that concepts
such as "monolingualism" and "bilingualism" are limited in their ability to represent these students' everyday language practices.

Jimmy (PR, Gen. 3, Gr. 12)

Jimmy, a Puerto Rican senior born in Chicago, is the boy whose interview I analyzed in detail in Chapter 2. His parents were born in Chicago, and all four of his
grandparents were born in Puerto Rico. In an interview that I conducted with
Jimmy during the fall of his senior year at NNHS, he described himself as a monolingual English speaker. Jimmy was the youngest in his immediate family. Both
of his older sisters graduated from the same four-year university in Chicago.[19] He
claimed that his oldest sister had the best Spanish out of the three of them, but
that she would mostly speak Spanglish as opposed to "perfect" Spanish. He said
that his other older sister, the "White one," who lived in the South Loop, spoke
the least Spanish.[20] Later that year, I accompanied Jimmy as he picked up his
prom tuxedo from a small rental shop near NNHS. While in the shop, Jimmy
spoke to the Mexican owners, a husband and wife, exclusively in English; they
spoke to him exclusively in Spanish. The nuanced English and Spanish vocabulary that this nonreciprocal bilingual interaction required, which included detailed discussion about his pants, shirt, vest, shoes, and bowtie, signaled Jimmy's
and the shop owners' receptive bilingual skills.[21]

In other interactions, Jimmy's self-identified monolingual English speech was
peppered with stereotypical Spanish lexical items and phonology. For example,
while wondering aloud about the sexuality of another male student at NNHS,
Jimmy questioned whether the student preferred "pincho," a Puerto Rican style
shish kebab that in this instance euphemistically referred to a penis. As described
in Chapter 3, Jimmy's standard phone greeting is, "¿Bueno?," which is stereotyped
in the Chicago context as the telephone greeting for Spanish-speaking Mexicans.
In one of our tutoring sessions, I asked Jimmy to choose a written character that
we could use as a variable when writing out algebraic equations. Jimmy chose
"ñ."[22] When I asked him why he chose a Spanish orthographic character despite
his self-proclaimed English monolingualism, he jokingly replied, "Spanish lives

in my soul, bro." In fact, his soul has been stirred! In a follow-up interview with Jimmy nearly a year after he graduated from NNHS and was finishing his first year in a Chicago-area junior college, he told me that he was becoming more confident in his Spanish skills because of his participation in a Humboldt Park softball league alongside many older Puerto Ricans who mostly spoke to him in Spanish.[23]

Victor (Mex[m]/PR[f], Gen. 3, Gr. 11)

Victor, a 16-year-old MexiRican junior, was born to a bilingual Mexican mother and a bilingual Puerto Rican birth father, but was taken in by a Spanish-dominant Puerto Rican foster family at the age of 10. While he had not seen his birth father since he was a baby, he visited his biological mother (a Chicago-born Mexican) regularly. Victor described himself as an English-dominant bilingual; he claimed that he could speak both Mexican and Puerto Rican Spanish but that he spoke more Puerto Rican Spanish because this was the dominant variety spoken in his foster home.

Victor told me that Puerto Rican Spanish is better than Mexican Spanish because Puerto Rican Spanish is "what's up" (i.e., cool) but Mexican Spanish is "more correct." When I prompted him to give me an example of Mexican and Puerto Rican Spanish, he told me that whereas Mexicans would pronounce the letter "s" when saying something like, "¿Cómo ustedes están? (How are you all doing?)," Puerto Ricans would "cut off the 's' or say it like an 'h.' "[24] In fact, Victor's placement of the pronoun "ustedes" before the verb "están" aligns even his impression of Mexican Spanish with stereotypical Puerto Rican syntactic patterns. Moreover, the /s/ aspiration/deletion that Victor sought to highlight in his Puerto Rican pronunciation was also somewhat aspirated/deleted in his Mexican pronunciation. He went on to explain:

> Hands on down, man, Puerto Ricans got that shit in the bag . . . they can knock out any Spanish thing, bro . . . like all these other languages, they ain't got nothing on Puerto Ricans. It sounds way better . . . because like the way it flows . . . like you be hearing some reggaeton music and you hear the way they got flow? Like that.

Victor associates Puerto Rican Spanish with reggaeton, which, as described in Chapter 3, is a music style with Spanish-language lyrics and Latin American/ Caribbean/hip-hop roots whose most successful artists are often Puerto Rican. His claims about Puerto Rican Spanish's "flow," a common term used to characterize one's lyrical prowess in hip-hop music (Alim 2006), were surely tied to reggaeton's increasing popularity among US Latinxs during the first decade of the 21st century (Rivera et al. 2009).[25]

Despite his strong valorization of Puerto Rican Spanish and his self-identification as a bilingual English-Spanish speaker, I never heard Victor speak Spanish with other students. In fact, I once heard him respond to a Mexican friend's Spanish-language greeting, "¿Que pasó, güey?" (What's up, man?), by telling him, "speak to me in English, I don't mess with that Spanish." It was initially unclear whether Victor was telling his friend not to speak Spanish at all or not to speak a particular kind of Spanish. He later clarified that he didn't like to be called "güey," an intimate, masculine term of address in Mexican Spanish (Bucholtz 2009). Victor told me that his friend should "take that güey and go on his way," playfully utilizing the homophony of Spanish "güey" and English "way."[26]

Jorge (Mex, Gen. 2, Gr. 9)

Jorge, a 15-year-old Mexican freshman, was born in Chicago; both his parents were born in Mexico. A self-described bilingual, Jorge said he spoke Spanish with his parents and mostly English with his younger siblings (he was the oldest). He was primarily socialized to and through Spanish language use until he entered elementary school and began learning English. In the classroom in which I observed him most closely, he sat with a boisterous group of Mexican students (three boys and three girls); he spoke English, Spanish, and Spanglish with these students, codeswitching intersententially and intrasententially (i.e., between and within sentences, respectively), but also playfully pronouncing Spanish words with English phonology, and vice versa. This prominent Spanish language usage, which was characteristic of ninth-grade NNHS classrooms, declined incrementally in 10th-, 11th-, and 12th-grade classrooms.[27]

When I asked Jorge about Mexican and Puerto Rican Spanish, he initially articulated an egalitarian perspective, simply claiming that every Latinx national subgroup has its own variety of Spanish. He pointed to my paleto-velar pronunciation of /ɾ/ as /l/ in the word "verdad" (really) as an example of how Puerto Rican and Mexican Spanish differ. On further questioning, Jorge said that Mexican Spanish is probably a little bit better than Puerto Rican Spanish because it is more correct. He said that he knew this because Mexican Spanish was the variety taught in NNHS language classes and the variety spoken on television and on the radio. He told me that he mostly listens to Spanish-language Mexican music, such as cumbia and durangüense, but also some reggaeton. He also joked with me about the fact that he had only recently learned from friends at NNHS that words such as "chévere" (cool/awesome) and "bochinche" (gossip) were stereotypically viewed in Chicago as Puerto Rican, *not* Mexican, Spanish terms.

Mayra (Mex, Gen. 1.5, Gr. 11)

Mayra, a 16-year-old junior, was born in Mexico City and came to the United States with her parents and baby brother at the age of 8. She described herself as bilingual, but she said that Spanish is her main language and she worried that she still had a "Mexican" accent when speaking English. Mayra characterized her parents as monolingual Spanish users and her brother, now 11, as bilingual. During an interview, she joked about how it is not fair that her younger brother can speak English without an accent; meanwhile, he played video games next to us and poked fun at his sister for being so excited about the opportunity to participate in an interview.

Mayra said that when she first came to Chicago it was very difficult for her to understand what was going on in school. There were some bilingual students who helped her to navigate English-dominant settings, but there were many other situations in which she acted like she understood the language in order to detract attention from her designation as an ELL.[28] I was struck by this account because it shed light on my observations of Mayra's behavior in the classroom. Although she came across as a reflective and thoughtful student in one-on-one interactions, in broader classroom interactions she frequently seemed aloof or goofy. While this behavior is commonplace among adolescents in US high schools, the extent to which it was shaped by her linguistic insecurity is unclear.

In contrast to Mayra's anxieties about her English language skills, she spoke confidently about her Spanish language abilities and about the Spanish language in general. She said that one of the main differences between Mexicans and Puerto Ricans is "the language." She provided examples such as the Mexican and Puerto Rican Spanish words for "sidewalk," "banqueta" and "concreto," respectively.[29] Mayra also talked about her appreciation of Spanish slang, such as "cuaderno" (notebook) for "friend," and idiomatic phrases such as "de bolón pin pon" (of a ping pong ball) to tell someone to hurry up. She said she used to think the best Spanish is spoken in Spain, but that changed when she heard the best Spanish is actually spoken in Mexico. She also said that she definitely would not go to Puerto Rico to hear good Spanish because Puerto Ricans "don't say the words right . . . they miss some words . . . like sometimes they lose the 'r,' sometimes they lose the 's,' and it's really weird . . . and with Mexicans . . . they know how to talk!" Mayra explicitly articulates the stereotype that Puerto Rican

Spanish is nonstandard. Similar to Jorge, she highlights the alternates of /r/ and /s/ in Puerto Rican Spanish. Mayra also describes ongoing debates about whether varieties of Spanish associated with Spain or Latin America should be taught in the United States.[30]

Lupita (Mex, Gen. 1, Gr. 10)

Lupita was born and raised in Mexico until the age of 15, when she joined her mother, father, and little brother permanently in Chicago and became a sophomore at NNHS. Lupita's family and I lived in the same apartment building, just a few blocks away from the school. Her father came to Chicago nearly 20 years before Lupita, initially migrating regularly between the United States and Mexico. Following Lupita's birth in Mexico he obtained legal status as a US resident and found a full-time job that he continued to work during the period of my fieldwork. Lupita and her mother joined him, but only her mother was able to acquire legal status as a US resident. They faced many difficulties in their efforts to find a legally permissible way in which to keep Lupita in the United States, which led them to ask a close family member to look after her in Mexico while they attempted to secure her status in the United States. During this time, Lupita's younger brother, Roberto, was born in Chicago. Her family eventually decided that it would be best for everyone if she lived with them in Chicago, even if this meant entering a new school, learning English, and becoming undocumented.

On her arrival in the fall of 2008, Lupita entered NNHS's transitional bilingual education program. When I first met Lupita, she said that she did not speak any English and that she was nervous about having to learn so many new things. A year later, as she prepared to enter her junior year, Lupita continued to describe herself as a monolingual Spanish speaker and lamented the fact that she was still in the "ESL" program. In the classroom, she was diligent and very quiet. She interacted exclusively with other students in the transitional bilingual education program. Outside of school, in a bilingual neighborhood where both Spanish and English linguistic practices were normative, Lupita was confident and personable. Her younger brother's English language skills did not prevent her from asserting herself as his older sister. Lupita's experience was unique in that not only was her US-born younger brother a confident English-Spanish bilingual, but both her parents also self-identified as bilingual users of English and Spanish. This means that Lupita interacted closely with the English language at school *and* at home, and that she would actually follow, not lead her parents in becoming bilingual in English and Spanish. Regardless of the fact that Lupita was surrounded by cultural reminders of Mexico in her family and neighborhood, she said that she still missed "home" (i.e., Mexico) and that she often felt like language made her an outsider not only in school but also in her own home.

Language Use Beyond "Monolingualism" and "Bilingualism"

There are several things to note in students' metalinguistic characterizations of their language use. Students' self-assessments of their linguistic status as monolingual or bilingual can be highly deceptive. Self-described English or Spanish monolinguals often interact intimately with both languages; meanwhile, self-described bilinguals interact with and draw on varieties of English and Spanish in a range of distinctive, idiosyncratic ways. In this sense, Latinx NNHS students demonstrate the ways that a person who self-identifies as monolingual and purports to be capable of using only language can in fact draw extensively on forms associated with other languages. Likewise, self-identified bilinguals should not simply be understood as people who use two languages "equally." Zentella points to the problematic way in which bilingualism is often framed as "two monolinguals stuck at the neck, that is, with one tongue in control of two inviolably separate systems" (Zentella 2003:53). Similarly, García suggests the need for a "plural vision for bilingual education, by which bilingualism is not simply seen as two separate monolingual codes—a vision that goes beyond 'one plus one equals two'" (García 2009:5). Problematizing standard conceptions of bilingualism *and* monolingualism, García proposes a framework of "translanguaging."[31] She builds from Bakhtin's notion of heteroglossia to suggest that a "translingual" approach can denaturalize presumed borders between and within languages and focus instead on the complex heterogeneity inherent in everyday language use. This approach makes it possible to reframe interrelations among varieties of English and Spanish in these students' language practices. That is, "translanguaging" is a helpful way to understand how self-identified monolinguals and bilinguals engage in linguistic practices that unsettle the boundaries between and within objectified languages. Thus, a translanguaging perspective is central to understanding the nature of Latinx NNHS students' "multilingual subjectivities" (Kramsch 2009).

It is also important to highlight local stereotypes of gender and Latinx national subgroups in the ideological spectrum from English-dominant to Spanish-dominant among these five students. The portraits highlight the stereotypical way in which Puerto Ricans and boys were generally more closely associated with English dominance, while Mexicans and girls were generally more closely associated with Spanish dominance. They also show the ways that students' linguistic practices constantly contradicted these stereotypes. Despite a multitude of opposing evidence, these ideological models provided NNHS students and employees with a set of assumptions to make sense of their heterogeneous linguistic repertoires. These students differ in terms of age, gender, (im)migrant generation, Latinx national subgroup, and self-described language proficiency. Yet, their language ideologies and linguistic practices demonstrate a shared investment in the ability to speak unmarked or "unaccented" English, as well as intimate familiarity with and affinity for Puerto Rican and Mexican varieties of Spanish. Specifically, they draw on local language ideologies that emphasize the "correctness" of Mexican Spanish and the "coolness" of Puerto Rican Spanish.[32] These ideologies challenge the notion that the Spanish language unifies US Latinxs in straightforward ways. A simultaneous commitment to demonstrating "unaccented" English ability and intimate Spanish familiarity presented Mexican and Puerto Rican students with the paradoxical task of signaling their Latinx identities by always sounding like they could speak Spanish *in* English, but never letting too much Spanish seep into their English. What linguistic materials might allow them to negotiate these competing demands? In the following section I show how Latinx NNHS students reconfigured Mock Spanish usages to reconcile these contradictory commitments.

Inverted Spanglish as Latinx Linguistic Dexterity

In dialogue with Hill's work on Mock Spanish (1993, 1998, 2008), which she describes as White Americans' incorporation of "Spanish-language materials into English in order to create a jocular or pejorative 'key'" (1998:61), such as "no problemo" and "buenos nachos," Zentella (2003) and Mason Carris (2011) provide evidence of Latinxs drawing on mock language practices to parody the speech of Whites. I build from both Hill and Zentella to suggest that in addition to the mocking quality of the voicing involved here, there is also the potential for Latinxs to use these language practices to meet the demand that they speak Spanish *in* English without being heard to possess an accent. These usages transform Mock Spanish into what I call "Inverted Spanglish," a register formation that is a unifying component of many US Latinxs' (generation 1.5 and beyond) linguistic repertoires.

Inverted Spanglish was ubiquitous at NNHS; it was used in interactions among Latinx teachers, among Latinx students, and between Latinx teachers and students. In broad terms, this US Latinx–based linguistic register consists of Spanish lexical items pronounced with English phonology; in less stereotypically technical terms, this might be described as "saying Spanish words in English." The particular type of

English phonology varied. In some cases, the Spanish word was pronounced with the same phonology that school-based actors conventionally used in their English speech. These usages generally took place in predominantly Latinx settings and involved in-group Spanish tokens (i.e., usages that are not familiar to most non-Latinxs and/or are not part of Mock Spanish repertoires). In one private classroom exchange, two sophomore boys, one Puerto Rican, Pedro (PR, Gen. 3, Gr. 10), the other MexiRican, Miguel (PR[m]/Mex[f], Gen. 2, Gr. 10), traded Inverted Spanglish insults:

PEDRO: What's up, *cuhbron*? /kʌbɹoʊn/ (Spanish, /kaβɾon/, "cabrón," "bastard")

MIGUEL: Not much, *pendayho*! /pɛndeɪhoʊ/ (Spanish, /pendexo/, "pendejo," "dumbass/asshole")

In this instance Inverted Spanglish transformed Spanish vulgarities that might otherwise operate as serious provocations into jovial play.[33] By pronouncing these words with English phonology, the would-be offenses took shape as jocular exchanges. The voicings involved here are more complicated, however, as "cabrón" and "pendejo" can index Latinx in-group knowledge of Spanish insults since they are often unfamiliar to non-Latinx Mock Spanish users. Inverted Spanglish, as opposed to Mock Spanish, allowed Pedro and Miguel to accomplish multiple goals simultaneously: (1) highlight a shared Latinx identity that involves critical distance from Whiteness, (2) lay claim to "cool" Americanness through English language dexterity, and (3) display their insider knowledge of Spanish.

Victor (Mex[m]/PR[f], Gen. 3, Gr. 11), one of the students whose sociolinguistic biographies is presented earlier in this chapter, used similar forms of Inverted Spanglish in one of my interviews with him:

JR: Does your birth mom speak Spanish?

V: Yeah.

JR: What kind of Spanish does she speak?

V: Regular Spanish, like she just learned it from *Inglace seen Buhrerus*. /ɪŋɡleɪs sin bʌɹɛɹʌs/ (Spanish, /iŋgles sin bareɾas/, "Inglés sin Barreras," "English without Barriers")

JR: And how is that regular Spanish?

V: To me, that's like a new breed thing right there. But my mom talks Spanish, she sound like a Mexican.

JR: Okay.

V: But my step-dad sounds like Puerto Rican when you hear him talk Spanish.

In this example, Victor references "Inglés sin Barreras," an English language learning course often advertised in Spanish language media. By pronouncing "Inglés sin Barreras" with his normative English phonology, with the most noticeable difference being his use of the English alveolar approximant /ɹ/ in the place of the Spanish trill /r/ and tap /ɾ/ in "Barreras," Victor jokingly suggested that his mother speaks generic Spanish like the variety spoken in the commercials for Inglés sin Barreras. Similar to the previous example, this indexicality requires Latinx in-group knowledge of language and culture.

NNHS students also used written forms of Inverted Spanglish that involved interlingual puns. Mayra (Mex, Gen. 1.5, Gr. 11), the self-identified Spanish-dominant bilingual student described earlier, showed me a notebook in which she and her friends wrote jokes to one another. The words "pink cheese, green ghosts, cool arrows," which when read aloud sound like the Spanish, "pinches gringos culeros," in other words, fucking American (or White) assholes, were written largely across one of the pages of her notebook. Mayra told me that she and her friends loved to trick their favorite White, monolingual English-using teachers into reading this aloud in front of the class. In this case, Inverted Spanglish takes the form of a coded message in which Spanish words are disguised as English graphemes to create an interlingual pun.[34] The written forms are intended to be pronounced with English phonology, and the humor is derived from most non-Latinxs' inability to recognize that these written English forms correspond to Spanish words when spoken aloud. Despite the surface appearance of animosity in this particular example, I witnessed students engage in this sort of public practice only with teachers around whom they felt the most comfortable.

Other Inverted Spanglish usages consisted of hyper-anglicized pronunciations of widely understood Spanish words in the course of English-dominant interactions. These tokens of Inverted Spanglish involved neither intimate Spanish vulgarities nor private conversations. In one case, a White teacher began the day in a sophomore study skills classroom by asking students to remind her of the date. One student yelled out, "November *quatro*" /kwɒtɹoʊ/ (Spanish, /kwatɾo/, "cuatro," "four"). Later in the class, another student responded to the teacher's request for a volunteer to answer a question on a worksheet: "I've got the answer to *numerow trace*" /numɚoʊ treɪs/ (Spanish, /numeɾo tɾes/, "numero tres," number three). These instances of inverted Spanglish differ from the previous examples because they appear to be similar to conventional Mock Spanish usages. That is, they do not index intimate knowledge of Spanish. Such usages, which involve Spanish words that are familiar to many non-Latinxs, more directly parodied the speech of Whites and others who might know and use stereotypically basic Spanish words such as "tres" and "cuatro." The parodic nature of this language use is signaled by the students' hyper-anglicized pronunciations, which in effect mock anglicized pronunciations of Spanish words. I commonly heard students engage in these kinds of linguistic practices outside of school, particularly in contexts that involved interactions between Whites and Latinxs.

One such context was a Mexican restaurant near NNHS. This restaurant became a popular destination for non-Latinxs because of the publicity it received on the Food Network's television show, "Diners, Drive-ins, and Dives" and on the popular online business review guide, "Yelp." From some Yelp reviewers' perspectives, the restaurant is not located in a desirable area. One reviewer states, "I took friends visiting from California on their first night in Chicago. The area surrounding the restaurant is scenic, but not in a good way!" Such comments signal that the restaurant is located significantly west of more gentrified areas. Language is also a frequent topic of these reviews, with comments such as, "You know it's authentic when the waitress speaks no English." Other reviewers combined these two topics: "If you rarely venture west of Western Ave like myself and don't speak a word of Spanish—go!"

The NNHS students who went to eat at this restaurant with me were annoyed by the way that White customers addressed Latinx employees. In a familiar scene in US restaurant settings (Barrett 2006), some of these customers were dismissive of waiters and waitresses and loudly expressed their annoyance at being forced to communicate in Spanish. Diana (Mex, Gen. 2, Gr. 12) and Walter (PR, Gen. 2, Gr. 12) drew on hyper-anglicized Inverted Spanglish usages in their parodies of these customers' behavior:

DIANA: *Donday esta el banyo?* /doʊndei ɛsta ɛl banjoʊ/ (Spanish, /donde esta el baɲo/, "¿Dónde está el baño?", "Where is the bathroom?")(Walter points in the direction of the bathroom.)

DIANA: *Moochus Gracias.* /mʊtʃʌs gɹɔsiʌs/ (Spanish, /mutʃas gɾasias/, "Muchas gracias.", "Thank you.")

WALTER: *Di nada.* /dɪ nɑdʌ/ (Spanish, /de naða/, "De nada.", "It's nothing."

Diana and Walter ostentatiously staged an impromptu performance that they intended to be overheard by the White people whose behavior they were parodying and the employees with whom they empathized. Unlike the previous examples of Inverted Spanglish, Diana and Walter did not use their normative English phonology when pronouncing Spanish words. Instead, they drew on the hyper-anglicized "Whitey voice" (Alim 2005). These students actively sought to make the disgruntled customers feel uncomfortable about their behavior by turning the linguistic tables and marking their language practices. To do so, it was crucial that the Spanish words referenced by Diana's and Walter's hyper-anglicized

Inverted Spanglish usages were widely recognizable by non-Latinxs and were even commonly part of Mock Spanish usages. Restaurants and other contexts in which perceived Spanish-dominant Latinxs provide services to non-Latinxs are prime sites for the production of these tokens of Inverted Spanglish. This is similar to Mason Carris' (2011) analysis of what she calls "La Voz Gringa," in which Latinx employees use "Valley-Girl-esque" phonology to perform in-group impersonations of the Spanish language use of a White employee in a southern California Mexican restaurant. An important distinction here is that Diana and Walter staged their performance in relation to White customers and Latinx restaurant employees, and their ability to speak perceived unaccented English was central to their performance and ongoing presentation of self.

Perhaps one of the most striking examples of a hyper-anglicized token of Inverted Spanglish is *Latino* /lætɪnoʊ/ (Spanish, /latino/), which some Latinxs playfully rhyme with hyper-anglicized pronunciation of the Spanish word, "platano" (plantain). They do so by pronouncing "Latino" in such a way that "Lat" sounds like the beginning of the English word "latitude," "in" sounds like the English word "in," and "o" sounds like the English word "oh." This contrasts with the "Spanish" pronunciation of "*Latino*," in which "La-" sounds like the beginning of the English word "Lollipop" and "-tino" sounds like the beginning of the English word "denote." As a word that is often pronounced in "English" yet understood as "Spanish," *Latino* is a quintessential token of Inverted Spanglish. Note that "Hispanic" does not have the same Spanish indexicality. It is no coincidence, then, that many self-identified Latinxs view "Hispanic" as a pro-assimilation term.[35]

Some tokens of Inverted Spanglish mix the patterns described previously. Recall that in the first set of examples of Inverted Spanglish, students used their normative English phonology to pronounce in-group Spanish lexical items among other Latinxs. In the second set of examples, students used hyper-anglicized phonology to parody non-Latinxs' pronunciation of widely recognized Spanish words in mixed Latinx and non-Latinx company. Examples such as "*cone pairmeeso*" /kon pɛɹmisoʊ/ (Spanish, /kon peɾmiso/, "Con permiso," "Excuse me") juxtapose in-group Spanish words with hyper-anglicized phonology. Similarly, Ms. Muñiz, one of the young Puerto Rican teachers described in Chapter 1, often asked her students to do something by saying "*pour fuhvor*" /pɔɹ fʌvɔɹ/ (Spanish, /poɾ faβoɾ/, "por favor," "please"). She used her conventional English phonology to pronounce a widely recognized Spanish phrase. Ms. Muñiz said that she talks like this "all the time" and that it is "just something that Latinos do." These examples show how Inverted Spanglish becomes a register of language through which US Latinxs create solidarity with one another. Diana and Walter said that they were comfortable using Inverted Spanglish with one another because they knew that they were not making fun of Spanish. In fact, when I asked them to explain their performance in the restaurant, they said that Inverted Spanglish allowed them to defend the employees and Latinxs in general.

Inverted Spanglish usages span the range of "figures" that Goffman suggests are central to the frame structure of talk. Ms. Muñiz positions herself as what Goffman calls a natural figure, "the only figures to physically emit on their own what is attributed to them" (Goffman 1974:524). Miguel and Pedro create "staged figures," or fictitious characters "in a strip of activity that is itself a make-believe" (1974:525). The students writing Inverted Spanglish jokes in their notebooks generated "printed figures," what Goffman describes as figures "constructed out of words, not out of live performers" (1974:529). In quoting a television commercial and "replaying . . a strip of experience," Victor's Inverted Spanglish involved a "cited figure" (1974:529). Finally, Diana and Walter (and the students responding to the teacher's request for the date and a volunteer to answer a question) employ "mockeries and say-fors" by "projecting an image of someone not oneself while preventing viewers from forgetting even for a moment that an alien animator is at work" (1974:534).

The Spanish-English enregisterment involved in these usages is unique in a number of ways. The usages that I am calling "Inverted Spanglish" were not celebrated or derided in the same way as documented cases of "Spanglish" code-mixing (Zentella 1997; Morales 2002; Stavans 2003; Lipski 2008). Often, the most contentious tokens of Spanglish consist of modified English lexical items pronounced with Spanish phonology within a strip of speech understood as "Spanish" (e.g., "lonche" for "lunch" or "rufo" for "roof"). Inverted Spanglish, which involves the use of Spanish lexical items pronounced with English phonology within a strip of speech understood as "English," is a linguistic reversal of Spanglish practices such as "lonche" and "rufo." Echoing the distinctions discussed in Chapter 3, these Spanglish practices are often characterized as ghetto. By shoring up anxieties about English language abilities, Inverted Spanglish avoids this stigmatization.

Perspectives on what constitutes Spanglish among Latinxs in Chicago often focus only on a small subsection of the practices analyzed as Spanglish in the literature cited earlier. When discussing Spanglish, Latinxs in NNHS and its surrounding communities frequently highlighted the insertion of Spanish lexical items pronounced with Spanish phonology into a strip of speech otherwise understood as English. Latinxs who spoke about Spanglish in this way offered examples of Spanish words that would commonly be inserted into English speech. These included familiar boundary-marking conjunctions such as "pero" (but) and "porque" (because), but also nouns such as "sala" (living room) and "chancla" (flip-flop). They offered distinct accounts of types of "Spanglish" usages. "Pero" and "porque" were described as another way of saying "but" and "because." This suggests the reduction of Spanish to a register of English. Alternatively, "sala" and "chancla" were described as possessing a particular cultural connotation that "living room" and "flip-flop" could not convey. In either case, these Spanish lexical usages operate not only as "emblems of ethnolinguistic identity" (Silverstein 2003b), but also raciolinguistic identity that position Latinxs as non-White. Inverted Spanglish's emblematicity is constituted by Latinxs' linguistic play on these popular conceptions of language and identity.

The English-Spanish enregisterment involved in Inverted Spanglish is related to Woolard's (1998) analysis of "simultaneity and bivalency," which points to the importance of moving beyond approaches that reify boundaries between codes.[36] In particular, she describes bivalency as "a simultaneous membership of an element in more than one linguistic system" (1998:6). Woolard's examples of bivalency include the verb form "saben," which she describes as "ambiguously Catalan or Castilian" (1998:7). This does not correspond directly to the particular mode of simultaneity at work in Inverted Spanglish usages. Whereas bivalency involves language use that is indeterminately suspended between codes, Inverted Spanglish derives its meaningfulness precisely by distinguishing between English phonology and Spanish lexical items. Woolard contrasts bivalency with "interference." If bivalency consists of the use of elements that can be interpreted simultaneously as standardized in more than one code, then interference is its nonstandardized counterpart. That is, interference involves the use of forms that can be recognized as belonging to more than one code without being standardized in either language. While interference would seem to closely approximate Inverted Spanglish's combination of Spanish lexicon and English phonology, a strict focus on linguistic features provides a limited account of this language use.

Rampton's framework of "language crossing" (1995, 1998, 1999, 2002, 2006) might also seem to apply to Inverted Spanglish. For Rampton, "'language crossing' refers to the use of a language which isn't generally thought to 'belong' to the speaker" (1998:291). Rampton provides examples of crossing such as "the use of Creole by youngsters of Anglo and Asian descent, the use of Punjabi by youngsters of Anglo and African Caribbean descent, and the use of Indian English by all three" (1999:362). In Inverted Spanglish, however, Latinxs make use of Spanish lexical items specifically understood to belong to them; the crossing comes not simply from this lexicon but also its pairing with English phonology. The combination of phonology associated with one language and lexical items associated with another suggests that Inverted Spanglish can in fact be understood as a complex kind of crossing. The full sociolinguistic implications of language crossing can be discerned only by analyzing the relationship between the various features of language involved and the models of personhood that they index (Wortham 2006; Agha 2007).

The enregisterment of Inverted Spanglish provides an alternative way of conceptualizing the negotiation of linguistic and social boundaries that the theory of crossing attempts to apprehend. That is, enregisterment, as an analytical tool, does not take for granted the relationship between particular linguistic forms and social identities. Rather, it directs attention to the ways that linguistic and other semiotic forms are endowed with cultural value as coherent sets. Whereas crossing risks naturalizing these form-identity relations, enregisterment points to the (re)production and transformation of these relations.

Perhaps the aspect of Woolard's and Rampton's approaches to linguistic simultaneity that is most applicable to this study is their broader framing of perceived hybrid language use in relation to Bakhtin's "translinguistic concept of 'double voicing' . . . in which an utterance can mix more than one linguistic consciousness" (Woolard 1998:17). The notion of voicing brings to focus the ways that images of "others" constantly figure into what might generally be received as unitary utterances (Bakhtin 1981). In Inverted Spanglish, double-voicing allows Latinxs to signal their intimate knowledge of English and Spanish by pronouncing in-group Spanish words with their own English phonology or by pronouncing widely recognized Spanish words with hyper-anglicized phonology. The erasure of Mexican-Puerto Rican Spanish difference in these usages introduces an additional voice to the equation—that of a US Latinx. In particular, this language use positions generation 1.5, 2, and 3 Latinxs as defining members of this category. Because its characteristic features are knowledge of Spanish lexical items, the ability to produce perceived unaccented English, and the presumption of one's Latinx identity, Inverted Spanglish mediates between the stigmatization that members of these generations face when speaking "English" or "Spanish" as separate codes. While Inverted Spanglish might be interpreted from some perspectives simply as a form of vestigial bilingualism (i.e., a sign of declining linguistic dexterity and the loss of an identity), it should now be clear that this language use operates in many other meaningful and productive ways.

The voicing involved in Inverted Spanglish is also reminiscent of language use in Basso's *Portraits of the "Whiteman,"* an account of linguistic play among the Western Apache. For Basso,

When Apaches switch from "Western Apache" to "English" for the purpose of imitating Anglo-Americans, they use the language in a special way; and it is this distinctive style of speaking—a style characterized by stock phrases, specific lexical items, recurrent sentence types, and patterned modifications in pitch, volume, tempo, and voice quality—that signals to those familiar with it that a particular form of joking has begun. (1979:9)

Basso shows how Apaches draw on these patterned switches between linguistic codes to momentarily take on an exaggerated "Whiteman" identity:

Apache jokers temporarily transform themselves into mock exemplars of the class of persons whose rightful members their behavior is modeled upon. Thus, they "become" Anglo-Americans, and it is this little miracle—the key element in all successful acts of impersonation—that warrants our attention. (1979:13)

In fact, some of Basso's examples of imitations of the "Whiteman" include young Apaches impersonating the White teachers they encountered in schools designed to teach them conventional academic subjects as well as "proper etiquette" (1979:24). Whereas the racialized linguistic play that Basso describes involves Apaches' imitation of Whites' English language use, Inverted Spanglish comprises Latinxs' imitation of Whites' *Spanish* language use. Thus, the meaningfulness of Inverted Spanglish is made possible only by the widespread US-based engagement with the Spanish language among Whites and non-Whites alike. This engagement results in part from the rapidly rising Latinx population, the contemporary mediatization of Spanish, and a long-standing history of US relations (and shared territories) with Latin America, but also from a multicultural ethos that promotes the embrace of particular forms of linguistic difference. This embrace includes the development of nominal Spanish language abilities that allow one to communicate in stereotypically "Latino" restaurants or to pronounce stereotypically "Latino" names. Inverted Spanglish pushes back against this form of multiculturalism by highlighting the characteristic cultural inappropriateness of non-Latinxs' Spanish language use.

In the context of NNHS, Inverted Spanglish takes on additional indexical meanings. If the category of Young Latino Professional corresponds to perceived English-dominant language use that somehow acknowledges Latinx identity, then Dr. Baez and students would seem to be on the same linguistic page. Yet, recall from Chapter 3 that the category of Young Latino Professional was stereotypically constructed in relation to stereotypes about lameness and ghettoness. How could one display English-dominant speech that points to one's Latinx identity without being subjected to the stigmatizing stereotypes associated with perceived lameness or ghettoness? Inverted Spanglish, which parodies speech associated with professionals, represents students' satirical response to Dr. Baez's project of transforming their identities. Insofar as a category such as Young

Latino Professional attempts to balance assimilation and cultural identity main-tenance, Inverted Spanglish is students' playful way of saying, "we get it." Inverted Spanglish dynamically voices not only racialized, US Latinx panethnic identities but also the principal's project of socialization within NNHS. Thus, the transfor-mation of Mock Spanish into Inverted Spanglish signals a complex set of inter-relations among US Latinxs.

Rethinking "Mock Spanish"

With the prior analysis of Inverted Spanglish in place, it becomes possible to re-think Jane Hill's formulation of "Mock Spanish" (1993, 1998, 2008). Again, Hill characterizes Mock Spanish as a set of discursive practices that involves the incor-poration of "Spanish-language materials into English in order to create a jocular or pejorative 'key'" (Hill 1998:682). Examples include Arnold Schwarzenegger's famous "Hasta la vista, baby" from *Terminator 2: Judgment Day,* and then-Ambassador to the United Nations Madeline Albright's characterization of Fidel Castro as having shown "not cojones, but cowardice" (1998:683). These examples demonstrate how the same "language mixing" that is heavily policed for some is received as legitimate (and even prized) for others. By achieving a particular footing (Goffman 1981) when using Mock Spanish, White actors concurrently position Latinxs as deviant foreigners and Whites as easy-going, mildly cosmo-politan, ideal Americans (Hill 2008).

In describing the "major functions" of Mock Spanish as "the elevation of Whiteness and the pejorative racialization of members of historically Spanish-speaking populations" (1998:682), Hill points to two important sets of issues. First, if users of Mock Spanish are understood to partake in "the elevation of Whiteness," then we must begin to consider both the broader social forces at work in the enactment of such a social stance and the potential for differently racialized subjectivities to be involved in this enactment. Reframing this point, is the eleva-tion of Whiteness exclusively enacted by the practices of White people (whom Hill sometimes glosses as Anglos)?[37] Second, if Mock Spanish is to be understood in relation to processes of racialization, then who exactly are the members of his-torically Spanish-speaking populations? Does Mock Spanish necessarily partici-pate in the racialization of all Spanish speakers? Is there a way in which one can be positioned simultaneously as a member of a historically Spanish-speaking popu-lation and White?

Hill's various analyses of Mock Spanish suggest how she might respond to these questions. Citing examples of Mock Spanish in texts such as *A Handbook for Travelers in Spain* and the blog of an American traveling through Spain, Hill explains the semiotic orders of indexicality involved in Mock Spanish

(Silverstein 2003a). On the first order, there is "the iconic association of qualities labeled in Spanish with qualities of Spanish persons" (Hill 2005:118), while the social qualities indexed by particular English speakers' usage of Mock Spanish constitute the second order. This analysis demonstrates the difficulty involved in understanding these linguistic practices in relation to the racialization of Latinidad. The ambiguity here in Hill's description of "Spanish persons" is a product of this difficulty. While it is in fact true that iconicity/rhematization (Irvine and Gal 2000; Gal 2005) is a semiotic process that often aligns stereotypical characteristics associated with populations and linguistic forms (e.g., Spanish as a "spicy" language, Latinxs as a "spicy" people, and Latinx cuisines as very "spicy"), the differing positionalities of Spain-oriented speakers of Spanish and US speakers of Spanish are confused in Hill's description. If racialization is to be a central part of understanding the function of Mock Spanish, then we will need a careful explanation of Latinx as a racialized category and the role that language ideologies play in positioning this category with respect to the Spanish language.

Hill describes Mock Spanish as a "covert racist discourse," explaining that, "it accomplishes racialization of its subordinate-group targets through indirect indexicality, messages that must be available for comprehension but are never acknowledged by speakers" (Hill 1998:683). In other words, Mock Spanish plays on assumptions about Latinxs without making these assumptions explicit. For example, "mañana works as a humorous substitute for 'later' only in conjunction with an image of Spanish speakers as lazy and procrastinating" (1998:683). The most profound aspect of this process, however, is not that it frames "Spanish speakers" (regardless of national background and ethnoracial identity) in particular ways, but that it specifically positions "Latinx" as a US racial category. Thus, Mock Spanish must be analyzed specifically in relation to US Latinxs rather than all Spanish speakers or "members of historically Spanish-speaking populations" in any national context. Note that the language ideologies involved need not correspond to empirical linguistic practices, even to the extent that the subjects who are racially stigmatized in this process might display no normatively defined Spanish language proficiency whatsoever. This is why Hill describes the individuals involved as members of "historically Spanish-speaking populations." Yet, the racializing effects of Mock Spanish do not apply to a large number of the individuals who would seem to fit into this category, namely many Spaniards, Latin Americans, and other "historically Spanish-speaking populations" who are not racialized as non-White in the ways that millions of US Latinxs are.[38] The complex nature of this interplay between ideologies of language and race makes linguistic practices such as

Mock Spanish difficult to parse in relation to broader questions about the (re) production of raciolinguistic categories in specific contexts.

In comparing Mock Spanish to African American English (AAE) "crossover" (Smitherman 1994; Rampton 1998), Hill points out that "while the 'Black' indexicality of 'What's happening' is easily suppressed, it is virtually impossible to suppress the 'Spanish' indexicality of 'Nada,' which has in 'Mock Spanish' the semantically pejorated sense of 'absolutely nothing, less than zero' " (Hill 1998:685). For Hill, this is a common difference between AAE and Spanish—that is, the frequent indeterminacy of AAE (i.e., the suppression of "Black" indexicality) as opposed to the explicit Spanish indexicality of Mock Spanish usages. Again, there is a great deal to unpack in this comparison. First, note the way in which AAE and Spanish are made comparable here (even if differentially so). While African American English seems to point toward particular speech communities within the United States, does Spanish do the same? Hill positions "Black" and "Spanish" as distinct and potentially analogous racial categories, which elides not only Afro-Latinidad but also the specificity of Mock Spanish as it participates in the racialization of US Latinxs rather than Spanish speakers in general.

These questions about crossover, indexical (in)determinacy, and the links between token linguistic usages and the identities they invoke require a firm semiotic reconsideration drawing on the analytical lens of *interdiscursivity*. That is, the interrelations among token linguistic practices and their social functions, such as the use of Mock Spanish and the ways in which it indexes identities, is an interdiscursive effect that emerges by way of the creation of particular contexts of usage (Silverstein 2003a). What sociolinguistic boundary-making and identity-making processes must take place in order for interdiscursive effects such as the "Spanishness"/"Latinidad" of Mock Spanish to become experienceable? It is also not by chance that Spanish and AAE are considered in relation to one another here. A larger racial imaginary is at play—namely, one in which the social roles that speakers inhabit through these "crossover" practices come to be meaningful only insofar as they interdiscursively cast an image of a broader social world (Irvine 2005). How does Mock Spanish racialize Latinxs by distinguishing them from and positioning them with respect to other racialized groups within different speech and language communities? In what ways might this powerful process involve the imagined calibration of the language practices of different racialized groups? Bonnie Urciuoli explains:

> The English of African American neighbors (from whom many Puerto Ricans learn their own English) is ... racialized, as is Puerto Rican Spanish when it is typified as a degenerate patois of Indian and African influences.... It is no accident that the Spanish and English of Puerto Ricans

and the English of African Americans are often said to be bastardized. (Urciuoli 1996:35)

There are competing forces of standardization tied to broader colonial histories at work in linking these linguistic practices to racial category-making processes. Zentella (1996) has pointed to differently positioned claims to standardized Spanish from in-group perspectives—that is, a complex system of competing Spanish standards. These competing systems of standardization and the colonial histories in which they are rooted structure the relationship between linguistic practices such as Mock Spanish and the regimentation of wider racial orders.

In Hill's formulation of Mock Spanish there is a tension between explaining these linguistic practices as products of particular identities and thinking of them as contributing to the very constitution of such identities or social stances associated with these identities. Can only Whites effectively use "Mock Spanish"? Non-Latinxs in general? Spaniards? More precisely, must we take for granted the ethnoracial position of the speaker in order to locate "Mock Spanish" usages? The theorization of Inverted Spanglish presented here helps to respond to these questions. Inverted Spanglish, which in many ways seems strikingly similar to Mock Spanish, is neither a straightforward contributor to the hegemonic position of Whiteness and monolingual English dominance nor a clear-cut critique of these hegemonies.[39] Instead, Latinxs transform Mock Spanish into Inverted Spanglish to meet fraught institutional demands that recruit them to speak Spanish *in* English without being heard to possess an accent.[40] Because US Latinxs always "look" and "sound" Spanish regardless of what language they are speaking or whether they are speaking at all, they must be careful not to signal Spanish too strongly. Inverted Spanglish allows Latinxs to make "the linguistic statement that they have acquired a practical insight or a linguistic mastery of their sociolinguistic environment" (Jaspers 2005:296; Gal 1988).[41]

The signaling achieved by Inverted Spanglish also sheds light on bilingual Latinx students' internalized linguistic stigmatization. Monoglossic US language ideologies and policies (García and Torres-Guevara 2010) devalue students' abilities in languages other than English, thus discouraging bilingual students from drawing on their Spanish language skills by interacting with students designated as ELLs. Students who identify as bilingual and English-dominant often avoid interactions with students designated as ELLs altogether to escape the stigmatization that these linguistically marginalized students face. Still, Latinx students who identify as English-dominant and/or bilingual feel an ongoing connection to the Spanish language, which suggests that their social networks might not be so rigidly defined in opposition to their peers who identify as Spanish-dominant.

Enregistering a Racialized Latinx Panethnicity

The debate surrounding the pronunciation of Sonia Sotomayor's surname with which this chapter opened points to the apparent tensions between assimilation and multiculturalism that surround Latinx raciolinguistic identities. That President Obama stressed the final syllable of "Sotomayor" in announcing her nomination, a pronunciation some proponents of assimilation—linguistic and otherwise—claimed is "unnatural" in English, might suggest that, as Nathan Glazer (1997) put it, *we are all multiculturalists now*. But analysis of the relationship between ideologies of assimilation and multiculturalism demonstrates that these cultural philosophies have much more in common than their surface opposition suggests. Both the opposition to and embrace of Latinx difference involve the naturalization of that very difference, as well as the forms of marginalization that correspond to it.

Remembering a preceding historical moment in the United States, Mexican American autobiographer Richard Rodriguez recalls hearing his name on the first day of Catholic school in 1950:

> The nun said, in a friendly but oddly impersonal voice, "Boys and girls, this is Richard Rodriguez." (I heard her sound out: *Rich-heard Road-ree-guess.*) It was the first time I had heard anyone name me in English (Rodriguez 1982:11, author's italics).

For Rodriguez, this was a formative moment that taught him to construct an ideological distinction between Spanish as a private language for use in the home and English as a public language for broader use in school and everyday American life. This rigid ideological distinction between Spanish as a private language and English as a public language informs Rodriguez's perspective on bilingual education:

> [B]ilingual education . . . a scheme proposed in the late 1960s by Hispanic-American social activists, later endorsed by a congressional vote . . . is a program that seeks to permit non-English-speaking children, many from lower-class homes, to use their family language as the language of school. (Such is the goal its supporters announce.) I hear them and am forced to say no: It is not possible for a child—any child—ever to use his family's language in school. Not to understand this is to misunderstand the public uses of schooling and to trivialize the nature of intimate life—a family's "language" (Rodriguez 1983:11–12).

The anxieties underlying the rigid distinction Rodriguez draws between public and private spheres, as well as his discussion of the relationship between language, class, ethnoracial identity, and schooling continue to echo in educational contexts such as NNHS. Importantly, while it is now widely acceptable and even celebrated for the President of the United States to pronounce a Supreme Court Justice's name "in Spanish," bilingual education has received little popular support as a mainstream educational policy for minoritized children. It is not by chance that the pronunciation of names "in Spanish" would be embraced at the same time that the Spanish-speaking abilities of the holders of those names are stigmatized. This is how multiculturalism and assimilation work hand-in-hand.[42]

I was reminded of these debates about the pronunciation of names during the NNHS graduation ceremonies I attended in 2008, 2009, and 2010. In these ceremonies, students' Division teachers announced the names of their graduating seniors.[43] While Latinx teachers were more likely than White teachers to use Hispanicized pronunciations (e.g., the surname Vazquez pronounced "Bazkez" /bazkez/ vs. "Vazkwez" /væzkwɛz/), almost all of the teachers alternated between the two. The difference is that the Latinx teachers' alternations were unmarked (i.e., there was little audience response to their pronunciations), whereas White teachers' anglicized and Hispanicized pronunciations prompted occasional giggles from audience members. Both Latinx and White teachers' pronunciations provided models of Inverted Spanglish. Depending on the voicing, these usages could be received as unmarked or as humorous. In either case, such usages brought attention to different ways of speaking English while positioning Spanish as a unified language.

Note also that Inverted Spanglish usages correspond to Krikorian's guidelines for assimilating Spanish to English. Yet, this correspondence is by no means straightforward. NNHS students did not simply suppress the aspects of their linguistic repertoires that deviated from English language hegemony. Instead, the voicing achieved by Inverted Spanglish satirically questioned the authority of those such as Krikorian who attempt to domesticate US Latinx language use.[44] Meanwhile, within the context of NNHS, Inverted Spanglish also satirically voiced the figure of the Young Latino Professional and revealed the contradictions that constitute it.

In the process of creating an emergent style of English, Inverted Spanglish erased Puerto Rican and Mexican Spanish difference. Whereas Spanish-dominant communication became a prime ideological site for the recognition of Mexican and Puerto Rican difference, English was imagined as a linguistic medium in which Puerto Rican and Mexican difference is much more difficult to perceive. As one ninth-grade girl (PR, Gen. 1.5, Gr. 9) explained to me:

You can tell when someone is Puerto Rican or Mexican from their accent in Spanish . . . you can hear when someone is Latino from the way they speak English [be]cause they got that something . . that spice! I don't know what it is, but you can hear it.

In this example, the student invokes the racialized, panethnic stereotype that "Latinos" are "spicy," similar to the mural advertising "latino flavors with the spice of life" in Figure 3.3. Importantly, she associates "Latino" panethnic spice with *English*. Thus, ideologies that locate Mexican-Puerto Rican difference within the realm of Spanish and flatten out this difference in English contribute to the fashioning of a racialized, panethnic Latinx subjectivity. The ability of Inverted Spanglish to signal knowledge of the Spanish language while simultaneously indexing one's English language dexterity positioned it as a linguistic vehicle for the production of racialized, panethnic Latinx identities in this institutional context. While Inverted Spanglish emerged as a way in which to construct shared Latinx identities, it did not necessarily allow students to escape the double-stigmatization mapped onto their English and Spanish language use by way of racialized ideologies of languagelessness.[45]

My focus on Inverted Spanglish is not intended to provide a general model of English-Spanish bilingualism among students at NNHS. There were many other ways in which students moved within and between perceived varieties of English and Spanish, many of which mirrored existing accounts of monolingual styleshifting and bilingual codeswitching. Like García (2009), who elaborates on Bakhtin's notions of voicing and heteroglossia to conceptualize hybrid language practices that she describes as "translanguaging," I seek to highlight the ways that NNHS students not only navigated but also transformed perceived linguistic boundaries. This perspective presents an analytical framework that can be used to understand the translingual practices of students who might otherwise be approached separately as monolingual or bilingual. The categories of monolingual and bilingual were crucial inside NNHS. Depending on the variety, perceived monolingual English use could signal one's stereotypical ghettoness (i.e., monolingual nonstandardized English) or one's stereotypical ethnoracial inauthenticity (i.e., monolingual standardized English). Meanwhile, perceived monolingual Spanish use was construed as lame and prevented full participation in everyday school life. Inverted Spanglish resolved this bind by voicing in-group knowledge of Spanish and English, while simultaneously parodying the category of Young Latino Professional and the views of those such as Krikorian.

This chapter demonstrates the complex relationship between language ideologies, linguistic forms, ethnoracial categories, and power-laden cultural contexts of usage. It highlights Latinx responses to stigmatizing ideologies of languagelessness and calls into question constructions of Latinx raciolinguistic authenticity. Latinxs' naturalized relationship with respect to the Spanish language manifests the ways that conceptions of authenticity can valorize and stigmatize languages and their users simultaneously. When understood in relation to ideologies of languagelessness, Inverted Spanglish, despite all its linguistic and cultural complexity, is by no means a straightforward signal of one's institutionally sanctioned Latinx personhood. Thus, ideologies of languagelessness and Inverted Spanglish demonstrate how the administrative projects, ethnoracial contortions, and metapragmatic models described in the first half of this book become linked to language ideologies and linguistic practices. Chapter 6 turns to a discussion of how these dynamics operate in relation to NNHS students' complex literacy practices. By allowing students to simultaneously signal multiple social affiliations, these practices challenge rigid distinctions between identities associated with "school" and "street."

6 "THAT DOESN'T COUNT AS A BOOK, THAT'S REAL LIFE!"

OUTLAW(ED) LITERACIES, CRIMINALIZED INTERTEXTUALITIES, AND INSTITUTIONAL LINKAGES

In this final chapter, I show how criminalized signs stereotypically associated with gang-related practices became linked to conceptualizations of standardized and nonstandardized literacies as mutually exclusive phenomena within New Northwest High School (NNHS). By situating students' modes of reading and writing as responses to their social worlds inside and outside of school, I explore the ways in which Latinx youth draw on semiotic practices to navigate and respond to experiences of stigmatization and marginalization across contexts.[1] Whereas Chapters 4 and 5 analyzed linguistic inversions and ambiguities structured by ideologies of languagelessness and contestations thereof, this chapter investigates literacy inversions and ambiguities structured by criminalized sign practices and contestations thereof. In each of these cases, students' economic and ethnoracial marginalization devalued their language and literacy practices, demonstrating "the power that social institutions have in shaping what gets to be constructed as literacy" (Baquedano-López 2004:246). Literacy inversions involve particularly high-stakes negotiations of identity. For NNHS students and many youth of color throughout Chicago, the felt need to draw on intertextual signs that simultaneously signal one's "school kid" and "street kid" affiliations can become a matter of life and death. These simultaneities are crucial components of the projected tension between assimilation and multiculturalism that I have analyzed throughout this book.

As described in Chapter 1, the number of Chicago Public Schools (CPS) students who were killed during the 2008–2009 school year reached a record-breaking 36, making Chicago the city with the nation's highest youth homicide rate.[2] The 36th killing was particularly chilling. On May 1, 2009, 15-year-old Alex Arellano was beaten with aluminum baseball bats, hit by a car twice, shot in the head, and burned.[3] His body was found on May 2, 2009, near 54th Place and South Sacramento Avenue in Gage Park, a Southside neighborhood known locally as "Crown Town" (a reference to the Latin Kings gang organization).

Police reported that gang members approached Alex Arellano and "checked him," or asked him about his gang affiliation. The experience of being "checked" is familiar to Black and Latinx youth throughout Chicago.[4] Specifically, young Black and Latino males are often involved on both sides of these encounters. Even if stereotypical signs such as one's clothing and hairstyle are not associated with gang membership, racial identification alone is often sufficient grounds for checking someone. In other cases, gang members stand on a particular street corner and check all passersby, regardless of race, gender, or even age.[5] These practices allow gangs to demarcate their territory. A person can be checked while walking or driving along streets that are claimed as gang territory. The former case is particularly problematic for students walking to and from school, although many times students themselves participate in the practice of checking.[6] While driving, individuals could be stopped and asked about their gang affiliation by someone standing on the street or by someone in another vehicle.

According to reports from the police and media, after Alex told the gang members who checked him that he was not in a gang, they lifted his shirt to search for gang-related tattoos and then warned him not to come around the neighborhood. They returned later in a car and demanded that Alex "throw up the crown," or use his hands to make the Latin Kings' gang sign.[7] When he refused, they beat him with baseball bats. Alex tried to run away, but they hit him with the car and continued to beat him. Again, he attempted to flee, but they chased him into the backyard of a vacant home. They resumed the beating, shot him in the head, and eventually burned his body. It is unclear whether the gunshot wound killed him before their having set fire to him.

In local print, television, and online news coverage of the killing of Alex Arellano, excruciating pictures of his family in mourning were juxtaposed with stories about the tragic loss of a "good kid" who refused to affiliate with a gang. His family told reporters that, to avoid the threats from gang members Alex experienced at the beginning of the school year, he had not attended school since September. Within a few weeks of Alex's killing, as the investigation surrounding this case unfolded, some people's sympathy waned. News stories emerged with titles such as, "Was Alex Arellano in a Gang? Does it Even Matter?"[8] In these stories, images from Alex's memorial were juxtaposed not with lamentations about the loss of a vulnerable teenager but with pictures from his MySpace social networking page that showed him using his hands to make gang signs. These skeptical news stories questioned whether Alex was actually in a gang or was simply pretending to be affiliated. Often more revealing than the stories themselves, however, were the debates that unfolded among readers who posted comments in response to the online coverage of Alex's killing and the ensuing investigation. These readers' comments point to the highly disparate perspectives from which people made sense of what seemed, to many observers, to be such a senseless case.

In response to an online news story written by popular *Chicagoland Television* (CLTV) host Garrard McClendon mourning Alex's death, several readers voiced their concerns about Alex's potential gang affiliation.[9] "Diego" wrote:

first off . . . he was a gang member . . . the house he was murder[ed] on is known for gang member[s] and drugs. . . [I] live on this block and [I] have reported gang activities many times . . . [I] dont feel sorry for him.

Another commenter, "Jay," agreed:

Hardly an angel . . . that sure looks like he's broadcasting some sort of gang affiliation. Are those "bunny ears" he's throwing up? And the left hand disrespecting who? . . . Granted, very few people deserve to get beaten, shot and burned like this kid was, but he wasn't some innocent child murdered out of the blue. He hadn't been to school since September 2008, didn't look like he was going to school any time soon, was running around a war zone . . . and represents [his gang affiliation] on a social networking site.

Taking issue with "Diego," "Jay," and others who were suspicious of Alex's potential gang affiliation, "Human" commented:

Have you ever thought of the fact that maybe he had those pictures and myspace to get the gang by his house off his back? . . . It just so happens that I have know[n] Alex for the last 8 years of his life, and know that he was a good kid. Was he an "Angel" of course not, which one of us was or is?

"Ghostwolf" concurred with "Human":

Some of you folks are incredibly insensitive. I grew up in a bad area, running home from school every night, hiding from "bad kids," missing school DUE to threats on my life and I'll tell you something right now. . . . You try to stay "cool," you try to look "cool" and you try to keep your head down. You most CERTAINLY attempt to "look" like you fit in cuz if you don't, you'll be tracked down like a rabid dog and beaten. The cops said he didn't have a rap sheet. According to people that knew him well, he was shy to the extreme and this issue about him not showing up at school? When you're afraid you'll be killed on your way to and from school, oft times you DON'T show up for school (yes, for months at time!).

Intervening in this debate between contrasting perspectives about whether Alex was actually a gang member, some participants in this exchange claimed to possess firsthand knowledge about his affiliation. According to "EL MALO" (my clarifications are in brackets):

ALEX WAS A 12st [street] PLAYER WISH [which] ARE MAMBERS [members] OF THE PEOPLE NATION AND SO ARE THE ALMIGHTY LATIN KINGS[.] HE WAS IN THE RUNG [wrong] HOOD OR SAD [said] THE RUNG [wrong] THINK [thing][.] HEY LIKE THEY SAY AROUND THIS PART OF THE SOUTH SIDE OF CHICAGO[:] GET RUN DOWN, GUN DOWN, AND BURN DOWN, IN KROWN TOWN[.]

For EL MALO, there was no question as to whether Alex was a gang member. He claimed that Alex was a member of the 12th Street Players, a gang on the South Side of Chicago. EL MALO explained that both the 12th Street Players and the Almighty Latin Kings were part of the umbrella organization, "People Nation."[10] In fact, the only question from EL MALO's perspective was what Alex did in order for fellow members of the People Nation to kill him.

I asked Luis, the brother of a former student of mine who grew up just a few blocks from where Alex's body was found, to talk to me about EL MALO's comments and the picture of Alex from MySpace. He explained that the 12th Street Players were "future Popes," or future members of the "Insane South Side Popes" gang. "Futures," he said, were prospective gang members who needed to prove themselves to achieve full membership. For Luis, the picture on Alex's MySpace was no mystery at all; Alex was clearly "throwing up" (representing for) the "Popes" and "throwing down" (disrespecting) the "Latin Counts." Luis claimed that Alex had been warned not to come to "Crown Town," and that it did not matter whether Alex was a part of the People Nation. He went on to say that the killing was not a reflection of a broader gang conflict as much as it was a matter of particular individuals who were deeply offended by Alex's apparent disrespect.

These differing perspectives on Alex's potential affiliation reflect the complex ambiguities that surround the interpretation of symbols understood to be gang-related. Recall the practice of "checking" described earlier, in which one is asked to identify one's affiliation, and the way in which it was framed in news coverage as an important exchange that led to Alex's eventual killing. The most complicated aspect of this practice is that one never truly knows the gang affiliation (if there is one) of the person who is doing the checking. This means that one must quickly assess the situation to determine whether it would be advantageous to affiliate with a particular gang or to claim that one is a "neutron," which means neutral and not affiliated with any gang. While displaying a gang sign certainly can signal gang membership, this is not always the case. One might "throw up" (i.e., represent positive affiliation with) a particular gang sign because one is a member of that gang, one wants to be in that gang, one knows someone who is in that gang, one lives in a neighborhood that is dominated by that gang, one frequently visits a neighborhood that is dominated by that gang, one jokingly wants to suggest gang affiliation, or one wants to check someone nearby (throwing up a sign at someone is often understood to require that person either to throw up an affiliated sign or throw down a rival sign).

This chapter positions the debate about whether Alex Arellano was a "gangbanger" or "just a good kid" as a discursive template in relation to which anxieties surrounding students' identities took shape within NNHS. Complex signs that structure recognitions of identity in each of these situations were rendered meaningful by way of presumptions about "school" and "street" as bounded, distinct institutional contexts rather than as interdiscursive concepts (Silverstein 2005). The circulation of ambiguous signs within and among these various contexts became linked to perspectives from which particular intertextualities were understood as criminal literacy or illiteracy altogether. I describe these practices as "outlaw(ed) literacies" to emphasize the rebelliousness and illegitimacy with which they are associated, as well as their potential criminalization. I argue that interrelations and interdiscursivities between "school" and "street" produced ambiguities that undermined efforts to distinguish between students' affiliation with one objectified sphere or the other. I point not only to the stakes of these ambiguous signs but also to the ways in which they became resources in everyday interactions and constructions of identity.

I also show how NNHS students' literacy practices were not simply devalued or erased but also criminalized. Students wrote their identities in complex ways, highlighting the competing forces that required them to simultaneously signal alignment with and opposition to the school's project of socialization. This project, as analyzed in Chapter 1, involved transforming students from (being seen as) "gangbangers and hoes" into "Young Latino Professionals." These categories correspond to the stereotypical conception that Latinx students in Chicago negotiate school-based socialization by becoming either "school kids" (who eventually graduate and become upwardly socioeconomically mobile (i.e., Young Latino

Professionals) or "street kids" who drop out and become part of the racialized American underclass (i.e., gangbangers or hoes). In contrast, I show how students at NNHS drew on intertextual literacy practices to signal school kid and street kid identities concurrently, thereby calling into question the principal's project of socialization and the school/street distinction more broadly.

Not All Writing is Literacy

At the beginning of the school day on a winter morning in February 2009, Mr. Thomas addressed his classroom full of ninth-grade students with uncharacteristic aggression:

> I need to talk to you guys about something serious that's been going on in this classroom, which is tagging.[11] I see it on the desks and even on students' work hanging on the walls. To me that's really disrespectful. How would you like it if I came into your house and wrote all over your stuff?

The students sat quietly and somewhat attentively as Mr. Thomas scolded them. Mayra (Mex, Gen. 2, Gr. 9) explained to me that someone had drawn a pitchfork—a common gang-related symbol—on the back wall of the classroom (see Figure 6.1 for a sense of what this looked like). Mr. Thomas continued,

> You guys know I don't like to get on your case, but that's how you know that this is important to me. Now let's put that behind us and get to work. Our focus for the next few months will be on one thing: writing. We have a school-wide problem with getting students to write, so we're going to work really hard on this for the rest of the year. I've got a prompt up on the board. I want you guys to write two paragraphs about your favorite class.

Mr. Thomas transitioned from reprimanding the students for tagging to noting the school's inability to get them to write, as though the two situations had nothing to do with one another. I looked around the room for confirmation of this ironic sequence of events from the other adult tutors who were present, but my gazes were met with blank stares. That some students were covertly composing text messages on their cellular phones while Mr. Thomas discussed their unwillingness to write was an added irony.[12]

Two days after Mr. Thomas' confrontation with these students regarding tagging in his classroom, the same class of students sat quietly in groups of four and worked on various homework assignments. After hearing a knock on the glass

FIGURE 6.1: Gang signs in a textbook. Jovani (PR, Gen. 3, Gr. 9) showed me these gang-related drawings inside his math textbook. These drawings were similar to those that Mr. Thomas found on the classroom wall. Note that some of the drawings are written on top of one another, while others have been erased. This is because students used the textbook to represent their alignment with and opposition to different gangs. By erasing or writing over previous drawings, the textbook became part of an ongoing symbolic battle over gang loyalties and rivalries. Several symbols from the larger picture are displayed below it to highlight some of the symbols that are recognizably gang-related. From *left to right,* the image of a diamond with three dots on a staff, which appears in several places in the larger picture, symbolizes the Insane Spanish Cobras and its "junior" group, the Young Latin Organization Cobras; the image of a pitchfork symbolizes the Maniac Latin Disciples and its "junior" group, the Young Latino Organization Disciples; the image of an eight-pointed star with dots on each point symbolizes the Insane Ashland Vikings; and the image of a crown generally symbolizes the Almighty Latin Kings. Note that the pitchfork is upside down, which means that it is being disrespected. This is how the different symbols in the drawing can be juxtaposed to align with or oppose one another. These gangs were associated with streets near NNHS and there were NNHS students who affiliated with each of these gangs. Photo by author.

window next to the classroom entrance, Mr. Thomas opened the door and welcomed into the classroom one of the two Chicago Police Officers stationed at the school. In full uniform, including his gun, baton, and handcuffs, Officer Pérez made his way to the back of the classroom to inspect the taggings that Mr. Thomas had reported. The students continued working and seemed to pay little attention to Officer Pérez. His presence was entirely unremarkable, which speaks to the naturalization of policing in the context of CPS and particular neighborhoods throughout the city (see Chapter 1 for a description of school-based police surveillance).[13] But was this tagging created by a "gangbanger" or just a "good kid"?

Contrary to Mr. Thomas' claims, the writing was not only on the wall, so to speak; countless other literacy practices were never recognized as such (Figure 6.2). Students' notebooks and textbooks were covered with words and symbols. Taggers created designs on US postal mailing labels and carried them around looking to place them in locations that would draw the most attention. These stickers were frequently marked with the identity of the individual tagger who created them and the tagging crew to which they belonged. In Figure 6.2, the tagging name is "CYKO" (psycho) and the tagging crew is named "DCM," which can stand for Da Criminal Minds, Da Chronic Mob, Da Crazy Motherfuckers, Da Criminal Motherfuckers, Da Crazy Mexicans, etc. I will analyze "CYKO" and "DCM" in greater detail later in this chapter. In contrast to taggers' efforts toward self-advertisement, some students (mostly girls) passed around anonymously coauthored "burn books" with titles such as "gossip n' drama" that served as cumulative records of their everyday experiences and described encounters with parents, teachers, and one another. Alongside notes they took during their classes, students wrote rap lyrics,[14] poems, jokes, and notes to share with one another. Cellular text messaging, although strictly prohibited, was rampant. Meanwhile, administrators patrolled MySpace and Facebook, online social networking websites where students created pages with the school's name that contained juicy gossip and various top-10 lists referring to students and school employees.

One student made a profile for NNHS on MySpace, which was once the largest social networking site globally. At the time, a MySpace profile allowed individuals to post pictures and music, provide a description of their interests, and become "friends" and exchange messages with other MySpace users. Some of the key features of a typical MySpace page were: a "profile picture," which is the image that other users saw when they visited or searched for a page; a "headline," which appeared next to the profile picture as a prominent statement about one's identity; and the "General Interests," "Music," and "Movies" sections of the profile, which were used to describe oneself and one's pop cultural tastes. On the MySpace page that a student created for NNHS, the profile picture was an image of the inside of the school taken from an online news article profiling NNHS. The headline

FIGURE 6.2: Students' literacy practices. The *upper left* image displays self-affirmations written on a girl's (PR, Gen. 2, Gr. 9) notebook including "Through the storm," "No day but today," and "Speak life!" This student, a devout Christian (nondenominational), said that church inspired these quotations. The *upper right* image is a tag on a postal sticker. This example includes the tagging name, "CYKO" (i.e., psycho), and crew name, "DCM" (i.e., Da Crazy Motherfuckers, Da Criminal Minds), that students used to "spread" their individual and group tagging personae as widely as possible. The *lower left* image is a notebook labeled, "Gossip-N-Drama: The Issues." Several female students (PR, Gen. 3, Gr. 11; Pr. Gen. 2, Gr. 11; and PR, Gen. 1.5, Gr. 11) co-authored this shared notebook anonymously to create a cumulative daily record of various events, experiences, and misgivings; it referenced situations at home and at school. Central characters included teachers, parents, and fellow students. The *lower right* image is a heart-shaped note written in Spanish and sent to a girl (Mex, Gen. 2, Gr. 9) from a boy (Mex, Gen. 1.5, Gr. 9). Inside, it reads, "Para La nena mas bonita de mis sueños TE QUIERO" (For the most beautiful girl of my dreams I love you). Twelfth-grade boys said that it was lame to write a note like this to a girl when you could just send her a text message using a cellular phone. See Ahearn (2001a) for an analysis of love letters and social differentiation. Photos by author.

stated "NNHS GOSSIP ALL THE WAY FROM JUNIORZ (i.e., 11th-grade students) 2 FRESHYZ (i.e., 9th-grade students)." The "General Interests" section listed gossip pertaining to the romantic lives of various 11th-grade NNHS students, the "Music" section listed similar gossip about 10th-grade students, and the "Movies" section profiled 9th-grade students' romantic drama.

Unlike the Facebook group titled "YOu know YOu went 2 NNHS When . . . " that I described in earlier chapters, which gained nearly 300 members within a week of its creation, the MySpace profile did not become a prominent topic of conversation among students and staff. Whereas the MySpace page was explicitly presented as an anonymous gossip forum, the Facebook group became a competitive comedic engagement in which students, whose names and pictures accompanied contributions to the group, sought to outdo one another with their quips about the school. It contained posts such as, "You know you went to NNHS when you spend a whole class on FB:]" (i.e., Facebook) and "You know you go to NNHS when you use this page to tell your life story." The majority of the students who participated in this Facebook group graduated from NNHS in 2008 and 2009. Many of them had been exposed to Facebook by friends in college and by older siblings. They often reported that Facebook was "more mature" and that MySpace was "ghetto." In this case, students distinguished between two social networking sites as a means by which to signal their transition from adolescence to young adulthood. As I described in Chapter 1, the irony is that while CPS banned the use of Facebook on school computers and Dr. Baez was greatly concerned by former NNHS students' creation of this Facebook group, students understood Facebook-based literacy practices as signs that they had become less "ghetto" and more like Young Latino Professionals.[15]

Whether by way of notes, tags, rap lyrics, text messages, MySpace, or Facebook, the same students who teachers claimed would not write seemed to be writing all the time. The negative valuation of low income, racialized students' language and literacy practices at NNHS is not particularly surprising. In her canonical language socialization study in the Southeastern US, Heath (1982, 1983) shows how the literacy practices of working-class White students from "Roadville" and working class African American students from "Trackton" are devalued in different ways. Based on their experiences of language socialization, Roadville students brought functional literacy skills with them to school, such as the ability to identify letters, numbers, and vocabulary labels of objects pictured in books. Such skills contributed to Roadville students' initial educational success in elementary school, but by the fourth grade these very same students foundered. In these later stages of elementary school, school-based literacy norms placed higher value on independence, creativity, and abstract thinking. In contrast, Trackton students brought independence, creativity, and abstract thinking with them to school from the beginning, as displayed by their embrace of audience-oriented presentations, poetic storytelling, and cross-situational analogizing. Because these skills were not valued in the early elementary school years, however, Trackton students were quickly identified as low-performing or deviant. By the end of elementary school, when their skills became valued, "they ha[d] not picked up along the way the composition and comprehension skills they need[ed] to translate their analogical skills into a channel teachers [could] accept" (Heath 1982:70). Similar to the communities in which Heath worked, NNHS students' everyday literacy practices were generally viewed as educational and cultural impediments rather than skills that could contribute to broader learning opportunities.

These literacy practices were not interpreted as such because they did not seem to have anything to do with increasing the school's scores on standardized reading and writing exams. In one after-school professional development workshop, the entire faculty came together to study the grading rubric for the writing portion of the ACT college entrance exam. They sat in groups according to their subject area, read through sample essays written by NNHS students, and discussed strategies for improving students' scores. Mr. Thomas used these strategies to introduce students to the scoring guidelines. Not surprisingly, the categories for assessing ACT essays did not seem to incorporate the skill sets students developed in their extracurricular writing practices. In fact these two realms were rendered incommensurable from the perspective of institutional authorities. The result? Probation. The criminalization of NNHS's students metaphorically mapped onto the entire school, which was placed on academic probation by CPS in part for its low reading and writing scores in the fall of 2008.

Outlaw(ed) Literacies

Whereas Heath (1982, 1983) focuses on the failure to recognize and build from the language and literacy skills that elementary school students bring with them to school, NNHS students' practices were not simply devalued but often criminalized. The locally constructed relationship between graffiti and tagging highlights the way this criminalization took place. While graffiti and tagging have long been associated with criminality nationally and internationally, they have been met with particularly harsh responses in the Chicago context. Not only are graffiti and tagging expressly outlawed, but since 1992 the sale of spray paint and certain markers has been illegal within Chicago city limits. Anyone in need of spray paint must travel outside of the city to acquire it. Rigo (Mex, Gen. 2, Gr. 11), a self-identified tagger at NNHS, explained to me that he made a lot of money by traveling to Chicago suburbs, purchasing spray paint and markers in bulk, and then selling them to fellow Chicago taggers at dramatically inflated prices. Tagging is outlaw(ed) literacy, and the implements involved become figured as criminalized weapons. This section focuses on the experiences of Rigo, a former NNHS student who took on the tagging name "CYKO" and became part of the tagging crew "DCM."

While the outlaw(ed) component of tagging is certainly part of the thrill for participants, students drew very clear lines of distinction between tagging and gang-related graffiti. In the spring of 2009, Rigo brought me around the neighborhood to show me his tags and explain what it meant to be in a tagging crew. I worked closely with Rigo throughout his sophomore year (2007–2008) and continued to correspond with him after he left NNHS during the fall of 2008. During the 2008–2009 school year, Rigo was supposed to be a senior, but his grades would not allow him to graduate on time. Thus, he was referred to as a "demo" (i.e., demoted) junior. When school counselors told him that he would need to spend at least an extra year at NNHS to graduate, he decided to leave school and attend a General Education Diploma (GED) program offered in the evenings at another local high school. Rigo is the student from Chapter 3 who suggested that if he were president he would require everyone in the country to be bald on Fridays. A self-identified "cholo," Rigo was particularly reflective about the genealogy of his sartorial style. In a book review of Luis Rodriguez's *Always Running* (2005[1993]), an autobiographical warning against the dangers of gang life in Los Angeles and Chicago (specifically, Humboldt Park) that Rigo wrote for class, he explained:

> In the early 1930s and 1940s what was known as the pachuco gang image later came to be known as the cholos. For example, the pachucos had a flashy style, with pin-striped suits, vests, canes, formal hats, suspenders, and dangling key chains. This look was known as the zoot suit. On the other hand, the cholo style includes baggy Dickies and Ben Davis pants, white t-shirts, extremely long belts, undershirts (in Chicago they are known as daygos), checkered flannel shirts, and bandanas. Pachucos and cholos represent different times and different styles but they are very similar lifestyles. It is this lifestyle that is passed on from generation to generation. The image is different but the barrio stays the same. I identify with the cholo style and I live in the hood, but I no longer see an interest or a family in the gang life.

In addition to identifying with a cholo style that opposed the push toward professionalism in NNHS, Rigo was chronically tardy and generally unenthusiastic about his mainstream academic studies. Yet, he endeared himself to several teachers and school counselors by earnestly engaging them in conversations about their lives and his everyday concerns. Rigo was oppositional in very particular ways. Whereas other students tested the limits of my camaraderie with them by suggesting that my lowly position as a classroom tutor made me nothing more than a glorified high school student, Rigo always referred to me—inside and outside of school—as "Teacher Jonathan." His displays of deference reflect not only the widely studied embrace of "respeto" (respect) in Latinx familial socialization (Valdés 1996; Zentella 1997) but also his experiences of socialization within explicitly hierarchical gang and tagging crews. In each of these organizations, there are clear distinctions in seniority between shorties/seniors/O.G.'s (least to most senior in gangs) and toys/members/legends (least to most senior in tagging crews).[16]

When Rigo was a freshman he became involved in a local street gang. He came to regret his participation in gang life, particularly the false sense of "family" that it created, and he eventually discouraged others from joining. In an interview, Rigo explained:

> In a way, you do see a family there. The streets were my house, the corners were our rooms, and they [fellow members] were my brothers, sisters, and cousins. I used to stand on a corner for like an hour or two every day. I would check different people passing by to see what they claimed. The reason I stayed in the gang life was because I actually saw it as a family for a while. I didn't see it as three or four people standing around without anything to do, and it was more than just selling drugs. It felt like these were the people who encouraged me to be who I wanted to be and taught me never to take shit from rival gangs. After a while, I started to see my brothers as backstabbers.

While Rigo came to see his fellow gang members as "backstabbers," he viewed his tagging crew as a more faithful organization. Rigo said that there were 16 or 17 full-fledged members of his tagging crew, DCM. Rigo's 29-year-old uncle, who went by the tagging name OREN, was the leader of the crew. Members ranged in age from 16 to 31. In addition to tagging, Rigo said that the crew was a group of people to "kick it with (i.e., hang out with), people who have your back." He suggested that the nature of members' participation depended on their age:

> People bombing [tagging most often] are ages 16–20. A lot of members in their early and mid-20s have [tagging-related] court [cases pending] or family shit, so they only hang out with the crew or come to meetings. Members in their late 20s mostly come out with their whips [cars] to give

us rides and will tag with us when there's a war [battle between tagging crews] or when they can't handle the itch [when they really miss tagging].

Crew members included high school pushouts, high school students, college students, and people who were trying to go to college. Rigo learned from his uncle that while DCM had been in existence since at least 1992, the crew went through a period when there were very few members. Rigo attributed this loss of "soldiers" [crew members] to deaths and incarceration. To revive the crew, Rigo said that DCM became more like a family. They took in "toys . . . the little kids who get dissed by big crews" and helped them to become full members. To become members, toys were required to go through a probationary period in which they had to show that they were "down for the crew only." To do so, they were not allowed to take on an individual tagging name, and they could only tag the crew's name. Upon becoming a member, one was allowed to tag one's individual tagging name and the name of one's crew. Hector (Mex, Gen. 2, Gr. 9), a student in Mr. Thomas' class, was one such aspiring member of DCM. Although he was not yet allowed to tag his individual name, he planned to take on the name USB. He practiced tagging this name constantly; of course, the crew name DCM always appeared near his tags of USB (Figure 6.3).

FIGURE 6.3: Practice tags in a notebook. This is Hector's notebook, in which he practiced writing his tag name, USB, as well as the name of the crew of which he hoped to become a member, DCM. Pages similar to this could be found in many NNHS students' notebooks. Photo by CYKO.

Rigo explained that he was once like Hector. He and many other students reported that they had been tagging their names since elementary school. Over time, OREN taught Rigo how to create tags with differing levels of complexity. These levels range from a basic tag, which consists of letters written with style, to a piece (i.e., masterpiece), which consists of complexly shaped letters with shadow effects and filled in with different colors. (See Figures 6.4 to 6.8 to get a sense of these levels of complexity in Rigo's tags.) After taggers develop the skills necessary to create tags with differing levels of complexity, they strategically decide where they will have the time and ability to create which tags. This involves a consideration of the potential for run-ins with residents, passersby, gang members, and police. The more conspicuous and daring the location, the more potential credibility and notoriety to be gained from creating a complex tag there.

Rigo said that tagging and gangbanging were completely different worlds. He explained:

> I am not in the corner standing, gangbanging at cars, throwing bottles at people because someone's baldheaded or has a tattoo on his neck. I don't sell drugs to kids on the corner. . . . I am not just waiting in a corner to get shot. It's stupid to fight for a corner that don't belong to me. It's stupid to shoot someone when there are kids around. And it's stupid to fight when all of us are Latino anyway.

FIGURE 6.4: Basic tag. This photo shows a basic tag, which consists of taggers' names (in this case CYKO and OREN) and the crew's name (DCM) written in a stylized way. Photo by CYKO.

FIGURE 6.5: Bubble letters. After a basic tag, one learns to create bubble letters, such as the letters DCM in this picture, which appear alongside a basic tag of CYKO. Photo by CYKO.

FIGURE 6.6: Bubble letters with shadows. Bubble letters can be made more complicated by adding shadow effects to them, such as the letters DCM in this picture. Photo by CYKO.

FIGURE 6.7: A "fill." This consists of shadowed bubble letters that are filled in with color. Photo by CYKO.

FIGURE 6.8: A "burner." This is one of the more complicated designs. It consists of highly stylized lettering, shadow effects, and several colors, such as the letters DCM in the picture. Photo by CYKO.

Rigo sought to narrate his transition from gangbanging to tagging as a maturation process of sorts, in which he came to realize the futility of violence and drug dealing, especially because it involved fellow Latinos. He distinguished between gangbanging and tagging not only during our conversations but also in the rap lyrics that he composed periodically:

> I'm not showin' your son crack-headed songs,
> or introducin' him to violence,
> or givin' him a bong,
> or makin' your daughter skip class,
> or makin' her stand in da corner to sell her ass,
> I'm jus' here, grab a can, bust a tag, and then I disappear.

Rigo's lyrics and his comments during our conversations demonstrated his awareness of the conflation of tagging and gangbanging. In these rap lyrics he addresses parents who do not want their children to engage in tagging or gang participation, for fear of their gendered connection to violence ("introducin' him to violence"), drug use ("I'm not showin' your son crack-headed songs"; "givin' him a bong"), truancy ("makin' your daughter skip class"), and sexual exploitation ("makin' her stand in da corner to sell her ass"). Instead, Rigo suggested that his tagging had nothing to do with these issues and that it should be viewed in a different light ("I'm jus' here, grab a can [of spray paint], bust [create] a tag, and then I disappear").

Whereas Rigo considered gang-related graffiti to be "stupid" and "a waste of time," tagging was for him an "art" and a way in which to "spread [his] name." As Rigo and I walked along several streets near NNHS, he explained some of the differences between gang-related graffiti and non–gang-related tagging.

He pointed to graffiti created by the YLODs, or Young Latin Organization Disciples (Figure 6.9). Unlike the tagging in Figures 6.4 to 6.8, gang-related graffiti generally signals a rivalry with a specific gang and seeks to stake out a particular set of streets as its territory. Non–gang-related tagging, however, is geared toward promoting the reputation of tagging crews and individual taggers by getting taggers' names up in as many places as possible. While gang-related graffiti uses stylized writing, the aesthetic quality is relatively unimportant for its creators and for rival gang members. The point of this graffiti is to play a functional role in delineating territory.

Rigo showed me many of the different buildings on which he placed his tagging name, CYKO, and other tags associated with his crew, DCM. He explained that the most meaningful tags were (1) those that were the most difficult to create, both in terms of their aesthetic complexity and their location (such as tags on buildings surrounded by elaborate fencing); and (2) those that would "spread" his name the farthest, such as tags created on delivery trucks that traveled throughout the greater Chicago area (Figure 6.10). Rigo proudly called me one day to share with me that someone had been taking pictures of his tags around the city and posting them on the Internet photo-sharing website, Flickr. He explained that it was his goal to make it to "12 ounce," an online forum for Chicago taggers and fans. When I first met Rigo (in the fall of 2007), he was just beginning to participate in DCM and was nowhere near as assertive about his potential to achieve fame. At that time, he was still a junior member, so he mostly tagged the crew's name. A postal sticker that he tagged and gave to me featured DCM in large bubble letters, surrounded by small tags of his name, CYKO, and the words: "WEN I Die ill JUZ B ANOther Memory" (Figure 6.11). This speaks to Rigo's awareness of the potential for an early death, like that of Alex Arellano described at the beginning of this chapter. More than two years later, he was not as concerned with death and instead boasted that the fame he could achieve through tagging was way better than anything he could get out of gangbanging. Similar to fame and the spreading of one's name that has been studied in canonical anthropological accounts (Malinowski 1922; Munn 1986), efforts toward the creation of social status by way of tagging were met with a range of societal perspectives about the meaning and value of these practices.

From the perspectives of school administrators, police, and city officials, gang-related graffiti and artistic tagging were the same thing. These symbolic conflations proved consequential. Rigo recounted a run-in with Chicago Police while he was out with his tagging crew on a weekend night. They were tagging a wall when a shooting took place nearby. Upon hearing the police sirens, they quickly got in their car so as not to get caught tagging. Rigo explained, "My

These are the letters "YLO," which stand for Young Latin Organization, the first part of the gang's name.

Crucially, the "O" consists of an upside down diamond on a staff containing a backwards "C." When this symbol is right side up, it represents the Insane Spanish Cobras and the Young Latin Organization Cobras. When it is upside down, these gangs are being disrespected.

The letter "D" and the upward facing pitchfork represent the Young Latin Organization Disciples and the Maniac Latin Disciples. Taggers do not use common gang-related symbols, such as pitchforks, crowns, and diamonds.

FIGURE 6.9: YLODs gang sign. This is a photo of graffiti created by the YLODs gang, or Young Latin Organization Disciples. This gang is for young people (roughly aged 10–17) who are prospective members of the Maniac Latin Disciples. Each of these gangs claimed territory near NNHS. The graffiti is typical in that it not only signals the YLODs' claims to a particular neighborhood, but it also disrespects a rival gang, the YLOCs, or Young Latin Organization Cobras. The "O" in YLOD is represented by an upside-down diamond on a staff with a backward "C" inside it. When this diamond is right-side-up with the "C" facing right, it is a symbol for both the Young Latin Organization Cobras and its "parent" organization, the Insane Spanish Cobras. The "D" and the pitchfork to the right of it symbolize the YLODs and the Maniac Latin Disciples. Taggers do not typically use common gang-related symbols, such as pitchforks, crowns, and diamonds. Photo by author.

stupid friend took the alley even though I told him not to. . . . I always seen people get caught in the alleys on [the television show] Cops." The police stopped their car and inquired about the shooting. The crew was forced to exit their vehicle. They admitted to tagging, but the police were more concerned with whether they knew anything about the shooting. They found no weapons in the car, just spray

FIGURE 6.10: Rigo/CYKO spreading his name. Rigo was particularly proud of the upper photo, a sticker with his tagging name, CYKO, and crew name, DCM, that he placed on a seat inside the courtroom where he was fighting charges of vandalism. The lower photo features Rigo's name spreading on a delivery van. Rigo created this tag, which contains the tagging name, CYKO, and crew name, DCM, on a delivery truck. He speculated that people all over the city and suburbs would see his name because of it. Photos by CYKO.

paint and markers ("streakers").[17] Rigo was arrested and charged with nine vandalism-related misdemeanor counts, but was he a "gangbanger" or just a "good kid"? Outlaw(ed) literacies link spray paint and markers to guns and knives, rendering the differences between gang-related graffiti and artistic tagging invisible. The actors involved are criminalized in similar ways, even if they draw clear distinctions between one another's practices.

It was not only from the perspectives of parental, school, and police authorities that gangbanging and tagging were related practices. When I asked Rigo whether there were, in fact, some similarities, he told me that he did not like it when people "try to sugarcoat it" by saying things like "art is not a crime." He emphasized that taggers do, in fact, commit criminal acts. He did, however, take issue with the extent of the criminalization of tagging. Rigo said that it was unfair that some taggers get locked up for six months or more. He also pointed out that tagging and gangbanging are similar in their organizational structures: "it kind of is a gang . . . a gang is just a crew that sticks together and clicks/cliques together."[18] In fact, one of Rigo's social media pages contained

FIGURE 6.11: DCM postal sticker. Rigo gave me this tagging sticker in the fall of 2007. At the top of the sticker he wrote "TEACH Jonathan," as a variation of "Teacher Jonathan," which was the way he typically addressed me in person or on the phone. The prominence of his crew's name, DCM, compared with the smaller tags of his individual name, CYKO, signal that he was still in the early stages of the process of earning enough credibility to represent his individual name. The teal blocked lettering of DCM is outlined with black shadowing and also contains royal blue "drips," a highly stylized feature that Rigo was just learning how to create. Above DCM, he tagged "WEN I Die ill JUZ B ANOther Memory." Photo by author.

a photograph of his crew, DCM, that is strikingly similar in structure to photographs of gangs that can be viewed on the website chicagogangs.org (Figure 6.12). Both tagging crews and gangs might hold up hand signs that represent their organization and use bandanas or photo editing to cover their faces to avoid legal troubles. Tagging crews and gangs might also proudly display the instruments that are associated with their respective collectivities. Whereas one of Rigo's social media pages displayed rows of spray paint cans, gang members posted pictures of their weapons caches on chicagogangs.org (Figure 6.12). Still, Rigo explained that tagging crews occasionally use their spray paint to "go to war" by crossing out or defacing the letters in one another's tags. This is similar to the language of "gang wars," which were a common topic of conversation at NNHS. Moreover, Rigo's tagging name, CYKO, was also a common nickname for gang members.[19]

Despite some of these apparent similarities, NNHS students and Latinxs throughout Chicago have no trouble distinguishing between gang-related graffiti and non–gang-related tagging. They know that gang-related graffiti contains symbols such as stars (the number of points is an important distinguishing feature between different gangs), pyramids (the number of bricks corresponds

FIGURE 6.12: Tagging crew vs. gang. The upper image is a photo of Rigo's crew, DCM. Note that their faces are blacked out and their hands are displayed in the shape of the letter "M" by holding out three fingers. The lower image diplays some of Rigo's spray paint supplies in front of a photo album that contains a catalogue of his crew's tags. As is demonstrated by Rigo's encounters with police seeking to identify gang members, spray paint cans can become associated with guns when they are held in the hands of young Latinxs. Photos by CYKO.

to different gangs), pitchforks (the number of points corresponds to different gangs), crowns (the number of points corresponds to different gangs), canes, top hats, and clusters of certain numbers of dots. In contrast, non–gang-related tagging does not contain such symbols. Instead, tagging crews write their names in highly stylized ways, with as many colors and as much complexity as possible.

The relationship between non–gang-related tagging and gang-related graffiti can be productively understood within a framework of genre and intertextuality.

In their influential analysis of these concepts, Bauman and Briggs (1992) explain that genre must be conceptualized as an intertextual phenomenon that "simultaneously renders texts ordered, unified, and bounded, on the one hand, and fragmented, heterogeneous, and open-ended, on the other" (1992:147). They point out that the process of linking a particular text to a genre "necessarily produces an intertextual *gap*" (1992:149, authors' italics) and that individuals can strategically bring attention to the "ordered" or "fragmented" relationship between texts by suppressing or foregrounding these gaps. Processes of suppressing or foregrounding these gaps reflect the perspectival nature of (mis)recognizing intertexual links (Agha 2005; Gal 2005; Irvine 2005). From Rigo's perspective, non–gang-related tagging and gang-related graffiti were distinct genres of activity. Rigo and other taggers were not particularly interested in maximizing or minimizing intertextual gaps between tagging and gang-related graffiti because they did not recognize tagging as part of a genre of gang-related graffiti. They did, however, understand that tagging crews and gangs were viewed as similar formations from various out-group perspectives. The previous examples show some of the ways that Rigo and others conceptualized and engaged with perceived similarities between participation in a tagging crew and participation in a gang. Rigo's arrest demonstrates his limited ability to manage this precarious relationship and shows how modes of authority privilege particular readings of intertextuality over others.[20] The police did not even need to see the particular tags that Rigo's crew created to link their tagging practices to gang-related graffiti. Thus, tagging and gangbanging were not simply intertextutally linked but also interdiscursively and institutionally anchored in relation to one another by way of racialized presumptions that position Latinxs as inherently criminal.

Not All Reading is Literacy

While gang-related indexicalities criminalized tagging crews from out-group perspectives, similar indexicalities shaped students' ideas about reading. Many students laughed when I asked them to name their favorite book. Most often they told me that they did not "read like that," reflecting the ideological dissociation of their reading practices from standardized literacy (i.e., literacy in the genres of text stereotypically associated with standardized registers of language). While previously working with schools and families in predominantly Latinx communities near NNHS, I noticed that many young people—current students, graduates, and pushouts alike—loved the book, *My Bloody Life: The Making of a Latin King* (Sanchez 2000), and its sequel, *Once a King, Always a King: The Unmaking of a Latin King* (Sanchez 2003). The events presented in these Chicago-based autobiographical accounts, written pseudonymously by Reymundo Sanchez, took place primarily in Humboldt Park, but kids all over the city knew about them and read them, often multiple times. When I asked students about these books, they often laughed and reported that of course they had read them. In light of this revelation, I pushed students to account for their purported lack of interest in books and reading. One student explained, "that doesn't count as a book . . . that's real life!" He and many others said that they read the books "every day." The books consist of first-person realist accounts of growing up Latinx in Chicago and the struggles involved in becoming a part of and then attempting to escape gang life. Despite students' claims that these are not "real" books, they are generally written using what from many perspectives would be viewed as standardized literacy forms. For example, the author recounts his arrival to Chicago from Puerto Rico as an elementary school student:

> We lived on the South Side of the city around Twenty-sixth Street. It was a predominantly Mexican neighborhood. For the most part they weren't very friendly to Puerto Ricans. Their favorite chant was "*Arriba Mexico, abajo Puerto Rico*" ("up with Mexico, down with Puerto Rico"). I think their dislike of Puerto Ricans stemmed from the fact that while we were citizens of the United States at birth, they had to literally sneak into this country. But that seemed to be predominantly an adult attitude; the kids didn't seem to care. I made friends who spoke Spanish as fluently as they did English. That helped my sisters and me learn English faster. (Sanchez 2000:5)

Students' intense engagement with this text was facilitated by its reference to people, places, and experiences that were familiar to them. They explained that this text contrasted strongly with almost everything they were asked to read in classrooms.

Knowledge of gang life among NNHS students was situated at the intersection of direct encounters with gangs throughout their lives, the everyday presumption that all students were potential gang members, and popular cultural representations that linked Latinxs to gangs. As Latinx youth throughout Chicago circulated these books among their families and friends, they participated in ritual literacy practices that validated and reproduced their socialization in relation to gang life. The underground circulation of *My Bloody Life*—inside and outside of schools and libraries—allowed students to performatively construct their identities in relation to practices associated with the oppositional stances detailed within it.

My Bloody Life was banned from most school libraries. Its overt association with gang life and graphic details of drug use and sex made it a highly controversial text, despite the fact that the author eventually escapes the gang. Because *My Bloody Life* spoke to their experiences, and because these experiences were defined in opposition to school, students imagined *My Bloody Life* and themselves outside of sanctioned literacy. Thus, hegemonic ideas about "real" reading and writing were not merely imposed externally. Students received and internalized these ideas, and drew on them to make sense of their everyday lives.

Interestingly, the things that many students said about *My Bloody Life*—that it "didn't count" as a book, that it was "real life," and that they read it every day—were the very same things that many evangelical Protestant students said about the Christian Bible.[21] While *My Bloody Life* was banned from many schools and libraries, a popular teacher at NNHS became infamous for throwing a Bible into the garbage after it was handed to him by a religious organization that was visiting the school. Many NNHS students regarded the Bible not merely as an abstract sacred text but rather as a guiding force that would allow them to transcend the violence and poverty that saturated their everyday lives. This teacher sought to encourage students to subject their religious beliefs to critical scrutiny, but he seemed to be unaware of the particular life circumstances in relation to which students interpreted his actions.

What could these texts and, by extension, the institutions to which they correspond, possibly have in common? *My Bloody Life* would seem to be a text for "bad kids" and the Bible a text for "good kids," so why would these texts be described and experienced in strikingly similar ways? In the remainder of this chapter, I argue that these kinds of similarities reflect a complex set of interrelations among institutions, identities, and ideologies. These interrelations produced ambiguous practices that simultaneously signaled multiple affiliations; meanwhile, the erasure of such interrelations sustained rigid distinctions between "bad kids" and "good kids."

School Kids and Street kids

In Flores-González's (2002) analysis of a predominantly Latinx Chicago public high school near NNHS, she shows how students come to be categorized as "school kids" and "street kids." She cites statistical evidence that as of 2000, 28% of 16- to 24-year-old Latinxs were high school pushouts, as opposed to 4.3% of Asians, 7.3% of Whites, and 12.6% of African Americans (2002:2). Tracking the variety of precarious paths toward students' identification with normatively defined educational success and failure, Flores-González effectively identifies the barriers that stand in the way of educational success for "ethnic and racial minorities in the inner-cities" (2002:24).

She is particularly interested in the seemingly contradictory paths students take toward leaving school before graduating. Florez-González provides examples of pushouts as different as "the homely 'good' girl," "the single mother of two," "the tough girl," and "the quiet, shy, and respectful student" (2002:xi). Students who were pushed out varied not only in personality but also in their academic abilities and family lives. Some students read at the college level, while others read at the fifth-grade level; some had college-educated white-collar parents, while others had parents who were factory workers; some had educationally successful siblings, while others had siblings who were pushed out, too. Flores-González describes a variety of factors that contribute to making "school kid" and "street kid" more and less plausible identities for these students; she also points to the ways in which social inequality systematically mediates students' identification with these categories. That these are the primary categories available to students of color in urban settings is one of the most striking aspects of Flores-González's analysis.

In analyzing the relationship between categories such as "school kid" and "street kid," it is crucial to remember that they are neither separate nor do they neatly map onto students' lives. The common promotion of "school kid" over "street kid" identities reifies this categorical binary. In an analysis of the incorporation of students' community and familial experiences into classroom learning, Johnson argues that "'street' does not need to be situated in opposition to 'school'" and that "communities, while containing dangerous elements, can also serve as educative spaces" (2008:14). "School kid" and "street kid" identities do not necessarily guarantee normative educational success or failure, respectively. Thus, the goal should not be to encourage the embrace of "school kid" identities, but rather to call into question the ways in which the categorical binary of "school kid" and "street kid" overshadows the nature of structural educational inequality, ethnoracial discrimination, and socioeconomic marginalization in this context. The operation of this binary is similar to the discussion of the categories of "Puerto Rican" and "Mexican" in Chapter 2, in which I pointed to Gal's argument that particular distinctions are "best understood as . . . discursive phenomena that, once established, can be used to characterize, categorize, organize, and contrast virtually any kind of social fact: spaces, institutions, bodies, groups, activities, interactions, relations" (Gal 2002:80–81). Taking Gal's cue, "school" and "street" can be understood not as objectively distinct spaces or biographical individuals but rather as discursive concepts that become associated with a variety of institutions, actors, and social practices.

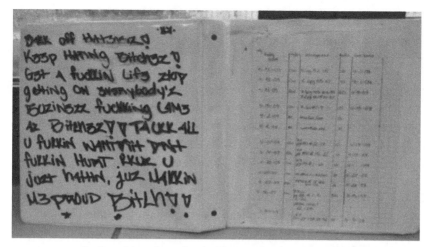

FIGURE 6.13: José's multivocal notebook. This notebook juxtaposes "school kid" and "street kid" voices. Note that my reference to school kid and street kid voices is not intended to suggest that these are biographical individuals, but rather characterological figures. Voicing involves a consideration of the dynamic interactional effects that take shape through invocations and arrangements of such figures (Bakhtin 1981; Silverstein 1999). Photo by author.

NNHS students' literacy practices demonstrate the discursive complexity of the concepts of "school" and "street." All NNHS students signaled their alignment with each of these concepts, albeit in different ways. One student's binder highlights the school/street distinction (Figure 6.13). José (Mex, Gen. 2, Gr. 9), a student in Mr. Thomas' class, kept one primary binder for all of his schoolwork. The right side of Figure 6.13 shows the front of the binder. It contains a sheet of lined paper that neatly lists José's class schedule and homework assignments. The left side of Figure 6.13 shows the back of the binder, which reads:

> BAKK off Hat3RZ! K33p HATINg Bitch3z! G3t A fuckkiN Lif3 ztop getting ON 3V3Rybody'z BUZiN3ZZ fuckking LAM3 AZ Bitch3Z!! TALKK ALL U fukkiN WANT! iit DNt fukkin HURT kkuz U juzt h4ttin, juz MAKKin m3 PROUD BitCh!!
>
> [Back off, haters! Keep hating, bitches! Get a fucking life . . . stop getting on everybody's business fucking lame ass bitches!! Talk all you fucking want! It don't fucking hurt because you're just hating, just making me proud bitch!]

José's notebook signaled his affiliation with school kid and street kid practices. The rant on the back of the notebook is intertextual with online instant messages and cellular text messages, demonstrated by the shifts between upper- and lower-case letters and the substitution of numerical characters for letters, such as the number "3" for the letter "E." Note also the standardized use of punctuation alongside nonstandardized spellings, such as the possessive apostrophe in the word "3V3Rybody'z" (i.e., everybody's) and the use of exclamation points throughout. José's nonstandardized usages are patterned alternations of standardized usages. For example, the word "buzin3zz," substitutes "z" for "s" and "3" for "e." What appears to be a straightforward "street kid" voice on the back of José's notebook in fact demonstrates that he has thoroughly mastered standardized practices, which allows him to play with these forms in systematic ways. That his rant is juxtaposed with the neatly written schedule on the front of his binder should come as no surprise. Distinctions that position school kids and street kids as separate biographical individuals do not capture José's practices.

Jose's juxtaposition of texts associated with "school kid" and "street kid" identities demonstrates several important features of this distinction. This binder is one of countless examples of the ways that "street" practices were circulated and even produced in school. While many educational researchers have rightfully argued that schools must value the literacy skills that students bring to the classroom (Freire 1970; Hull and Schultz 2002; Mahiri 2004; González, Moll, and Amanti 2005), it is important to consider how purported "out-of-school" literacies can actually be created and circulated within school. In other words, interactions within school contribute to the production, circulation, and general engagement with "out-of-school" literacies. How helpful is the notion of "out-of-school" literacies, if these literacies are often developed inside school? In this sense, we must rethink the notion that "school" and "street" correspond to distinct spaces and practices. In fact, the structure of the "street" literacy displayed on the back of José's binder, which includes many systematic variations of standardized forms (e.g., 3V3RYBODY'Z for everybody's and BUZIN3ZZ for business), reflects his engagement with and mastery of "school" literacy. Alternatively, the positioning of these texts on the front and the back of José's binder might suggest that these two voices exist in uncomfortable relation to one another. Is the voice on the back of his binder in fact confronting the voice on the front? Either way, José's literacy practices show how "school kid" and "street kid" become voices that can be signaled in close proximity to one another.

In a related example, David (PR, Gen. 3, Gr. 12) also signaled his "school kid" and "street kid" affiliations simultaneously. He was emphatic about his opposition to gangs, which he described as "so lame." I sent him a text message to ask him to clarify something he stated in an interview that I conducted with him. As described in Chapter 5, David said that he was playing Xbox 360 Live, an Internet-based multiplayer video game system that allows opponents to hear one another's voices, when an opponent told him, "Shut the fuck up, you Mexican!" While David, a proud Puerto Rican, was confused by this provocation, he concluded that his opponent identified him as Mexican based on his voice. I was unsure whether this opponent truly identified David as Mexican solely because of his voice, so I exchanged text messages with him to ask what other information his opponents might have had about him. I was interested in two potential signals: (1) the physical appearance of the avatar that David chose to represent himself on the screen and (2) his "gamertag," the username he created for himself (see Figure 6.14 for a sense of what David's profile screen looked like):

JR: In our interview you said that you were playing xbox live and someone told you to "shut the fuck up, you Mexican!". . . you said you thought they said that because of your voice . . .
    Here are my questions: (1) What does your avatar look like? Does it have white or brown skin? (2) What is your Gamertag? Does it "sound" Spanish? I'm giving a presentation today and I want to be able to play part of our interview.
D: It has like a golden brown skin. My gamertag is ps3killa360love.
JR: And now I have to write a chapter about your Gamertag . . . that's amazing
D: Lmao ok kool

In response to my question about his gamertag, David wrote that it was "ps3killa360love," or PlayStation 3 killer, Xbox 360 love. This means that he opposed Sony's PlayStation 3 video game console and aligned with Microsoft's Xbox 360

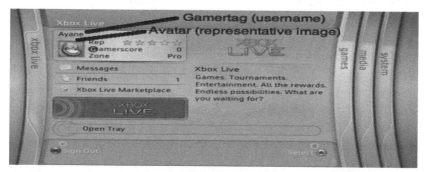

FIGURE 6.14: Xbox 360 Live profile screen. This profile displays one's "gamertag" (username) and "avatar" (image used to represent the player).

console. What is interesting here is that he drew on the structure of a common gang-related refrain that signaled affiliation with one gang and opposition to another (e.g., Cobra killer, King love). Students used this structure constantly. A common example was "ONHS killer, NNHS love," which meant that they opposed ONHS and positively represented NNHS. Countless categorical distinctions could be invoked using this structure. In David's case, he used a gang refrain to signal a rivalry between two video game systems. In particular, he made it clear that he affiliated with Microsoft's Xbox 360 and wanted nothing to do with Sony's PlayStation 3. An example that might be more familiar to mainstream academic audiences would be "PC killer, Mac love." Latinx students all over Chicago play with this refrain in similar ways.

David distanced himself from gangs, which he described as lame, yet he represented himself by signaling his knowledge of gang practices. Again, David's literacy practices do not fit neatly into "school kid" or "street kid" categories. He simultaneously drew on practices associated with each of these categories to fashion shifting identities.[22] Moreover, David's interweaving of "school kid" (i.e., video game-related) and "street kid" (i.e., gang-related) discourses shows how he did not simply seek to maximize or minimize intertextual links, the two overarching intertextual strategies that Bauman and Briggs (1992) identify. Instead, he drew on ambiguity and bivalency (Woolard 1998) to signal his joint engagement with each of these categories.

Beyond the School/street binary

The relationship between "school" and "street" as a set of discursive concepts and institutional contexts contributed to many contradictory situations for NNHS students. When Rigo began high school, he identified as a member of a gang. When he transitioned to night school, he identified as part of a tagging crew. When night school did not work out and he put his education on hold, he became part of a banda (folkloric Mexican music/dance) crew. Rigo went from being a student and a gang member to being a pushout and an expressive cultural performer. These apparent contradictions are structured into the discursive distinction between "school" and "street." Questions about whether Alex Arellano was a "school kid" or a "street kid," from the beginning of this chapter, were also structured in relation to the discursive distinction between these categories and the way in which it was mapped onto interrelated institutions, identities, and practices. Like Rigo and virtually all of the students with whom I interacted at NNHS, Alex likely signaled his affiliation with each of these categories.

Students at NNHS were faced with the complex task of configuring identities that would allow them to signal multiple, frequently contradictory allegiances simultaneously. Students' outlaw(ed) literacy practices provide insights into this situation by demonstrating the ways that (1) students' reading and writing skills were not simply erased but frequently criminalized; (2) the distinctions that students drew between practices such as gangbanging and non–gang-related tagging to distance themselves from criminality were rendered invisible; and (3) students simultaneously affiliated with "street kid" and "school kid" categories to manage competing pressures. These practices and processes demonstrate the perils involved in the negotiation of Latinx identities at NNHS and in schools throughout the United States (Zentella 2005; Mendoza-Denton 2008).

On the surface, the distinction between "school kids" and "street kids" echoes previous ethnographic studies of class-based categorical distinctions in schools (Willis 1977; Eckert 1989, 2000). Whereas these studies focus on educational contexts in which students' differential economic positions and access to resources organize categorical distinctions such as "jock" and "burnout," NNHS students inhabited shared positions of economic and ethnoracial marginality. Not only were they recruited to identify with "school" and "street" in similar ways, but they also faced similar perils associated with their negotiations of these joint identifications. The case of Alex Arellano described at the beginning of this chapter demonstrates how the stakes of the distinction between "school kid" and "street kid" involves the legitimation of life and death. Thus, the cultural distinction between school and street becomes a powerful structuring logic through which disparity is reproduced and rationalized.

The culturally valorized distinction between communicative repertoires associated with "school" and "street" masks what is actually a range of register usages and ideological perceptions by framing them as mutually exclusive standardized and nonstandardized practices. Recall José's binder, which reflects his joint engagement with different registers, yet runs the risk of being interpreted solely as a gang-related tag. This explains how students could claim that texts such as *My Bloody Life* do not count as "real" books. Attempts to encourage or require students to identify only as "school kids" are held in tension with the broader "street"-based anchoring of their everyday, racialized experiences; these fraught power dynamics are characteristic of the relationship between literacies and social identities. Efforts to enhance mainstream educational achievement by building on practices associated with extracurricular domains often reify social and linguistic boundaries and reproduce troublesome hierarchies that position such practices as useful only insofar as they are understood to contribute to normative learning in straightforward ways. Rather than replicating these distinctions, our theories and practices alike would benefit from a reconsideration of the boundaries that circumscribe language, identity, and institutionality. Indeed, the socialization to and through vast languages, literacies, and other forms of knowledge production in various extracurricular contexts suggests that we would be well-served by reimagining communities *as* campuses in their own right (Rosa 2017).

CONCLUSION

HEARING LIMITS, VOICING POSSIBILITIES

In June 2010, I attended New Northwest High School's (NNHS's) third annual graduation ceremony. The Puerto Rican valedictorian rapped his entire speech, which included celebratory lyrics about "freshy Friday" (the semi-mythical day toward the beginning of each school year when ninth-grade students were the victims of pranks initiated by sophomores, juniors, and seniors), the ACT (college entrance exam), prom, and how P.E. (physical education) classes at NNHS used to be same-sex but shifted to co-ed. The Mexican salutatorian greeted the audience in Spanish before delivering the majority of his speech in English: "¡Buenas tardes y bienvenidos a todos en este día maravilloso!" (Good afternoon and welcome to everyone on this wonderful day!). After the assistant principal, Ms. Torres, read the graduating students' names, pronouncing most of them "in Spanish" (i.e., with stereotypical Spanish phonology), Dr. Baez kissed each student individually and had her picture taken with them holding their diplomas.

From out-group perspectives, the ubiquitous June graduation parties—with abundant decorations, food, and attendees—that Latinx and African American families throw in residences, city parks, and forest preserves throughout the Chicago area are often mistaken for high school graduation celebrations. In fact, many of these families are celebrating elementary school graduations (i.e., eighth-grade graduations) with the knowledge that there is no guarantee that Chicago Public Schools students will graduate from high school. In contrast, at the third annual NNHS graduation ceremony described previously, nearly 100% of the school's seniors graduated, as was the case for each of the previous graduating classes.

I took a Chicago Transportation Authority bus from Humboldt Park downtown to Navy Pier, where the graduation ceremony was held. As I stepped onto the bus, I saw Roberto (PR, Gen. 3, Gr. 10) and Edgar (Mex, Gen. 2, Gr. 11), students whom I tutored during the 2008–2009 and 2007–2008 school years, respectively. A friend of theirs from NNHS was able to get them a couple of tickets to the graduation; the staff at Navy Pier required the tickets for entry to the event. Roberto and Edgar were both wearing their NNHS uniforms, which consisted of short-sleeved maroon polo shirts with the school's name embroidered on them, khaki pants, and "Vans" brand shoes. They pointed to my fresh haircut and said that they wished they had time to go to the barbershop or at least to change their clothes before the ceremony. Edgar pinched his shirt, lamenting, "everyone will look so fresh over there and we're here in our uniforms." Shifting topics, they mentioned that they were looking forward to "fun day" at school later that week. Each year at NNHS, the last day of school was called "fun day." A carnival was set up on the large field next to NNHS, and it was the only day when students could wear their "street clothes" to school. On previous "fun days," I joked with teachers about the possibility that street clothes would make the school's walls fall down. For Dr. Baez, the informal nature of the day made it reasonable to allow the students to wear informal clothes. For the rest of the school year, however, students had to dress like Young Latino Professionals.

Roberto, a "cool" Puerto Rican who was the object of many NNHS students' attraction, told Edgar not to worry about wearing the uniforms to the graduation and quickly changed topics to discuss the religious initiation—he called it his "celibacy"—that he was undergoing as part of his church youth group. I remembered that Roberto strongly identified as Christian. In particular, I recalled that during one of our tutoring sessions when I asked him what kind of music he liked, he said that he only listened to Christian music. Roberto explained to Edgar that as part of his celibacy he was not allowed to date girls for three months. He could not even exchange cellular text messages with girls because this might lead to something more serious. Roberto told Edgar that he no longer said vulgar words such as "F-A-G-G-O-T"[1] or "H-E-L-L" (he spelled them out loud), unless he was talking about the Bible. He explained to Edgar how sure he was that God would bless him at the end of his celibacy. Edgar asked Roberto to bring him to the church so that he could check it out.

Like many other NNHS students, Roberto attended a church called Rebirth.[2] The church had thousands of members in its congregation. At the time, its services were held in the auditorium of a large, predominantly Latinx high school in Humboldt Park.[3] This included five separate services on Saturdays and Sundays (one of which was in Spanish, but the English language services were peppered with Spanish words and phrases) and a youth service called "Motivated" on Thursday evenings. I attended the youth service once with Jimmy (PR, Gen. 3, Gr. 12), one of the students whose experiences I have described throughout this book. Jimmy asked me to accompany him to the service so that he could talk to his girlfriend, Iris (PR,

Gen. 3, Gr. 11), an NNHS student and active participant in the church. After hearing a rumor from an acquaintance at NNHS that Iris was planning to cheat on him with a young man at the church, Jimmy wanted to find out whether it was true. Allegedly, Iris sent a text message to a boy at the church telling him that she wanted to be in a relationship with him after his celibacy was over and that she was going to wait for him. Jimmy was excited to finally be in what he thought was a good relationship, so he took this news hard. He said that if he went to the church with one of his friends from NNHS, the youth pastors would think that he was trying to start trouble; on the contrary, he suggested that he would be less likely to get in trouble if I went with him.

When we arrived at the church I was surprised to encounter so many students from NNHS. In particular, I was shocked to see Keyla (PR, Gen. 3, Gr. 10/out of school), a young woman with whom I had worked at NNHS but had not seen since she stopped attending school. Keyla was known to hang out with the gang-affiliated youth who lived on her block (the same block where Jimmy lived); she was also the only young woman I encountered at NNHS who openly expressed her attraction to other young women at the school. Based on my perception of Keyla, I could not figure out why she would attend an evangelical youth service at a church that was well known for its homophobic leadership and clean-cut image. After the service, I checked out the church's website and discovered that it has programs geared toward "young women in the Humboldt Park community who have been physically and spiritually broken." The site featured the testimony of a young woman who was transformed from "gangbanging" and "living a lifestyle of homosexuality and sexual immorality." Her testimony states that God changed her life "from the inside out . . . down to [her] hair and choice of clothing." The testimony is accompanied by before and after pictures that symbolize her new outlook. Was Keyla seeking to experience a similar transformation?

NNHS students simultaneously negotiated various efforts geared toward transforming their identities, expressive practices, and social realities. Students carefully responded to and even sought out these makeover projects. The situations analyzed throughout this book demonstrate how institutional projects of transforming marginalized Latinx youth shape students' expressive practices, along with their identifications of themselves and others. The intersectional mobility project of transforming (recognitions of) students from gangbangers and hoes into Young Latino Professionals at NNHS was linked to other local transformation projects, such as those at Rebirth Church, as well as to broader anxieties concerning the status of Latinx identities.

While Dr. Baez was interested in creating Young Latino Professionals—figures carefully positioned between assimilation and multiculturalism—students were engaged in balancing acts of their own. Their identifications with categories such as Mexican, Puerto Rican, Hispanic, and Latina/o became infused with the anxieties built into the projected tension between assimilation and multicultural authenticity. These anxieties prompted students to engage in various ethnoracial contortions to orient themselves in relation to categories over which they ultimately had limited control. Yet, students' fundamentally shared experiences of marginalization and socialization, when apprehended in light of popular cultural, governmental, and local representations of Latinidad, contributed to the creation of Latinx as a racialized, panethnic category. This category-making process involved the navigation of structural inequities associated with racial, spatial, and class exclusion on the one hand, and the creative remapping of national borders through diasporic imaginaries that project a more expansive vision of the Americas on the other. The creation of US Latinx identities corresponds to the emergence of communicative indexes that signal students' comprehension of the multiple allegiances that are required of them. In the context of NNHS, stereotypical Spanish and English language forms became enregistered as Inverted Spanglish usages as a way of contesting racialized ideologies of languagelessness. This register of language also parodied the category of Young Latino Professional. Meanwhile, in the realm of literacy, students carefully, yet precariously, signaled their affiliation with both "school" and "street" through the deployment of outlaw(ed) literacies.

In this book I have shown how categorical distinctions across realms of theory and practice can be productively analyzed as interrelated sets. The projected tension between multicultural identity maintenance and assimilation organizes distinctions such as neighborhood high school vs. selective enrollment high school, gangbanger/ho vs. Young Latino Professional, race vs. ethnicity, Latina/o/x vs. Hispanic, Latin American vs. American, bilingualism vs. monolingualism, Spanish vs. English, Inverted Spanglish vs. Mock Spanish, legitimate reading/writing vs. outlaw(ed) literacies, and school vs. street. Experiences within NNHS demonstrate how these categories become intertwined in countless, indeterminate ways. These categories can be productively understood in relation to a raciolinguistic perspective, which attends to the historical and contemporary conaturalization of language and race. Such a perspective can play a crucial role in illuminating the dynamic processes through which populations come to come to look like a language and sound like a race.

Beyond this local scene, it is important to consider the dynamic interplay between racialized, panethnic category-concepts and semiotic practices across differing nation-state contexts. As I have argued, Chicago's long-standing panethnic Latinx population uniquely positions it as a geopolitical and sociocultural space in which to track these dynamics. While the historical and contemporary racialization of Latinxs is met with creative panethnic responses, we must continually consider the ways that efforts toward contestation can disrupt, reconfigure, and rearticulate long-standing colonial relations. From this perspective, it is crucial to interrogate how an exclusive focus on mainstream measures of success such as upward socioeconomic mobility and educational achievement legitimates racial capitalism as a mode of governance and the colonial power relations out of which it emerged. The public education system is a particularly concrete example of the institutional structures through which these power relations are reproduced. While Dr. Baez created an institutional project that facilitated the graduation of nearly all of her students, these students were not guaranteed anything beyond high school. As it turns out, efforts to achieve a high school diploma, like those to master the English language or obtain citizenship, by no means provide straightforward access to the range of societal opportunities understood to be available to anyone who works hard enough to earn them in an imagined American meritocracy. Still, Latinxs' strategic engagement with marginalizing institutional frameworks and contestations of their everyday experiences of exclusion suggest that broader transformations are possible. Insofar as NNHS became a context in which to challenge the terms of Latinx exclusion, it is a sign of the broader ways in which particular institutional sites can serve as crucial platforms for unsettling ethnoracial, geopolitical, and linguistic borders that arbitrarily circumscribe various identities, rights, and communicative practices. The reimagining of these borders within NNHS and its surrounding communities demonstrates that worlds beyond these borders are not just possible, but in fact already in existence and waiting to be recognized as such.

NOTES

INTRODUCTION

1. Kara Spak and Dave Newbart, "Our Baby Boom: Growing Up with Multiple National Identities Gives Chicago's Young Hispanics a Unique Perspective—and Opportunity," February 19, 2010, *Chicago Sun-Times*, http://www.suntimes.com/news/metro/2060425,nuevo-chicago-hispanics-022010.article (accessed March 6, 2010).

2. I seek to emphasize the perspectival nature of the Latinx category, its everyday interactional production, and the particular ways that individuals are interpellated by it. While this category is associated with US-based Latin American (im)migrants and their descendants, people who fit this description are not necessarily interpellated as Latinx (Chapter 2 includes a discussion of a student who self-identified as African American and Latina, but who was often recognized only as African American); conversely, people who do not fit this description can be interpellated as Latinx (Chapter 5 includes a discussion of a Filipino teacher who was often recognized as Latino). Moreover, the political territories associated with Latinidad are highly contested, including the shifting US-Mexico border and questions surrounding the ethnoracial identities of Central American, South American, and Caribbean populations.

3. Throughout the book I use the term "ethnoracial" when I am explicitly addressing both race and ethnicity, as well as when I am referring to the relationship between the construction of Latinx national subgroups (e.g., Mexicans, Puerto Ricans) and the racialization of Latinidad as an umbrella category.

4. Bucholtz (2011) demonstrates how a key feature of Whiteness as a racial and linguistic power formation is its alternate homogeneity and heterogeneity. One the one hand, Whiteness is homogenized through its position as an unmarked norm; on the other, Whiteness is differentiated through heterogeneous instantiations that afford White individuality in contrast to people of color, whose practices are conventionally

understood as collective rather than individual phenomena. These patterns become highly consequential insofar as they exceptionalize perceived deviance by individual White people and essentialize perceived deviance by individual people of color.

5. Mexican philosopher José Vasconcelos (1997) famously predicted that a superior "cosmic race" would emerge in Latin America as a result of miscegenation in this context.

6. In the chapters that follow, I analyze the troublesome stereotypes surrounding each of these "problems."

7. This focus on naturalization is inspired by the theorization of linguistic and social boundary-making within influential work on language ideologies. In their conceptualization of the semiotics of sociolinguistic differentiation, Irvine and Gal note that, "linguistic differentiation is not a simple reflection of social differentiation or vice versa, because linguistic and social oppositions are not separate orders of phenomena" (2000:76). The crucial point is that social and linguistic boundaries must be understood as situated semiotic configurations and perceptions rather than empirical realities. Relatedly, Silverstein's (2003a) framework of indexical order points to the dynamic semiotic processes through which social and linguistic relationships come to form and undergo transformations through situated instances of communication.

8. Shankar (2013) and Carbado (2005) have also productively theorized racial and linguistic naturalization in relation to advertising and legal domains, respectively. Their important work demonstrates the ways that these distinctive domains are organized by historical and contemporary modes of racialization.

9. Makoni and Pennycook (2007) theorize linguistic boundary-making phenomena in relation to colonial histories. From a contemporary political and economic perspective, such boundary-making practices are often organized by the logics of "pride" and "profit" that circumscribe the values associated with particular modes of communication for particular populations (Duchêne and Heller 2012). For Shankar and Cavanaugh (2012), the commodification of communicative phenomena underscores the ongoing importance of attending to the co-constitutive nature of language and materiality in the ways that contemporary workings of global capitalism rearticulate long-standing structures of language and political economy (Gal 1989; Irvine 1989).

10. Racial theorists have invoked this interplay between linguistic and social differentiation, such as Bonilla-Silva's (2011) notion of "racial grammar." However, rather than viewing linguistic structure simply as a metaphor for the organization of racial dynamics, I am interested in exploring the co-naturalization of language and race.

11. Bucholtz (2003) has also challenged conceptions of authenticity within the field of sociolinguistics, and the ways that such conceptions replicate stereotypes about language and identity, rather than analyzing the production of these stereotypes.

Relatedly, Bucholtz and Hall (2005) propose "authentication" and "denaturalization" as a central dynamic in the sociolinguistic analysis of identity and interaction.

12. Throughout the book I use the phrase "students designated as English Language Learners" rather than simply referring to students as "English Language Learners" in an effort to emphasize that this label is an institutional attribution rather than an objective fact about one's language proficiency.

13. See Heller and McElhinny (2017) for a stunningly comprehensive overview of the relationship between language, capitalism, and colonialism.

14. My analysis of emblematic forms of Spanish and English involves attention to the interplay between linguistic structures and social contexts. I take my cue here from practice-based approaches to communication, which recognize that "language has radically systematic features, and yet these appear to be almost constantly locked into the kinds of activities that speakers carry on with speech" (Hanks 1996:9). Thus, I investigate the register formation that I call "Inverted Spanglish" as a scalar phenomenon whose meaning takes shape in specific contexts. In the context of New Northwest High School, this involves the invocation of the institutional identity of Young Latino Professional.

15. My conception of "looking like a language" and "sounding like a race" is inspired by Fanon's (1967) discussion of the interplay between language and race in "The Negro and Language," the opening chapter of *Black Skin, White Masks*. For Fanon, "the Negro of the Antilles will be proportionately Whiter—that is, he will come closer to being a real human being—in direct ratio to his mastery of the French Language" (1967:18). To theorize this raciolinguistic dynamic in the context of US Latinxs, I build from Anzaldúa's suggestion that "ethnic identity is twin skin to linguistic identity—I am my language" (1987:81). See González (2006) for a borderlands-oriented linguistic ethnography of education that also draws inspiration from Anzaldúa.

16. Ethnicity has been a long-standing concern among sociolinguists and linguistic anthropologists, including the recent theorization of "ethnolinguistic repertoire" (Benor 2010). My conception of raciolinguistic enregisterment (i.e., looking like a language and sounding like a race) seeks to contribute to more recent theorizations of language and racialization (Urciuoli 1996; Hill 2008; Alim and Reyes 2011; Bucholtz 2011; Dick and Wirtz 2011; Wirtz 2014). I take my cue from Alim and Reyes (2011) in drawing attention to the ways that American society is hyperracial and hyperracializing, as well as in seeking to problematize the presumptions associated with dialect-based and group-based approaches to the analysis of language and race. I contribute to these modes of analysis by theorizing strategies for "languaging race" (Alim and Smitherman 2012:2) and "racing language."

17. Enregisterment is also a crucial analytical tool for understanding the invention of languages and the populations to which they are understood to correspond. As such, this concept contributes a great deal to broader efforts toward denaturalizing

languages and combating the stigmatizing effects of regimes of standardization (Makoni and Pennycook 2007).

18. Inoue (2003, 2006) demonstrates how similar interconnections play out in the notion of Japanese "women's language." The fact that most women do not speak "women's language" does not prevent the widespread circulation of the belief that they do as a language ideology. She points to practices of translation as productive and complicated vehicles for the reproduction of this ideology by arguing that translation calibrates "women's language" in relation to cultural categories such as race and class. For example, working-class Black women in the Japanese translation of *Gone with the Wind* do not speak "women's language," whereas middle-class White women do. "Women's language" in Japan is similar to "Spanish" for many Latinxs in the United States; that is, Latinxs can be imagined to speak "Spanish" regardless of whether they are speaking English or have no Spanish language proficiency whatsoever. As Eisenlohr points out, "there is no necessary relationship defined between the valuation of a language as an emblem of group identity and its use as a predominant medium of interaction" (2004:36). This is similar to Lo's analysis of codeswitching, in which "outgroup talk contextualizes . . . stances as characteristic of a given ethnic category, projecting category memberships for each of the participants and assumptions about speakers' positions as animators or authors of the stances" (Lo 1999:475). Thus, stance-taking and the recognition thereof (Kockelman 2004; Jaffe 2009) become central to the process of raciolinguistic enregisterment that I describe.

19. Chun notes "the importance of attending to how racialized language is a negotiated process, how this process intersects with local ideologies of race, gender, class, and authenticity, and how reading race often achieves more than racial classification alone" (2011:404).

20. Dick and Wirtz (2011) examine how this remapping is often enacted through "covert" racializing discourses.

21. The name of the school as well as all school employees and students are pseudonyms.

22. Each Chicago public school has a Local School Council, which consists of parents, teachers, community residents, a student representative, and the school's principal. In Chapter 1, I describe Local School Councils in more detail.

23. Chapter 1 analyzes the relationship between ideologies surrounding race, class, gender, sexuality, and educational achievement.

24. The phrase "sin papeles," often glossed in English as "without papers" or "undocumented," indexes solidarity with those whose US migration status is unauthorized. This stands in contrast to the term "illegal," which has come to index anti-immigrant perspectives. Plascencia (2009) and Rosa (2012) explore debates surrounding these usages, and De Genova (2004) traces the historical emergence of the notion of "illegality" as it pertains to US Latinxs, specifically Mexicans.

25. The Census counts all people residing in the United States regardless of migration status.

26. In Chapter 2, I analyze situations in which distinctions were drawn between "Latino" and "Hispanic," but even the people who drew these distinctions alternated between using both terms to identify themselves and others.

27. This approach involves viewing language not simply as a window through which to analyze social life or as a cognitive capacity distinct from culture, "but, above all, as a cultural practice, that is, as a form of action that both presupposes and at the same time brings about ways of being in the world" (Duranti 1997:1).

28. Dr. Baez framed this transformation project in a range of ways, sometimes substituting "at risk youth" for "gangbangers" and "hoes" and other times using "professionals" as shorthand for "Young Latino Professionals"; she also used combinations thereof, including the statement, "we are transforming at risk youth into young Latino professionals." I capitalize "Young Latino Professional(s)" to emphasize the paradigmatic nature of this category for my analysis.

29. In linguistic terms the principal's project of transforming students into Young Latino Professionals could be understood as a call for them to be *articulate while Latinx*. This is akin to Alim and Smitherman's (2012) analysis of language, race, and the politics of respectability in the context of discourses surrounding President Barack Obama and African Americans more broadly.

30. It is crucial to emphasize the deceptive nature of the distinction between assimilation and multiculturalism. Indeed, as Brown (2006) and others have shown, the multicultural embrace of difference often aligns with the very assimilatory ethos it purports to oppose.

31. Chow (2002) refers to this required embodiment of authentic difference as "coercive mimeticism" and highlights the roles that members of marginalized groups play in reproducing these dynamics through the policing of authenticity. Similarly, Reyes (2002) analyzes the ways in which multicultural authenticity is constructed in particular institutional settings and performatively renegotiated in everyday discourses and interactions.

32. Deportation and detention are linked to many other contemporary examples of racist, often specifically anti-Latinx, sentiments and policies, such as the continued creation of a 2,000-mile security fence and surveillance regime along the US-Mexico border, as well as calls for the abolishment of the 14th Amendment in order to prevent the US-born children of unauthorized migrants from becoming US citizens. De Genova (2004) analyzes the production and political effects of "illegality" and "deportability" in the context of Mexican migration to the United States. Hernández (2008) historicizes detention as a particular, racialized US immigration enforcement strategy. Rosas (2012) explores the interpellating and criminalizing effects of US border surveillance, as well as the uptake and cooptation of this criminality. These theorizations shed light on the surge in deportations during the Clinton, G. W. Bush, and Obama administrations. By 2014, the number of people deported under the Obama administration surpassed two million, making Obama

the president with the highest rate of deportation in US history. This has led some immigration reform activists and Latinx civil rights organizations to dub Obama "deporter in chief." Meanwhile, those opposing comprehensive immigration reform, particularly an expansion of migration rights and access to citizenship for unauthorized migrants, claim that Obama was in fact too weak on immigration enforcement. These debates involve questions about the distinction between "returns" and "removals" as distinctive modes of repatriation. Anti-Latinx racism also played a central role in immigration discourses surrounding the 2016 US Presidential campaign and subsequent election of Donald Trump.

33. In Rosa (2014b), I show how these signs are structured as ideological bundles that link the United States, Whiteness, and the English language, on the one hand, and Latin America, Brownness, and the Spanish language, on the other.

34. For an extended analysis of the contradictory ethnicization and racialization of Latinx identity and the problematic nature of efforts to resolve these contradictions by creating a coherent Latinx subject, see Viego (2007).

35. "U.S. Future 'Unthinkable' Without Hispanic Population," May 2012, *Latin American Herald Tribune*, http://www.navigationpartnersllc.com/u-s-future-"unthinkable"-without-hispanic-population/ (accessed September 26, 2017).

36. Kristian Ramos, "Latino Children are This Country's Future," May 21, 2012, *NBC Latino*, http://nbclatino.tumblr.com/post/23476898511/opinion-latino-children-are-this-countrys-future (accessed September 26, 2017).

37. Sara Inés Calderón, "The Census, English, Spanish, and the New U.S. Latino," April 12, 2011, *NewsTaco*, http://www.newstaco.com/2011/04/12/the-census-english-spanish-and-the-new-u-s-latino/ (accessed September 26, 2017).

38. David Morse, "The Sound of the Latino Future?: It's English," September 18, 2012, *AdAge*, http://adage.com/article/the-big-tent/reach-hispanics-moving-forward-speak-english/237157/ (accessed September 26, 2017).

39. Ramos-Zayas (2004) frames US Latinxs' recruitment to perform desirable citizenship in relation to a "politics of worthiness" that continually reproduces their marginalization.

40. Semiotic approaches to racialization (Urciuoli 1996; Bucholtz 2011; Wirtz 2014) provide an alternative to analyses of race that privilege "pigmentocratic logics" (Bonilla-Silva 2004) rather than attending to the multiple, dynamic sign processes through which race is rendered visible. Thus, my approach to analyzing the racialization of US Latinxs from a semiotic perspective is distinct from efforts to move beyond the "Black-White Binary" (Perea 1997) or posit a "Latin Americanization" (Bonilla-Silva 2004) of US racial concepts. Rather than staking claims to a new racial paradigm, I track the ways that racial categories are invoked, circulated, embodied, enacted, and transformed institutionally and interactionally. As Chun (2011) demonstrates, a semiotic approach can reframe the notion of moving beyond Black and White, not by displacing these categories altogether, but by attending to the

shifting, multiple, and indeterminate ways they are invoked in context. For Wirtz, this involves asking "what semiotic ideologies drive this indexical anchoring of racialization in the body" (2014:16).

41. Elsewhere I explore this remapping of linguistic and ethnoracial borders as a form of "diasporization" (Rosa 2014a). In his analysis of US-based Dominicans, Bailey (2002) examines similar negotiations of race and language across (im)migration cohorts.

42. Gal theorizes the concept of "axis of differentiation" to understand the allocation of "contrasting values to linguistic forms" (2012:22), as well as the ways that these values "distinguish and rank linguistic forms and forms of personhood" (2012:23).

43. Indeed, these practices involve the enactment of alternative social relations and symbolic orders, what Povinelli (2012) calls an *otherwise*.

44. While the idea of governmental intervention into the lives of the populace through compulsory education might conjure images of a unified locus of power, Foucault emphasizes the importance of understanding governmentality without attributing undue weight to the concept of the state. To overemphasize the role of the state is to reduce it to essential functions, such as the "development of productive forces and the reproduction of relations of production" (Foucault 1991:103). This reduction both misunderstands the differential forms that power takes in its dispersion and creates the illusion that the state is the sole institutional location of power. In a contrasting take on the dispersion of power, Althusser argues that institutions such as schools, families, and churches ("Ideological State Apparatuses") can be understood as plural only because "the unity that constitutes ... [them] as a body is not immediately visible" (Althusser 1994[1979]:111). For Althusser, this unity is manifested in the hailing of subjects through interpellation. Thus, schools become part of a structure of interlocking, authorized institutions of interpellation. Insofar as these institutions operate in coordinated ways to interpellate subjects, it is important to resituate Foucault's claims about the institutional particularity of power.

45. Like Paris (2011), I attend to the ways that students contest naturalized relationships between language and ethnoracial identity. Whereas Paris pursues this line of analysis by exploring the linguistic repertoires of students who are racialized in relation to distinctive categories, I focus on the interplay between the sociolinguistic production of a particular ethnoracial category and the range of institutional contexts and scales that organize this process. My specific interest is in the production of notions of difference as they pertain to communication and categories of identity.

46. In Chapter 3, I analyze the ways that qualia of "ghettoness" and "lameness" structure the embodiment and enactment of Puerto Rican, Mexican, and Latinx identities.

47. I draw on Rymes's repertoire-based approach to the analysis of communicative practices that "investigates the possibility for productive heterogeneity across diverse social domains" (2011:210). This approach is central to the analysis of often

mass-mediated language use that is characteristic of "late modernity" (Rampton 2006). These approaches correspond to calls for "an account of language that explores its modernity (Urla 2012:7). Central to this effort is attention to the ways that language practices and populations are positioned as (il)legitimate in particular institutions and contexts, as well as the modes of mediation that link broad political and economic dynamics to everyday interactions. Heller (2006) points to the ways that schools become key sites in which to track processes of linguistic minoritization and the political and economic structures that organize them.

48. Jeffrey S. Passel, D'Vera Cohn, and Mark Hugo Lopez, "Hispanics account for more than half of nation's growth in past decade," March 24, 2011, *Pew Hispanic Research Center*, http://www.pewhispanic.org/2011/03/24/hispanics-account-for-more-than-half-of-nations-growth-in-past-decade/ (accessed July 27, 2014).

49. Ibid.

50. Ibid.

51. Mark Mather and Patricia Foxen, "America's future: Latino Child Well-Being in Numbers and Trends," April 28, 2010, *National Council of La Raza*, http://publications.unidosus.org/bitstream/handle/123456789/1200/AMERICA_S_FUTURE_Latino_Child_Well_Being_in_Numbers_and_Trends.pdf?sequence=1&isAllowed=y (accessed September 26, 2017).

52. Rodríguez-Muñiz (2015) cautions against viewing demographic predictions as straightforward reflections of empirical population shifts. Instead, he argues that we must attend to the performativity of statistics and the ways that they structure both popular anxieties and Latinx political organizing.

53. The 19th-century US-based claims to neocolonial control over the Americas were contested by counter-hegemonic pan-Latin American movements that included figures such as Simón Bolívar, José Martí, and Eugenio María de Hostos (Ramos 2001).

54. In addition to Cruz (2007), see De Genova and Ramos-Zayas (2003) and Fernández (2012) for a historical overview of Mexican and Puerto Rican migration to Chicago.

55. "Hispanic Population in Select U.S. Metropolitan Areas, 2011," *Pew Hispanic Research Center*, http://www.pewhispanic.org/2013/08/29/hispanic-population-in-select-u-s-metropolitan-areas-2011/ (accessed July 27, 2014).

56. Ibid.

57. "Country of Origin Profiles," April 22, 2010, *Pew Hispanic Research Center*, http://pewhispanic.org/data/origins/ (accessed May 21, 2010).

58. Ibid.

59. Here I follow Richland's crucial point that while "prevailing anthropological theories that treat claims to cultural distinctiveness as binaries of resistance-hegemony—as either liberatory or reifying, autochthonous or other determined . . . [are each] accurate to [an] extent, a more nuanced picture emerges by attending to the semiotic 'microdetails' of actual social practice," where instances "of cultural difference,

always informed by but never identical to each other, are deployed over the course of sociocultural events" (2007:541).

CHAPTER 1

1. "508 Chicago Kids Shot in Just 16 Months," *Chicago Sun-Times*, March 9, 2009, http://www.suntimes.com/news/commentary/1466791,CST-EDT-edit09.article (accessed August 4, 2009).

2. Eric Zorn, "Killings of Students Provides a Grim Tally," *Chicago Tribune*, March 17, 2009, http://archives.chicagotribune.com/2009/mar/17/local/chi-zorn-17-mar17 (accessed August, 4, 2009).

3. Andrea Billups, "36 Chicago Area Students Killed Sets Record," *The Washington Times*, May 13, 2009, http://www.washingtontimes.com/news/2009/may/13/ record-36-students-killed-this-school-year-across-/ (accessed August 4, 2009); in Chapter 6, I analyze the news coverage, online message board postings, and local discussions surrounding the 36th killing.

4. I join Ralph (2014) in seeking to develop an analysis and portrayal of structural inequality in Chicago that avoids the pathologizing tendencies that are characteristic of scholarly analyses of urban contexts.

5. Andrea Billups, "Chicago: Murder Rate Sparks Political Spats," *The Washington Times*, July 25, 2008, http://www.washingtontimes.com/news/2008/jul/25/ spiraling-murder-rate-sparking-political-spats/ (accessed August 4, 2009); more recently, there have been debates about the use of the term "Chiraq," a reference to Chicago's warlike rates of violence, in political commentary, social media, and popular representations, including the name of a 2015 Spike Lee film. For example, the website Chicagoist.com featured a June 10, 2013 article by Samantha Abernathey titled "Is the Term 'Chiraq' Offensive?" (http://chicagoist.com/ 2013/06/10/hbo_vice_chiraq_chicago.php, accessed June 3, 2014). Similarly, a May 30, 2014 story by Adrienne Samuels Gibbs in the *Chicago Sun-Times*, titled "Attack on Chiraq: Activists Want The Word to Die" (http://www.suntimes. com/news/27541587-418/attack-on-chiraq-activists-want-the-word-to-die.html#. U43XrP3VSoo, accessed June 3, 2014), highlights perspectives from which terms such as "Chiraq" sensationalize and naturalize violence in Chicago. Ralph (2014) presents an incisive analysis of the logics surrounding violence and the experience of its aftermath in Chicago.

6. During the summer of 2009, another 15-year-old CPS student was shot and killed in almost the same exact location. He was riding his bike on a Thursday afternoon when a bullet struck him in the back; he was rushed to the hospital and died shortly thereafter.

7. They said that the Almighty Latin Devils are "lame" because they attempt to appropriate the school's mascot, the blue devil, as a gang symbol. For these girls, the fact that the school would let them wear the school uniform (with a blue devil on it)

despite the possible link to gang symbolics meant that this gang is not much of a threat. I have changed the name of this gang and the school mascot in order to protect the school's anonymity. In Chapter 6, I analyze patterns in gang names and symbolics.

8. In Chapter 6, I highlight students' shifting proximity to what are often imagined and analyzed as distinct "street kid" and "school kid" identities. I call such distinctions into question by analyzing the slippery ways in which *all* students could be recognized in relation to these identities.

9. Rios (2011) and Mendoza-Denton (2008) have explored similar Latinx gender dynamics in their studies focused on Latino and Latina youth, respectively.

10. I use the pseudonyms "New Northwest High School" and "Old Northwest High School" to signal the distinct ways in which the schools are positioned temporally with respect to educational reform efforts.

11. The Logan Square Neighborhood Association (LSNA) has worked with schools in the Logan Square community on Chicago's Northwest Side since the 1960s. Most recently, LSNA worked with teachers at ONHS to create the ONHS Social Justice Academy. The Social Justice Academy was designed to provide ONHS freshmen with an alternative to participation in the school's popular JROTC military program by allowing students to take on leadership roles in a range of community-based service learning projects.

12. I am highlighting the statistics from 2003–2004 because NNHS opened the following year.

13. It is crucial to note that these designations are ideologically situated, institutionalized assessments rather than objective representations of students' identities. For example, African American and Latinx students constitute nearly 90% of Chicago Public Schools students, yet they are represented as racial minorities in official district statistics and media portrayals thereof. Thus, it is productive to understand minoritization as a process of marginalization rather than a straightforward numerical assessment.

14. Racial/Ethnic Survey, *Chicago Public Schools*, http://cps.edu/Performance/Documents/DataFiles/FY04_Racial_Ethnic%20Survey.xls (accessed July 28, 2014).

15. Racial/Ethnic Survey, *Chicago Public Schools*, http://cps.edu/Performance/Documents/DataFiles/FY05_Racial_Ethnic%20Survey.xls (accessed July 28, 2014).

16. In the 2007–2008 school year, Chicago Public Schools students were designated as 46.5% African American, 39.1% Latinx, 8.0% White, 3.3% Asian/Pacific Islander, 2.9% Multiracial, and 0.2% Native American. Note that the figure of 8.0% White students includes a sizeable Polish population, including many who were classified as English Language Learners. Shedd (2015) explores African American youths' acute analyses and experiences of these patterns of segregation and exclusion in Chicago.

17. Humboldt Park has been undergoing rapid gentrification for the past several decades, which is part of a broader history of the displacement of Puerto Rican communities throughout Chicago (Mumm 2014).

18. I worked in an after-school program at ONHS in conjunction with the National Puerto Rican Forum from 2003 to 2006. I also tutored and taught at two nearby alternative schools that served many students who were pushed out of ONHS. Based on the high rates at which particular racialized groups leave school, Fine (1991), Tuck (2012), and others have persuasively argued that it is important to understand these students as "pushouts" rather than "dropouts." Whereas discourses of dropping out are often associated with the notion that students choose to leave school of their own volition, the concept of pushout is intended to draw attention to the systematic, institutional processes that make schools accommodating contexts for some students and uninhabitable for others. Throughout the book, I use "pushout" rather than "dropout" except in statistical designations, direct quotations, and analyses of stereotypes and popular views.

19. Elizabeth said that this was a "nation war," not just a regular gang fight. Individual gangs in Chicago are part of larger umbrella organizations called the "Folks Nation" and "People Nation." See Chapter 6 for a description of these structures.

20. According to the Centers for Disease Control and Prevention (http://www.cdc.gov/mmwr/preview/mmwrhtml/ss5806a1.htm, accessed June 4, 2014), the 2004 nationwide pregnancy rates for Latinas and African Americans between the ages of 15 and 19 years were 132.8/1,000 and 128.0/1,000, respectively. The rate for Whites was 45.2/1,000. Despite these stark differences in rates of teen pregnancy based on race, it is crucial not to draw simplistic conclusions about the causes or results of these disparities. Indeed, scholars have questioned the ways that moral panics surrounding "teen pregnancy" position a vulnerable age cohort as a convenient scapegoat for a broader range of societal issues, a profitable marketing ploy, and a strategic political discourse (Luker 1996; Males 2010).

21. Editorial Projects in Education Research Center. 2009. "Closing the Graduation Gap: Educational and Economic Conditions in America's Largest Cities." April 2009. http://www.edweek.org/media/cities_in_crisis_2009.pdf (accessed August 18, 2009).

22. Center for Labor Market Studies (Northeastern University, Boston, MA) and The Alternative Schools Network (Chicago, IL). 2009. "Left Behind in America: The Nation's Dropout Crisis." May 5, 2009. http://www.northeastern.edu/clms/wp-content/uploads/CLMS_2009_Dropout_Report.pdf (accessed June 4, 2014).

23. There are also many community-based alternative and independent high schools in the city, such as those that are part of an organization called the Alternative Schools Network. Many of these schools are rooted in long-standing, post-civil rights struggles and are geared toward presenting Black and Latinx pushouts with opportunities to graduate.

24. Sara Karp, "Top Schools Grow Less Diverse," *Catalyst Chicago*, November 1, 2007, http://www.catalyst-chicago.org/news/2007/11/01/top-schools-grow-less-diverse (accessed June 3, 2014).

25. Will Okun, "Disparities." *New York Times Online Edition*, December 21, 2007, http://kristof.blogs.nytimes.com/2007/12/21/disparities/ (accessed June 3, 2014).

26. President Barack Obama's educational reform plan, "Race to the Top," was announced in the summer of 2009, shortly after I concluded my second year of fieldwork in NNHS. With its emphasis on performance-based standards and embrace of privatization, Race to the Top reproduces and in fact amplifies many problematic features of No Child Left Behind. See Lipman (2011) for an analysis of the forms of inequality associated with these neoliberal education policies.

27. Malcolm X College is one of seven City Colleges of Chicago.

28. Laura was unique in that she gained access to and openly discussed her use of contraception. My conversations with young men and women NNHS students who were involved in pregnancies reflected students' limited knowledge of birth control options. Additionally, students were unsure of medical facilities that would help them with these issues. For example, Felix (PR, Gen. 3, Gr. 11), whose girlfriend had a miscarriage, and Victor (Mex[m]/PR[f]), whose girlfriend believed that she was pregnant at one point, regularly consulted with me about what clinics would be willing to provide free/low-cost prenatal services. These experiences reflect the ongoing failures of sexuality education and the disparate ways that these failures negatively affect the lives of urban youth (Fine 1988; Fine and McLelland 2006).

29. As mentioned previously, Dr. Baez invoked this transformation project and the categories involved in it in a range of ways, sometimes substituting "at risk youth" for "gangbangers" and "hoes" and other times using "professionals" as shorthand for "Young Latino Professionals"; she also used combinations thereof, including the statement, "we are transforming at risk youth into Young Latino Professionals." I capitalize "Young Latino Professional(s)" to emphasize the paradigmatic nature of this category for my analysis.

30. For a comparative distinction, see Rivera-Servera's (2012) discussion of the interplay between "chusma" and "fresa" as potent, class-differentiating concepts in his analysis of queer Latinidades. That is, "chusma" is analogous to gangbanger and ho in its class-negative connotations, and "fresa" is analogous to Young Latino Professional in its connotation of aspirational upward mobility.

31. Higginbotham (1993) coined the term "politics of respectability" in reference to African American women's promotion of characteristics such as politeness, cleanliness, chastity, and temperance during the Progressive Era, specifically in conjunction with their participation in the Baptist Church. Higginbotham emphasizes the significance of in-group (African American) and out-group (White) audiences for respectable presentation of self. An African American politics of respectability is also associated with Booker T. Washington's (1901) philosophies of self-help, accommodation, and economic advancement at the turn of the 20th century.

32. These identity management projects are not particular to African Americans and Latinxs. Sarroub (2005) and Fader (2009) discuss the competing attachments that Muslim and Hasidic Jewish youth, respectively, navigate as they are socialized to marked gender, religious, and ethnoracial identities.

33. These include reality television programs such as MTV's "From G's to Gents" and VH1's "Charm School," each of which focuses primarily on professionalizing and civilizing contestants through lessons in etiquette, speech, and dress, among other topics. Not unlike the transformation from a "gangbanger" or "ho" into a "Young Latino Professional," these programs are produced and consumed in relation to popular ideas about the ways in which race, class, and gender constitute personhood. In fact, the second season of MTV's "From G's to Gents" included a contestant named "Macho," a Puerto Rican from Chicago with a purported history of gang participation (http://www.mtv.com/global/music/shows/ajax/castsByFranchiseHTML.jhtml?seriesID=24724, accessed October 2, 2017).

34. http://www.chicagolatinonetwork.com (accessed June 6, 2010).

35. Students at this charter school play sports such as lacrosse and rugby, which are generally understood as middle-class, elite, and collegiate activities in the US context. This speaks to the charter school's efforts to create a college-like atmosphere.

36. The only day when the uniform policy did not apply was the last day of school, which was called "fun day."

37. Boys' earrings, particularly when worn in one ear and not the other, were understood as potential indexes of gang affiliation.

38. I analyze the symbolic value of these hairstyles in detail in Chapter 3.

39. "Lining" describes the use of a straight razor to outline the edges of a haircut all the way around the head. In the context of many Latino and African American barbershops, it is one of the final elements of a haircut and considered to be an important element of looking and feeling "fresh" (i.e., cool or in style) and clean. In Chapter 3, I analyze the meaningfulness of qualia (Chumley and Harkness 2013) associated with haircuts as a way of conceptualizing Latinx embodiment.

40. Dr. Baez was consistent in her implementation and application of this policy; on more than one occasion she admonished me for coming to the school with my shirt untucked.

41. It is no mistake that concerns about sexuality would enter into the conversation about Jimmy's clothing and embrace of hip-hop style. There are fervent debates about hip-hop fashions, including anxieties surrounding the incorporation of "tight" clothing and "queer-inflected style" into hip-hop aesthetics (Penney 2012).

42. I analyze gang-related "checking" in detail in Chapter 6.

43. Advanced Placement (AP) courses are generally understood at NNHS and in high schools throughout the United States as college-level courses. Students can earn college credit for these courses by scoring high enough on the annual Advanced Placement exam that is administered for each individual course.

44. During my two years of fieldwork at NNHS, I worked primarily as a tutor/mentor in the AVID program.

45. In Chapters 4 and 5, I explore the language ideologies and policies that informed the school's orientation to bilingual education and students' linguistic responses to this orientation.

46. In "The Fact of Blackness," Fanon (1967) explores the racial overdetermination of Blackness, its always already recognizability, and the knowledge that is presumed to be accessed through these recognitions. I am similarly interested in these issues of overdetermination, recognition, and knowledge creation in the racialization of US Latinxs.

47. Dr. Baez uses race and ethnicity interchangeably to analyze predominantly African American communities' investment in African American school leaders and predominantly Hispanic communities' investment in Hispanic school leaders.

48. Don Babwin, "Cameras Make Chicago Most Closely Watched U.S. City," *Associated Press*, April 6, 2010, http://www.huffingtonpost.com/2010/04/06/cameras-make-chicago-most_n_527013.html (accessed June 3, 2014).

49. In the fall of 2009, a suburban Chicago police officer working as a resource officer in a school for special needs students broke the nose of a 15-year-old African American student who would not tuck in his shirt; the incident achieved national notoriety. See Nicole Orichula, "Video Shows Cop Assault on Student," *NBC Chicago*, October 8, 2009, http://www.nbcchicago.com/news/local/Cop-Caught-on-Video-While-Pushing-Special-Needs-Student-63688407.html (accessed June 3, 2014).

50. Scholars such as Devine (1996) and Noguera (2003) have explored how these modes of discipline systematically link urban schools and prisons. In fact, many education scholars view racialized disciplinary procedures and policing as part of the "school-to-prison pipeline" (Kim, Losen, and Hewitt 2010; Bahen, Cooc, Currie-Rubin, Kuttner, and Ng 2012; Nocella, Parmar, and Stovall 2014) and processes of hyperincarceration of racialized populations associated with the "new Jim Crow" (Alexander 2012).

51. In Chapters 4, 5, and 6, I present an in-depth analysis of the politics of language and literacy in this context.

52. These discourses reflect anxieties about gender and race disparities, specifically higher rates of educational achievement among girls of color than boys of color, across urban US contexts (Lopez 2003).

53. My use of the terms "Chicanidad," "Chicano," and "Chicana" is intended to signal gender nonbinary perspectives (i.e., Chicanidad), critiques of positioning masculinity as default (i.e., Chicano), and the particularity of feminist perspectives (i.e., Chicana).

54. See Vázquez (2011) for an analysis of modes of triangulation through which Latinx authors navigate, reject, and reconfigure existing binaries of identity.

55. Brown argues that, "the call for tolerance, the invocation of tolerance, and the attempt to instantiate tolerance are all signs of identity production and identity management in the context of orders of stratification or marginalization in which the production, the management, and the context themselves are disavowed. In short, they are signs of a buried order of politics. . . . [D]epoliticization involves construing inequality, subordination, marginalization, and social conflict, which all require political analysis and political solutions, as personal and individual, on the one hand, or as natural, religious, or cultural on the other. . . . [D]epoliticization involves removing a political phenomenon from comprehension of its historical emergence and from a recognition of the powers that produce and contour it" (Brown 2006:14–15)

56. In the second half of the book I draw on Fanon's (1967) analysis of language and race to analyze language ideologies and linguistic practices within NNHS.

57. The "Obama effect" has been studied in relation to the implications of an African American role model for the educational achievement of Black students (Marx, Ko, and Friedman 2009), as well as implicit prejudice toward and stereotyping of Blackness among non-Blacks (Plant et al. 2009).

58. The apolitical nature of new paternalism is in many ways similar to the promotion of "grit" or the development of "non-cognitive skills" (i.e., skills such as perseverance rather than conventionally conceived academic skills) as a strategy for the educational success of urban youth of color (Tough 2012). These approaches frame underachievement as a matter of remedying individual students' behaviors rather than addressing systemic structural inequities.

CHAPTER 2

1. My theorization of ethnoracial contortions is in dialogue with Candelario's (2007) analysis of "strategic ambiguity" in the context of Dominicans' shifting racial identifications, Godreau's (2008) notion of the "slippery semantics" that characterize Puerto Ricans' race talk, and Roth-Gordon's (2013) theorization of the "racial malleability" that Brazilian male youth demonstrate through their engagement with hip-hop cultural forms. However, I emphasize the fraught nature of the interplay between institutional constructions and interpersonal enactments of ethnoracial categories. Specifically, I seek to highlight the institutional constraints on one's ability to deploy strategic ambiguity, slippery semantics, or racial malleability.

2. Here I am thinking of Williams' (1989) argument: ". . . any identity formation process . . . must be understood in relation to the societal production of enduring categorical distinctions and not simply in terms of individuals adopting and 'shedding' particular manifestations of those categorical identities" (428).

3. This is the most selective college to which any student from NNHS's first two graduating classes gained acceptance. Yesi was one of four students in her class to leave

the state of Illinois for college. Her college acceptance was facilitated by her participation in a college preparatory program at an elite local university throughout high school, which encouraged students to apply to highly selective schools. She also received a full scholarship from the Posse Foundation, which supports students from "disadvantaged urban backgrounds" in cities such as Chicago, New York, and Los Angeles. In Chapters 3 and 4, I describe Yesi's transition to college and analyze the relationship between the linguistic stigmatization she faced in Chicago and at college. Despite these challenges, Yesi went on to become the first person in her family to graduate from college.

4. See Chapter 1 for a more detailed description of these demographic disparities.

5. Similar colorblind perspectives have been widely analyzed inside (Ladson-Billings 1994; Pollock 2004a) and outside (Bonilla-Silva 2003; López 2006) of school contexts.

6. While there are no official statistics on the Mexican and Puerto Rican localities from which Chicago-based Latinxs emigrate, previous research has analyzed transnational relationships between Chicago and Michoacán, Mexico (Farr 2006), as well as Chicago and San Sebastián, Puerto Rico (Pérez 2004).

7. The reclaiming of Chicago as part of Puerto Rico is characteristic of what Rúa (2012) describes as the "grounded identitdad (identity)" that Puerto Ricans have been constructing in Chicago since the 1940s.

8. Scholars such as Ramos-Zayas (2003) and Rinaldo (2002) have analyzed strategic efforts on the part of Puerto Rican political activists to resist gentrification by imbuing the landscape with signs of Puerto Rican identity.

9. See Arredondo (2008), Fernández (2012), De Genova (2005), and Ramírez (2011) for accounts of the emergence of "Mexican Chicago."

10. For more on place-making in Latinx communities, see Rios and Vazquez (2012).

11. Here I am invoking Gupta and Ferguson's (1992) theorization of reterritorialization as a process in which space becomes a site for the rearticulation of identity and contestation of inequality.

12. Fernández (2012) effectively frames these joint histories of struggle as follows: "I analyze Mexicans' and Puerto Ricans' experience in postwar Chicago as interrelated and overlapping struggles over *place*—both an imagined position in the local social order and a concrete, physical location within the city's geography" (8).

13. Talk of national identification cards also took place in the weeks leading up to the annual NNHS prom. Students who brought dates from other schools were required to have their dates register at NNHS prior to the prom. This was a safety mechanism to keep track of everyone who attended the event. Photocopies of the identification cards of students from other schools were kept in a binder that was then used to verify identities at the prom. While most students from schools other than NNHS used identification cards from their respective schools, I noted that there were multiple Mexican national identification cards in the notebook while

working at the registration table on the night of the prom. One could imagine that for many other schools such an identification card would be questioned or potentially disallowed, but in NNHS this was an entirely unremarkable practice. A Mexican national identification card was perfectly legitimate in this Chicago context.

14. Dávila (1997), Ramos-Zayas (2003), Negrón-Muntaner (2004), and others have explored the gendered, classed, and racialized politics of this representation and its strategic deployment.

15. Torres-Saillant (2003) argues that Latinxs often identify as an ethnic group to avoid the stigmatization associated with racialization (specifically, the stigmatization of Blackness). He suggests that by fusing race and ethnicity into a racialized, panethnic conception of Latinx identity, Latinxs would be in a better position overcome tensions between Latinx subgroups and combat White supremacy.

16. Williams (1989) articulates the relative legitimacy of ethnicity vis-à-vis race as follows: "Thus, to understand the material and symbolic interconnection between the production and maintenance of racism and the quest for ethnic distinctiveness, we must consider that in the process of nation building as race-making, while the blood of some citizens courses through the mainstream of civil society, accreting the state foundation, other bloods spill in the soil. If citizens are aligned through their blood but not their class position with the ruling members of the historical bloc, they may expect that their blood spills on fertile ground destined to produce lasting and worthy contributions" (436).

17. Ngai (2004) powerfully demonstrates the ways that distinctions between race and ethnicity have been codified and institutionalized in immigration laws, and how Asians and Latinxs, in particular, have been continually faced with "racial ineligibility" for citizenship (42).

18. He was referencing the popular reality television weight loss show, "The Biggest Loser."

19. These students' intimate orientation to and skepticism of Americanness demonstrates the persistence of the "ambivalent Americanism" in relation to which Sanchez (1993) characterizes second-generation, Los Angeles–based Mexican Americans in the mid-20th century. In more recent Chicago-based research, Flores-González (2017) frames this as a dynamic in which Latinx youth come to understand themselves as citizens but not Americans.

20. This interaction reflects the ways that Latinx/Hispanic, as well as Puerto Rican and Mexican, were conceptualized and experienced as distinct from and yet related to African American/Black within NNHS. Out of the hundreds of students with whom I interacted during my two years of fieldwork, only one student identified as African American and Latinx. This student, Elizabeth (AA[m]/PR[f], Gen. 3, Gr. 12), hung out with a group of African American girls and was viewed by most students simply as African American. However, her Spanish surname sometimes led people to inquire as to her ethnoracial identity. In one lunchroom encounter

I observed, Elizabeth overheard a group of Latinas speaking in Spanish about her and her friends. She interrupted them to let them know that she could understand what they were saying. The Latina students quickly changed the subject, and one of Elizabeth's African American friends inquired, "Your dad's Puerto Rican, right?" Elizabeth nodded in agreement. She told me that her parents were divorced and she was raised primarily by her mother, so she identifies more strongly as African American. Elizabeth was an exception to stereotypical conceptions of Black and Hispanic as discrete categories within NNHS.

21. Fernández (2012) uses "Brown" as a way of capturing the distinctive racial positioning of Mexicans and Puerto Ricans in Chicago, but she also clarifies: "the term *brown* does not represent a universal *color* of all Mexicans and Puerto Ricans. Rather, in the racial taxonomy of the United States, *brown* stands in as a placeholder that captures the malleable meaning assigned to the social difference most Mexicans and Puerto Ricans are believed to embody" (17).

22. Mora (2014) explores the negotiated nature of the creation and incorporation of the Hispanic category in the US Census. Specifically, she emphasizes the interplay among the Census Bureau, media executives, and activists with a range of political, ethnic, and racial affiliations. Thus, "the [Hispanic] category was not simply a label imposed by the government" (117). The ambiguous construction of "Hispanic" as an ethnic category that could be also be used as a racial category satisfied the Census Bureau's investment in maintaining continuity in its race statistics across censuses (which would have been disrupted if Hispanic were included as a new racial category). This effort also resonated with non-Hispanic racial interest groups that sought to prevent a decrease in their numbers (if Hispanic were included as a new racial category), as well as Mexican, Puerto Rican, and Cuban political groups that sought to make claims as a collective demographic while also maintaining their distinctiveness.

23. See Fernández (2012) for a historical account of the post–World War II emergence of Puerto Ricans' and Mexicans' shared location in Chicago's geography and social order.

24. Fernández's (2012) analysis of Puerto Ricans' and Mexicans' migration to and shared positioning in Chicago explains, "in postwar Chicago, Mexicans' and Puerto Ricans' parallel stories intertwined and resembled each other significantly and therefore must be told together. Chicago was unique in its ability to attract such large numbers of Mexicans and Puerto Ricans in the years during and after World War II, and it was the only major city in the country that contained such a distinctive ethnoracial mix" (12).

25. Some students claimed that individuals with one Puerto Rican and one Mexican parent would most likely claim that they were Puerto Rican since it was "cooler." In fact, I found that this happened in both directions and that it frequently involved identifying in the same way as the parent with whom individuals understood themselves to share the closest relationship.

26. In his analysis of queer Latinx performance, Rivera-Servera conceptualizes "friction as a theory in practice invested in the encounters that constitute queer Latinidad while insisting on its provisional and negotiated nature" (2012:175).

27. It is also no coincidence that one of the strongest recent advocates for immigration reform in the US Congress has been Chicago's own Luis Gutiérrez (D-IL, 4th District), a Puerto Rican raised on the city's Near Northwest Side. Gutiérrez was a former university student of the director of Chicago's Puerto Rican Cultural Center and also the former Alderman of Chicago's 26th Ward, which contains Paseo Boricua (pictures of Humboldt Park and Paseo Boricua adorn his congressional webpage, https://gutierrez.house.gov/, accessed October 28, 2017). To be clear, Gutiérrez, like all Puerto Ricans born on the island and in the US mainland, is a US citizen by birth. His longtime immigration rights advocacy is not simply informed by a short-lived, strategic political calculation. His socialization to immigration rights advocacy came in part by way of the Puerto Rican Cultural Center's long-standing commitment to this expressly panethnic Latinx effort. In fact, the Puerto Rican Cultural Center's board of directors is composed of Puerto Ricans *and* Mexicans.

28. In the weeks after Arellano entered sanctuary, affiliates of the Puerto Rican Cultural Center stood guard outside the church with a large Puerto Rican flag to ensure her safety and keep the community informed of her well-being. During one late night shift that I held alone, I received many words of encouragement and expressions of support for Arellano from passersby. See Rodríguez-Muñiz (2010) for an account of Chicago Puerto Ricans' support of Arellano and the proimmigrant rights movement, and Pallares (2010) for an analysis of Arellano and the importance of ending family separation as part of broader efforts toward immigration reform. After remaining in sanctuary for 12 months, Arellano left Adalberto United Methodist Church to begin touring the nation as an advocate for immigration reform. She was apprehended by Immigration and Customs Enforcement authorities and deported on August 20, 2007.

29. Note that in her description of the different challenges that Puerto Rican and Mexican students face, particularly with regard to their socioeconomic status, Dr. Baez focuses on unauthorized migrant Mexican students. In fact, the majority of the Mexican students at NNHS were US citizens. While unauthorized migrant students and their families face countless challenges in their everyday lives based on their lack of US citizenship (Gonzales 2015), it is important to note that overall Puerto Ricans and Mexicans face nearly identical poverty rates in the United States.

30. Chapter 3 explores these stereotypes in detail.

31. In two Chicago-based ethnographies, Rúa (2012) explores the "limitations of Puerto Rican citizenship" and De Genova (2005) shows how Mexicans' labor participation is racialized as "illegal" regardless of their citizenship status.

CHAPTER 3

1. As in earlier chapters, I invoke Fanon's (1967) notion of the "fact of Blackness" to think about the racialization of Latinidad, the naturalization of its recognizability, and the stereotypes associated with this identity.

2. I approach "ghettoness" and "lameness" as qualia (Chumley and Harkness 2013) that structure the embodiment of Latinidad among NNHS students. These qualia are culturally mediated ways of structuring everyday experiences and evaluations thereof. Importantly, when viewed in relation to the institutional axis of differentiation between gangbangers/hoes (ghetto) and Young Latino Professionals (lame), qualia such as ghettoness and lameness can be understood as part of a political economy of identity and embodiment.

3. Jimmy also references Blackness, which underscores the local distinction between Blackness, on the one hand, and Mexicanness and Puerto Ricanness, on the other.

4. "Hispanic Foods" and "Asian Foods" are both commonly labeled sections in grocery stores, which demonstrates the ways that Asianness and Hispanicness can be simultaneously racialized and ethnicized. That is, their ethnicization is reflected in the legitimate public invocation of difference in relation to food products. In contrast, other public displays of "Hispanic" and "Asian" difference, such as those associated with language (as I show in detail in the chapters that follow), are often heavily policed and thereby racialized.

5. Jewel-Osco is a prominent mainstream grocery store chain throughout the Midwest; its headquarters are in the Chicago suburb of Itasca. Students typically referred to the store as "Jewels." Yesi (PR, Gen. 1.5, Gr. 12/first year of college) noted this vernacular linguistic practice by explaining that, "everyone adds an 's' to 'Jewel,' even though it doesn't have one."

6. Cermak Produce is a chain of grocery stores throughout Chicago that sells products associated with Mexican and Puerto Rican cuisine, as well a range of other items. Stores such as Cermak Produce, Armitage Produce, and Central Park Fruit Market are midsize establishments, somewhere between smaller bodegas with more limited merchandise and larger mainstream grocery stores. Notably, the produce is typically significantly cheaper at stores such as Cermak Produce than at larger grocery stores such as Jewel-Osco. In wealthier parts of the city, these hierarchies are reproduced between stores such as Mariano's (formerly Dominick's), Trader Joe's, and Whole Foods.

7. It is also important to note that Jimmy's joke invokes Whiteness rather than Blackness. Whereas "Hispanic" was distinguished from other foods in the store in a way that "White" and "Black" were not, Jimmy's invocation of Whiteness points to his awareness of its status as the unmarked norm (compared with Blackness).

8. Jacobs-Huey (2006) has also focused on hair as an important site for linguistic anthropological examinations of race, gender, and embodiment. In her analysis of discourses and practices surrounding African American women's hair care, she argues that by understanding "Black hair care as a linguistic and cultural engagement" with

"African American women's ethnic and gender identities," we can develop "insights into the discursive and corporeal dynamics of African American women's being and becoming" (2006:4–5). I am similarly interested in discourses and practices surrounding hairstyles as sites for the production, socialization, and embodiment of Latinx identities.

9. A fade is generally a short haircut in which the hair on top of the head is gradually "faded," or blended, into a shorter length on the sides and back of the head. Fades can be "high," "medium," or "low," depending on where one wants the barber to begin to blend the length of the hair on the top into the hair on the sides and the back. Thus, an example of a request for a fade might be, "a low fade with a 2 and a 1." The numbers refer to the length of the attachment that barbers place on their electric clippers to cut the hair on the top and the back of the head. There are also names for particular fades, such as a "bald fade," in which there is no hair on the back of the head. From the perspectives of people not familiar with such hair-grooming practices, the difference between styles of fades and lengths of hair involved might be completely unperceivable. However, from in-group perspectives, minute differences in hair length—in some cases eighths of an inch—could be felt acutely. After a week or so of not having a haircut, male students often remarked that they felt "lame" because of the length of their hair. While fades are sometimes associated with a military-style haircut, they are often understood as stereotypically masculine Black and Latino aesthetic styles. Thus, there are many barbershops in Chicago geared toward African Americans and Latinos with the word "fade" in their name, such as "Fade Factory," "The Fade Inn," "Ace of Fades," and "Platinum Fades."

10. My interview with Francisco demonstrates the deceptive nature of stereotypes about the recognizability of Mexican-Puerto Rican difference. I interviewed him with two of his Puerto Rican friends, Marie (a sophomore) and J.C. (a junior). When I asked them how they identified themselves in terms of race and ethnicity, I thought I heard all three of them say they were Puerto Rican. From my perspective, nothing about Francisco's speech or physical appearance contradicted my assumption that he was Puerto Rican. I had only heard him speak English, which sounded similar to many Chicago-born Latinxs; nothing about his skin color, hair texture, or other physical features placed him outside of my ideas about what a Puerto Rican looks like. Later in the interview, when the three students told me where they were born, I discovered that Francisco is Mexican. He was born in Acapulco and had resided in Chicago as an unauthorized migrant since the age of 2. Thus, Francisco undermined stereotypes about the recognizability of Puerto Rican–Mexican difference *and* citizens/noncitizens. Additionally, despite the fact that soccer was constantly identified as the sport for Mexicans, Francisco was a member of the NNHS basketball team.

11. Such hairstyles are often stereotypically associated with African Americans, but in the context of NNHS and predominantly Latinx communities throughout Chicago, these were understood as part of a range of possible Latinx styles.

12. Many male students rejected this gendered stereotype by getting fades and other haircuts from female stylists/barbers.

13. This approach builds from Reyes' (2007) and Wortham and Reyes' (2015) analyses of the ways that ethnoracial stereotypes become important resources in everyday communication. Specifically, Reyes shows how these stereotypes are invoked and transformed, thereby mediating between microsocial interactional role inhabitances and macrosocial identity formations.

14. I analyze stereotypically Puerto Rican, Mexican, and Latinx indexical qualities of language in detail in Chapters 4, 5, and 6.

15. These include stereotypes about family size (e.g., Mexicans have larger families), vehicles (e.g., Puerto Ricans drive smaller cars), and local stores (e.g., Mexican vs. Puerto Rican produce markets).

16. I have encountered several other Chicago Puerto Ricans who use "¿Bueno?" as a playful telephone greeting. The stereotypical telephone greeting for Spanish-speaking Puerto Ricans is "hey-lo" (/xeɪlo/), a conventional English language telephone greeting ("hello") pronounced with stereotypical Puerto Rican Spanish phonology.

17. After she graduated from NNHS, Leti reconnected with her biological father, who is a US citizen. When I last spoke with her, she did not yet have citizenship but had obtained legal residency status.

18. Juke is often referred to as "ghetto" house music and is characterized by its rapid tempo and pounding beat. There are similar forms of music in other cities, such as Baltimore ("club" music) and Detroit ("jit"), but each region has a distinct style. While juke is most closely associated with African American youth in Chicago (i.e., most juke DJs are African American, and there are many predominantly African American footwork crews throughout the city), Latinxs are also active participants in this form of music and dance. The gendered dancing that goes along with juke music includes elaborate forms of stereotypically masculine "footwork" and equally elaborate forms of stereotypically feminine "bobbing." Like other popular youth-oriented music genres, juke dancing can also involve highly sexually suggestive partnering. Many Chicago Public Schools students learn the juke version of the cha-cha slide (called the "ghetto" slide or "juke" slide) in elementary school. Freshmen and sophomore students in particular would often talk about their desire to have a "juke" party or share stories about juke parties that they attended. They would also collect and trade juke compact discs with music by Chicago disk jockeys such as DJ Chip, DJ Slugo, and DJ V.

19. Like salsa and reggaeton, durangüense is a distinctively diasporic music genre, in this case linking Durango, Mexico to Chicago. The first breakthrough durangüense group, Grupo Montéz de Durango, achieved international notoriety with their 2003 album "De Durango a Chicago," which debuted at number two on the Top Latin Albums chart. They also had a number one album on the Top Latin Chart in 2010, with "Con Estilo . . . Chicago Style."

20. Hutchinson (2007) and Chavez (2017) have explored Mexican and Mexican American music and dance as importance sites of diasporic identity formation. Relatedly, Ines Casillas (2014) analyzes the powerful way in which Spanish-language radio functions not simply as a platform for Latinx musical consumption, but also for the forging of political subjectivities.

21. Tasha interpreted this situation in relation to her broader complaint that Latinx students were favored at NNHS. Ms. Ginsberg, the popular White teacher described earlier, agreed with Tasha's perspective. She felt that African American students were generally ignored. Ms. Jackson, the widely embraced school librarian and one of the few African American staff members (also described earlier), disagreed strongly. She pointed out that when African American students talked to her about feeling neglected she asked them to give her examples of what they saw as the problem. Ms. Jackson said that the students' inability to answer this question led her to conclude that the students were simply concerned with the fact that they were an overwhelming demographic minority in NNHS, but that this did not necessarily mean that they were being treated unfairly within the school.

22. The style of dance that is most directly associated with reggaeton is called perreo, which essentially translates to "doggy-style." This references the simulated sexual moves stereotypically performed by those who dance to this music with one another.

23. Carter (2014) analyzes the interdiscursive construction of "Spanish" across scales and institutional contexts, with a particular focus on a middle school in the "New Latino Diaspora" (Wortham, Murillo Jr., and Hamann 2002) of North Carolina.

CHAPTER 4

1. Ms. Díaz's standardized Dominican Spanish was somewhat of a novelty in the predominantly Mexican and Puerto Rican Midwestern Latinx context. In fact, Ms. Díaz emphasized her Dominicanness and often spoke of her participation in DAMA, the Dominican-American Midwest Association. Despite the stigmatization of Dominican Spanish alongside other Caribbean varieties from many non-Caribbean Latinx perspectives (cf. Zentella 2009), Ms. Díaz's close association with Dr. Baez and her exclusively Puerto Rican administrative staff placed her in a position of institutional power within NNHS. This allowed Caribbean varieties of Spanish to serve as the default variety in formal events such as the graduation. In Chapter 5, I explore the ideologies surrounding different varieties of Spanish in detail.

2. In her statement to the audience, Dr. Baez claimed to occasionally forget words in Spanish, which implied that she knew them at one time. This confession did not necessarily position her as linguistically incompetent, but rather as someone with whom many generation 1.5, 2, and 3 Latinx audience members might identify strongly (linguistically speaking). In this sense, Dr. Baez's switch from English to

Spanish could be interpreted as the opposite of what Bourdieu (1991) describes as "strategies of condescension," in which persons in positions of power draw on stigmatized language practices to appeal to marginalized audiences or to seem like they are just everyday people. Alternatively, her statement could be interpreted as an effort to explain how difficult it is to translate for oneself in realtime.

3. Indeed, language standardization is a chronotopic phenomenon that ideologically locates linguistic practices spatially and temporally (Silverstein 2005). Often, this involves imagining linguistic practices in relation to particular national pasts, presents, and futures.

4. Bonfiglio (2002) shows how race has anchored the historical construction of these models in the United States, such that conceptions of the American East Coast as the center of contaminating immigrant otherness position the West and Midwest as sites of ideal American language use and personhood.

5. This expectation that US Latinxs should act like monolingual English users and monolingual Spanish users is what Heller (2006) describes as "double monolingualism."

6. As described earlier, AVID (Advancement Via Individual Determination) is a study skills class that all students at NNHS took during their freshman, sophomore, junior, and senior years. Students designated as English Language Learners who took their core classes in the sheltered transitional bilingual education program were mainstreamed into AVID classes with the rest of the student body.

7. This spatialized icon of the marginalization of students designated as ELLs was shaped by a stratification of language use similar to Silverstein's (2003b) aforementioned conical model of ethnolinguistic hegemony.

8. Previous studies of Latinx students in Chicago have found collaborations among children with varying Spanish and English language skills, with children frequently developing their skills as "language mediators" (Olmedo 2005; Potowski 2005). These important studies were conducted with students at a different developmental life stage from the students at NNHS (i.e., elementary school) and in a very particular language learning educational context (i.e., dual-language schools that promote bilingualism for all students).

9. Scholars such as Bailey (2002), Mendoza-Denton (2008), and Shankar (2008) have explored these dynamics in a range of geographical and institutional settings, and in relation to a range of ethnoracial groups, throughout the United States.

10. LEP (Limited English Proficiency) is a common designation in US governmental, juridical, and educational contexts.

11. My invocation of "full" bilingualism demonstrates the ways that scholars of language can reproduce stigmatizing language ideologies that problematically position different linguistic repertoires as comparatively "full" or "incomplete."

12. More than 40 years ago, Fishman and Lovas (1970) pointed out the ironic tendency toward defining one-way English language transitional programs as "Bilingual Education."

13. The total student population during both the 2007–2008 and 2008–2009 school years was roughly 980. Based on my observations, the majority of these students regularly engaged in both English and Spanish linguistic practices.

14. The process that Fishman characterizes as "Anglification" captures some of the linguistic and cultural dimensions of assimilation, but it is crucial to emphasize the racialized nature of these dynamics.

15. Later in this chapter, I discuss the ways that mainstreamed Latinx students (i.e., those who were not designated as ELLs) were able to draw on and develop their Spanish language skills in Spanish language classrooms that were curricularly positioned within the broader US model of "foreign language education." In many of these classroom contexts, bilingual Latinx students discovered that their Spanish language use was viewed as incorrect and in need of remediation from the perspective of standardized Spanish language curricula.

16. Blommaert, Collins, and Slembrouck (2005) discuss how constructions of linguistic and communicative competence create perspectives from which some people are understood to speak no language properly.

17. ACCESS stands for Assessing Comprehension and Communication in English State-to-State for students designated as ELLs. It is the name of the English proficiency test that is used in more than half of the nation's states. It was created in 2002, following the implementation of President George W. Bush's comprehensive educational reform plan, No Child Left Behind.

18. Aparicio (2000) suggests that "foreignness," as it pertains to the Spanish language and US Latinxs, is a racialized notion that contributes to the "dispossession" of Spanish. García (2014) interrogates the "foreignness" of US Spanish from an alternative perspective, that of Spain. She shows how depending on context, Spanish has been strategically positioned as a nationalized, minoritized, or globalized language. Meanwhile, Macías (2014) analyzes the discursive and ideological production of Spanish as the "second language" of the United States, and Paris explores the implications of Latinx students' perception that "Spanish is becoming famous here in the United States" (2011:51).

19. García and Mason show how racialized conceptions of Spanish as the "language of the conquered and the colonized" (2009:80), as well as the "uneducated and poor" (2009:84), make transitional bilingual education the only imaginable model in which the Spanish language could be used in the education of students designated as ELLs.

20. This stratified dynamic can also be reproduced in dual-language settings (Valdés 1997). Flores and García (2017) explore similar dynamics in their analysis of the

ways privileged populations have metaphorically—and sometimes literally—relocated bilingual education from basements to boutiques.

21. The presumption that people have a single, "first" language is part of broader monolingual ideologies that are characteristic of modern nation-states. These ideologies are reflected in concepts such as "mother tongue" and "native speaker" (Bonfiglio 2010).

22. While states and districts are required to provide accommodations to students designated as ELLs, their approaches vary dramatically. There are four major approaches to providing resources for students designated ELLs that meet the requirements of the Lau decision: transitional bilingual education, maintenance bilingual education, two-way bilingual education, and English as a Second Language (ESL). In transitional bilingual education (the most common approach), students receive content area instruction in their "native" language while learning English as a second language, and after 3 to 5 years are "mainstreamed" out of the program into monolingual English classes. Maintenance bilingual education is a more comprehensive approach in which students receive content area instruction in their "native" language while learning English as a second language, with the ultimate objective of comprehensive proficiency in both languages. In contrast to transitional bilingual programs, no limit is set on the time that students can participate in maintenance bilingual education programs. In a two-way bilingual program, students designated as ELLs are integrated with "native" English speakers under the guidance of bilingual teachers, with the goal of developing bilingual proficiency among all students. Finally, in ESL programs, ESL aides are often provided to assist students designated as ELLs within the mainstream classroom, and pull-out programs are sometimes included throughout the day, giving students English language lessons separate from mainstream classes (Nieto 2002). The predominance of transitional approaches reflects not only English language hegemony but also the particular constraints placed on educational programming in the context of No Child Left Behind (NCLB), the national educational reform scheme introduced by President George W. Bush in 2002. NCLB required schools to administer an annual standards-based assessment of students designated as ELLs in order to demonstrate "adequate yearly progress" (AYP). Similar to NCLB's other test-based efforts toward creating educational "accountability," schools that failed to demonstrate AYP were placed on probation; subsequently, schools that consistently failed to meet AYP could be shut down and reorganized. With their sole emphasis on English language skills, transitional and ESL programs aligned most closely with the annual testing required by NCLB. Maintenance and two-way bilingual programming might not produce the sorts of results that would be readily reflected in annual NCLB testing.

23. In 2016 California voters overturned Proposition 227 by voting in an overwhelming majority for Proposition 58, the California Non-English Languages Allowed in Public Education Act. While this represents an important step toward unsettling monolingual educational norms, scholars have warned that we must be attentive to the ways in which efforts toward embracing linguistic diversity are conceptualized and implemented (Flores 2013; Valdés 1997).

24. Silverstein (2003b) points out that "glottonyms," such as "English," "Spanish," and "French," are themselves highly naturalized constructions with long-standing ties to nation-building projects. Elsewhere (Rosa 2014a), I have explored the ways that notions of rigidly bounded languages are constructed and deconstructed in contexts such as NNHS and its surrounding communities.

25. Flores (2013) shows how the contemporary promotion of plurilingualism in particular liberal settings is tied to forms of neoliberalism that reproduce inequality while purporting to embrace difference.

26. Mark Saxenmeyer, "Inside the 'Spanish Bubble': Chicago's Language Divide," *Fox News Chicago*, June 14, 2010. http://www.myfoxchicago.com/dpp/news/special_report/chicago-spanish-bubble-20100614 (accessed June 15, 2010).

27. In response to critiques of this classification by the American Anthropological Association's Committee on Language and Social Justice, the US Census Bureau has ceased its use of the label "linguistically isolated." There are ongoing discussions about possible replacements, as well as alternative ways of recognizing and valuing bi/multilingualism.

28. Hyon B. Shin and Rosalind Bruno, "Language Use and English Speaking Ability: 2000," October 2003, http://www.census.gov/prod/2003pubs/c2kbr-29.pdf (accessed July 12, 2014).

29. Leeman (2004) has examined the racialization of language throughout the history of the US Census.

30. US Latinxs are also the targets of other forms of linguicism, such as what Baugh (2003) calls "linguistic profiling." In May 2010, a Puerto Rican man who was born on the island and raised in Chicago was detained by Immigration and Customs Enforcement officials who suspected that he was an unauthorized migrant. After the man was released, he told reporters, "[The Immigration and Customs Enforcement Agent] did not believe I was Puerto Rican because of the way I look and the way I talk . . . I guess I have a Mexican accent." In another example, police officers in Dallas, Texas issued dozens of traffic citations between 2007 and 2009 to people for being "non English-speaking drivers." The citations, which were issued almost exclusively to Latinxs, were later invalidated when it became clear that there was no law requiring police to monitor drivers' English language proficiency. These officers, literally the language police, demonstrate the ways that linguistic profiling targets Latinxs and their language practices.

31. Allard, Mortimer, and Wortham (2008) show how Mexican students in a "New Latino Diaspora" setting are subjected to this double-stigmatization through the stigmatizing stereotype that they speak "Hillbilly Spanish" and "Tarzan English."

32. Recall from Chapter 2 that Yesi was one of only two students in the two graduating classes I followed who went on to attend a Tier 1 college.

33. Urciuoli (2008) explores the forms of inequality that structure the experiences of Latinx undergraduate students in university-level Spanish language courses, as well as the neoliberal politics of "diversity" that recruits these students to display their Latinx authenticity.

CHAPTER 5

1. Mark Krikorian. 2009. "Assimilated pronunciation." *National Review Online*, May 26, 2009. http://www.nationalreview.com/corner/182339/assimilated-pronunciation/mark-krikorian (accessed July 9, 2014).

2. Mark Krikorian. 2009. "It sticks in my craw," *National Review Online*, May 27, 2009. http://www.nationalreview.com/corner/182354/it-sticks-my-craw/mark-krikorian (accessed July 9, 2014).

3. Krikorian's views on pronunciation mirror those analyzed by Silverstein (1999) as modes of "Linguistic NIMBYism." Similarly, the parenthetical statement about the unmodernness of gender marking in Spanish nouns is what Silverstein calls "a language-shapes-thought Whorfianism," in which "certain people . . . reason that using languages other than ours could not possibly think about the world the way we speakers of English do" (2003b:531).

4. While Krikorian distinguishes between English and Spanish pronunciations of the vowels in the second and fourth syllables of Sotomayor (i.e., he writes them as "SO-tuh-my-er" and "so-toe-my-OR," or "tuh"/"toe" and "er"/"or"), he directs most of his attention toward syllable stress (he uses uppercase letters to highlight particular syllable stress patterns). Interestingly, Obama's pronunciation was not particularly Hispanicized. Were he to have produced a dental as opposed to an alveolar /t/ in the second syllable (for many English speakers, this would sound similar to the difference between pronouncing a "d" and "t") or an alveolar tap /ɾ/ in the final syllable, as did Sotomayor herself when she was sworn in by Chief Justice John Roberts, this might have become even more linguistically offensive and worrisome for Krikorian. Note that one particularly interesting linguistic feature of the structure of the swearing-in ceremony is that it requires the appointee to echo the Chief Justice as they administer the judicial oath, including the statement of the appointee's name. When Sotomayor was sworn in on August 8, 2009, Roberts pronounced her name Sonia Sotomayor /soʊnjʌ soʊtoʊˈmeɪɔːr/. She repeated Roberts, providing an alternative pronunciation: Sonia Sotomayor /soʊɲʌ soʊt̪oʊmaɪˈɔːɾ/. Note the differences in Sotomayor's palatalized /ɲ/ in her first name, and dental /

t/, diphthong in the penultimate syllable /aɪ/, and stress on the final syllable of her surname. Surely there have been phonetic differences between the speech of the administrant and appointee in prior Supreme Court swearing-in ceremonies, but the indexical meanings of these differences take shape in relation to the identities that are understood to produce them. As such, anxieties surrounding the meaning of Sotomayor's Latina identity were sufficiently potent to position syllable stress as a powerful threat to the nation's character. Krikorian's linguistic imprecision in characterizing language use in this situation is not so much a reflection of his phonetic naïveté as it is evidence that ideas about personhood shape the interpretation of language use. Sotomayor's Latina identity, in conjunction with this identity's imagined embodiment of the Spanish language, creates the potential for her English language use, as well as the English language use of other Latinxs, to become perpetually linked to Spanish.

5. In fact, the examples he uses of a monophthong ("freed") and a diphthong ("fried") are both diphthongs (/iy/ and /ay/, respectively).

6. Andrew Leonard. 2009. "How to pronounce Sotomayor," *Salon.com*, May 27, 2009. http://www.salon.com/tech/htww/2009/05/27/pronouncing_sotomayor/ (accessed July 9, 2014).

7. Leonard's reference to degrees of diversity demonstrates the perspectival nature of such characterizations. That is, English is no more inherently "diverse" than any other language. Recent theorizations of language and "superdiversity" draw on similar presumptions about degrees of diversity (Blommaert and Rampton 2011; Blommaert 2013). See Reyes (2014) for a reconsideration of the ways that perceptions of degrees of diversity reflect the ideological perspectives of listening subjects (Inoue 2006).

8. The simultaneous stigmatization and embrace of Latinx identity reflected in these blog postings is no coincidence. It echoes the negotiation with respect to the recurring dichotomy explored throughout this book between "Latino threat" (Chavez 2008) and "Latino spin" (Dávila 2008). Again, these joint discourses allow seemingly opposing characterizations of Latinxs such as "illegal, tax burden, overly sexual, patriotic, family-oriented, hard-working, and model consumer . . . [to] circulate in concert" (Dávila 2008:1). This apparent contradiction is in fact a product of the nature of stereotypy. The danger is that each of these characterizations is fundamentally anchored in the stigmatization of Latinx difference.

9. Flores (2014) demonstrates the long history of stigmatization jointly reproduced by apparently opposing sides of debates over linguistic diversity in the United States.

10. The equation of Spanglish with Latinx identity also erases the important role of indigenous languages across the Americas. Similarly, the definition of Latinxs' as a "mixed-race culture" is linked to forms of anti-Indigeneity and anti-Blackness that problematically locate Latinxs in the "racial middle" (O'Brien 2008).

11. See Ocampo (2014) for a discussion of the complex ways that Filipinos navigate their racialization as part of Asian and Latinx panethnic groups.

12. This is the same student who claimed that Mexicans are Hispanic and Puerto Ricans are Latino, as described in Chapter 2.

13. There are also important distinctions between the status of French vis-à-vis Creole languages in the postcolonial French Caribbean and English vis-à-vis Spanish in a settler colony such as the United States (cf. Garrett 2012; Managan 2008; Schieffelin and Doucet 1994).

14. He claimed that Puerto Rican Spanish sounds "cool, like salsa [music]," whereas Mexican Spanish sounds "lame, like banda [music]."

15. It is important to note that the ideologies of correctness associated with Mexican Spanish are in many ways particular to this context. In NNHS and throughout Chicago, Mexican Spanish is positioned as the unmarked Spanish norm vis-à-vis Caribbean varieties, specifically Puerto Rican Spanish. In many other contexts, such as the US Southwest and West Coast, there is a long history of stigmatization associated with Mexican American/Chicanx/"Pochx" Spanish. Fought (2003) and Martínez (2006) explore this stigmatization and provide alternative accounts of the complexities of Chicanx English and Spanish.

16. In addition to Slobe (2018), Bucholtz (2011) tracks the circulating figure of the stereotypical White "valley girl" and its linguistic construction.

17. Chun (2009) and Shankar (2008) explore similar dynamics of in-group linguistic mocking.

18. This is similar to the pride/profit axis of differentiation that Gal (2012) describes. In this case, Spanish is associated with cultural pride, and English is associated with institutional profit.

19. In that both of Jimmy's sisters graduated from college, his family was extremely unique in the context of NNHS. No other students whom I interviewed were able to name an immediate family member who graduated from college.

20. Jimmy draws a connection between race, language, and class. The middle child, the sister closest in age to Jimmy, lived in the South Loop, a part of the city associated with young, middle-class professionals. Jimmy said that she was White and that she could not speak Spanish. This demonstrates the common conception that Whiteness, middle-class socioeconomic status, and English monolingualism coincide with one another. When I asked Jimmy to clarify what he meant when he described his sister as White, he suggested that her behavior and mannerisms are stereotypically White. This demonstrates the ways that race was invoked and perceived in relation not only to physical appearance but also a broader set of signs and practices. It is also interesting to note that Jimmy's characterization of his family's differing linguistic proficiencies contradicts the expected pattern in which heritage language skills decrease in order from oldest to youngest child. In this case, Jimmy claims that the middle child possesses the least Spanish proficiency. As described earlier, Jimmy was quick to attribute this to her Whiteness, an interesting play on

Fanon's aforementioned (1967) well-known description of the Black Antillean who becomes Whiter through mastery of the French language.

21. Such two-way receptive bilingual situations have been promoted throughout Europe as a desired model of multilingualism and multiculturalism (Thije and Zeevaert 2007).

22. As Urla notes, "letters can operate as condensed signs of differing political ideologies [and] imagined geographies (2012:89).

23. Jimmy described his fellow softball participants as "viejos" [old people], and said that he might not have been speaking the "cleanest" (i.e., least profane) Spanish, but that he was learning nonetheless.

24. This /s/ aspiration/deletion is characteristic of Caribbean Spanish and takes two forms here. In syllable final placement before a consonant, as is the case with the first /s/ in "ustedes" as well as in "están," /s/ is realized a laryngeal fricative /h/. In absolute word final position, such as the second /s/ in "ustedes, /s/ is realized as an alveolar sibilant.

25. While many NNHS students were reggaeton fans, others, such as Jimmy (a self-proclaimed hip-hop fanatic) wanted nothing to do with it. Jimmy claimed that reggaeton is lame and that it only has one beat. He also said that he could not understand the highly vernacular Puerto Rican Spanish lyrics. From many other perspectives, however, reggaeton was viewed as "ghetto" Puerto Rican music. Much to Jimmy's dismay, his best friend, Michael (PR, Gen. 3, Gr. 12), listened to reggaeton all the time.

26. Victor's alternate valorization of Puerto Rican and Mexican Spanish corroborates the findings of Rúa (2001), Potowski and Matts (2008), and Torres and Potowski (2008) in their research focused on the complex language practices and modes of identification among MexiRicans/PortoMexicans in Chicago.

27. It interesting to consider the trajectory of decreasing prominence of Spanish language use within mainstream classrooms in relation to the trajectory of increasing rigidity in ideas about Mexican-Puerto Rican difference discussed in Chapter 2. These joint shifts reflect students' engagement with competing institutional demands in which language and identity were linked in various ways. That is, to be Puerto Rican, Mexican, or Latinx could correspond alternately to any number of varieties of English and Spanish. Toward the end of this chapter, I explore these correspondences further.

28. She employed strategies similar to those described by Monzó and Rueda (2009), such as head nods and other paralinguistic cues, in their account of how emergent English-Spanish bilingual Latinx children "pass" for English fluent.

29. She provided other examples, such as "pato," which is Puerto Rican slang for "gay," but simply means "duck" in Mexican Spanish; she also pointed out the counter-example of "puñal," which means "gay" in Mexican slang, but simply means "knife" in Puerto Rican Spanish.

30. García (2014) and Del Valle (2014) explore the politics of globalization, power, and legacies of colonialism that shape ideologies surrounding the teaching of varieties of Spanish associated with Spain and Latin America.

31. Later in this chapter, I discuss Kathryn Woolard's (1998) framework of simultaneity and bivalency to examine formulations of "translingualism" that might be more familiar to linguistic anthropologists. In particular, I use these notions to analyze NNHS students' syncretic English-Spanish language practices.

32. These ideologies remap stereotypes about the correctness of so-called "White English" and the coolness of so-called "African American English." A complete analysis of the remapping of racial, ethnic, and linguistic borders is beyond the scope of this chapter, but I explore these issues elsewhere (Rosa 2014a, 2014b).

33. One student told me about an uncle of his from Puerto Rico who got into a fight with his Mexican employer who called him a "cabrón" (bastard). The revalorization of "cabrón" from an insult to a term of solidarity was not communicated in the shift from Mexican Spanish to Puerto Rican Spanish. The use of "cabrón" in Inverted Spanglish avoids these conflicts.

34. Martínez (2010) and Martínez and Morales (2014) explore the potential pedagogical benefits of using Spanglish to develop literacy skills, as well as Latinx students' creative engagement in profane bilingual wordplay.

35. Another instance of Inverted Spanglish involved demographic categories. While filling out the Scantron form for the ACT (American College Testing), the standardized college entrance exam that is used most often in Illinois, Mexican and Puerto Rican students laughed at the option to identify themselves as "Chicano," a subcategory of "Hispanic." Several students jokingly asked one another, "Are you a *Chickahno* /tʃɪkɔnoʊ/ (Spanish, /tʃikano/)?" For these students, the ACT form's inclusion of "Chicano," a categorical descriptor associated with politically progressive/anti-assimilation West Coast US Mexicans, was an example of White people trying too hard to be politically correct. In his stand-up routines, Mexican American comedian George Lopez plays with similar hyper-anglicized pronunciations of "Chicano."

36. Fader (2009) analyzes similar forms of simultaneity and bivalency among Hasidic Jewish youth.

37. Use of the term "Anglo" is stereotypically associated with the southwestern United States.

38. See note 45 in this chapter for a demonstration of the ways in which US Latinxs' language use is racialized from particular Spain-oriented institutional perspectives.

39. Martínez (2013) analyzes the alternately hegemonic and counter-hegemonic ideologies associated with Latinx middle school students' conceptions of Spanglish.

40. Again, this is the inverse of the type of language learning that is valued within middle-class and upper-class educational communities. In these contexts of

socioeconomic privilege, speaking Spanish (and other languages) *without* an anglicized accent is often idealized.

41. In addition to Woolard's and Rampton's accounts of language play, Jaspers'
(2005) analysis of Moroccan boys' "linguistic sabotage" and "doing/being ri-
diculous" in Belgium presents another framework for understanding Inverted
Spanglish. The experience of looking like a language in the Belgian context
involves presumptions about Moroccans' inability to speak Dutch. Jaspers shows
how a group of young Moroccan boys combat these racialized ideas by playfully
"upkeying" (Goffman 1974) to Standard Dutch. In contrast, the use of Spanish
lexical items to "upkey" in Inverted Spanglish demonstrates the distinct history of Latinxs and the Spanish language in the United States compared with
Moroccans in Belgium.

42. In "Hegemonic Multiculturalism," Garza and Crawford (2005) show how assimilation and multiculturalism become joint projects in educational contexts that simultaneously embrace diversity and bilingualism as abstract concepts yet define success
only "in terms of immigrant students' level of assimilation and fluency in English"
(2005:616).

43. "Division" is the Chicago Public Schools equivalent of what is called "Home Room"
in many other educational contexts.

44. In many ways, Inverted Spanglish allowed Latinx NNHS students to reclaim the
Spanish language in the face of linguistic hegemony that strongly discourages
its use. Aparicio (2000) frames this linguistic hegemony as a mode of Spanish
"dispossession."

45. The Madrid-based Real Academia Española (Royal Spanish Academy), whose
motto is "limpia, fija, y da splendor" (cleans, sets, and casts splendor), draws clear
distinctions between US Latinxs and other Spanish speakers. The Academy added
the word "espanglish" (Spanglish) to its 2014 edition of the Spanish language dic-
tionary, defining it as "modalidad del habla de algunos grupos hispanos de los
Estados Unidos, en la que se mezclan, deformándolos, elementos léxicos y gramati-
cales del español y del ingles" (mode of speaking among some US Hispanic groups
in which they mix, thereby deforming, lexical and grammatical elements of Spanish
and English). This demonstrates the precarious nature of US Latinxs' simultaneous
use of Spanish and English. Del Valle (2011) has explored the fraught relationship
between the Real Academia Española and US Latinxs, namely the effort to simultaneously include and stigmatize this population as part of a global community of
hispanohablantes (Spanish speakers).

CHAPTER 6

1. Cintron (1987) explores similar dynamics of marginalization and expressive practices in his analysis of Chicago-area Latinx youth.

2. Andrea Billups, "36 Chicago area students killed sets record," *The Washington Times*, May 13, 2009, http://www.washingtontimes.com/news/2009/may/13/record-36-students-killed-this-school-year-across-/ (accessed August 4, 2009).

3. Marquez (2012b) analyzes the ways in which the killing of Alex Arellano was framed as the product of racialized pathology rather than structural inequity.

4. Rymes (2001) analyzes the similar phenomenon of being "hit up" in the Los Angeles context. There are subtle differences between checking and hitting up. Unlike "hitting up" in Los Angeles, "checking" in Chicago generally focuses on one's potential gang affiliation more so than the particular streets with which one is associated.

5. One student's mother, a conservative middle-aged Mexican woman, described the experience of being checked on several occasions not far from where Alex Arellano was killed.

6. Young people also playfully "mock check" one another by asking, "What you on?" or "What you is?" These questions are understood as the most common way in which checking is initiated. Clever, often humorous responses in these situations vary from mock invocations of the names of actual gangs to many non–gang-related categories.

7. Many Latinx youth throughout the city learn a number of gang signs at a young age from friends and family members.

8. Regina Waldroup, "Was Alex Arellano in a gang? Does it even matter?" *CLTV*, May 5, 2009, http://weblogs.cltv.com/news/local/chicago/2009/05/was_alex_arellano_in_a_gang_does_it_even_matter.html (accessed August 7, 2009).

9. Garrard McClendon, "Murder was the case: Alex Arellano is dead." *CLTV*, May 4, 2009, http://weblogs.cltv.com/news/opinion/mcclendon/2009/05/murder-was-the-case-alex-arell.html (accessed August 6, 2009).

10. The two overarching gang families in Chicago are the People Nation and the Folks Nation. There is widespread knowledge of this gang structure throughout Chicago, particularly within predominantly Latinx and African American neighborhoods and among those associated with law enforcement. Students often joked about the potential gang affiliations of teachers who unknowingly used the words "people" and "folks" in everyday classroom situations.

11. From students' perspectives, tagging could refer to gang-related or non–gang-related sign practices; from most mainstream institutional perspectives, all tagging was viewed as gang-related behavior. I will explore different types of tagging later in this chapter.

12. Garcia (2017) explores the politics of and pedagogical strategies for incorporating various technologies into mainstream classroom spaces.

13. The students' responses to the officer's presence could also be interpreted as a sign of their familiarity with him or their performance of obedience to avoid confrontation.

14. Alim (2011) explores the educational implications of such hip-hop literacies, characterizing these practices as "ill-literacies."

15. Students used Internet proxy sites to view websites that were banned by CPS.
16. The structural correspondence between membership hierarchies in gangs and tagging crews is not by chance. Later in this chapter, I point to the interdiscursivities that precariously link these organizational forms from in-group and out-group perspectives.
17. Rigo called the large, thick markers that he carried "streakers."
18. I asked Rigo to clarify whether he meant "clicks together," as in "vibes" together, or "cliques together," as in constitutes a "clique" or social group. He said both interpretations apply.
19. Many other nicknames for gang members and names of gangs themselves invoked mental instability, such as "insane," "maniacs," and "crazy."
20. This also demonstrates the ways that power over contextualization, or lack thereof, is a central component of the relationship between language and agency (cf. Ahearn 2001b; Duranti 2004).
21. Meanwhile, Rigo referred to his catalogue of photographs of DCM's tags as "the bible."
22. In other research on literacy, this kind of simultaneity has been framed as "hybrid literacies" (Jocson 2005) and "syncretic literacies" (Duranti and Ochs 1997; Gregory, Volk, and Long 2013).

CONCLUSION

1. Since the church Roberto attended was widely regarded as homophobic, it is interesting that he identified a homophobic epithet as an example of the vulgar language that he ceased using while undergoing this religious ritual. This reflects the broader conservative distinction between more and less acceptable forms of homophobia.
2. The name "Rebirth" is a pseudonym.
3. Since 2010, the church has opened its own building or "campus" and has also purchased several other nearby properties.

REFERENCES

Agha, Asif. 2004. Registers of language. In *A companion to linguistic anthropology*, ed. Alessandro, Duranti, 23–45. Malden, MA: Blackwell Publishing.

———. 2005a. Voice, footing, enregisterment. *Journal of Linguistic Anthropology* 15(1):38–59.

———. 2005b. Semiosis across encounters. *Journal of Linguistic Anthropology* 15(1):1–5.

———. 2007. *Language and social relations*. Cambridge, UK: Cambridge University Press.

Ahearn, Laura M. 2001a. *Invitations to love: Literacy, love letters, and social change in Nepal*. Ann Arbor, MI: University of Michigan Press.

———. 2001b. Language and agency. *Annual Review of Anthropology* 30:109–137.

Ahmed, Sara. 2012. *On being included: Racism and diversity in institutional life*. Durham, NC: Duke University Press.

Alcoff, Linda Martín. 2006. *Visible identities: Race, gender, and the self*. Oxford: Oxford University Press.

Alexander, Michelle. 2012. *The new Jim Crow: Mass incarceration in the age of color-blindness*. New York: The New Press.

Allard, Elaine, Katherine Mortimer, and Stanton Wortham. 2008. Hillbilly Spanish and Tarzan English: Ideologies of Mexican immigrant language and identity in the Latino diaspora. Paper Presented at the American Educational Research Association Annual Meeting, New York, NY, March 2008.

Alim, H. Samy. 2005. The whitey voice: Linguistic agency, (anti)racism, and the discursive construction of whiteness in a black American barbershop. Paper presented at New Ways of Analyzing Variation 34 Conference, New York University, New York, October 2005.

———. 2006. *Roc the mic right: The language of hip hop culture*. New York: Routledge.

———. 2011. Global ill-literacies: Hip hop cultures, youth identities, and the politics of literacy. *Review of Research in Education* 35(1):120–146.

Alim, H. Samy, and Angela Reyes. 2011. Complicating race: Articulating race across multiple social dimensions. *Discourse & Society* 22(4):379–384.

Alim, H. Samy, and Geneva Smitherman. 2012. *Articulate while black: Barack Obama, language, and race in the U.S.* Oxford: Oxford University Press.

Althusser, Louis. 1994 [1979]. Ideology and ideological state apparatuses (notes towards an investigation). In *Mapping ideology*, ed. Slavoj Zizek, 100–140. London: Verso.

Amaya, Hector. 2007. Dying American or the violence of citizenship: Latinos in Iraq. *Latino Studies* 5(1):3–24.

Anzaldúa, Gloria. 1987. *Borderlands/la frontera*. San Francisco: Aunt Lute Books.

Anyon, Jean. 2005a. What "counts" as educational policy? Notes toward a new paradigm. *Harvard Educational Review* 75(1):65–88.

———. 2005b. *Radical possibilities: Public policy, urban education, and a new social movement*. New York: Routledge.

Aparicio, Frances. 2000. Of Spanish dispossessed. In *Language ideologies: Critical perspectives on the official English movement*, ed. Roseann Dueñas González and Ildikó Melis, 248–275. Urbana, IL: NCTE.

———. 2003. Jennifer as Selena: Rethinking Latinidad in media and popular culture. *Latino Studies* 1(1):90–105.

Aparicio, Frances, and Susana Chávez-Silverman, eds. 1997. *Tropicalizations: Transcultural representations of Latinidad*. Hanover, NH: University Press of New England.

Appadurai, Arjun. 1996. *Modernity at large: Cultural dimensions of globalization*. Minneapolis, MN: University of Minnesota Press.

Arredondo, Gabriela. 2008. *Mexican Chicago: Race, identity, and nation, 1916–39*. Champaign, IL: University of Illinois Press.

Bahena, Sofía, North Cooc, Rachel Currie-Rubin, Paul Kuttner, and Monica Ng, eds. 2012. *Disrupting the school-to-prison pipeline*. Cambridge, MA: Harvard Educational Review.

Bailey, Benjamin. 2002. *Language, race, and negotiation of identity: A study of Dominican Americans*. New York: LFB Scholarly Publishing.

Bakhtin, Mikhail. 1981. *The dialogic imagination*. ed. Michael Holquist and Caryl Emerson. Austin: University of Texas Press.

Baltodano, Marta P. 2004. Latino immigrant parents and the hegemony of Proposition 227. *Latino Studies* 2(2):246–253.

Baquedano-López, Patricia. 2004. Literacy practices across learning contexts. In *A companion to linguistic anthropology*, ed. Alessandro Duranti, 245–268. Malden, MA: Blackwell Publishing.

Barrett, Rusty. 2006. Language ideology and racial inequality: Competing functions of Spanish in an Anglo-owned Mexican restaurant. *Language in Society* 35(2):163–204.

Basso, Keith H. 1979. *Portraits of the "whiteman": Linguistic play and cultural symbols among the Western Apache*. New York: Cambridge University Press.

Bateson, Gregory. 1972. *Steps to an ecology of mind*. Chicago: University of Chicago Press.

Baugh, John. 2003. Linguistic profiling. In *Black linguistics: Language, society, and politics in Africa and the Americas*, ed. Sinfree Makoni, Geneva Smitherman, Arnetha F. Ball, and Arthur K. Spears, 155–168. London: Routledge.

Bauman, Richard, and Charles Briggs. 1992. Genre, intertextuality, and social power. *Journal of Linguistic Anthropology* 2(2):131–172.

———. 2003. *Voices of modernity: Language ideologies and the politics of inequality*. New York: Cambridge University Press.

Benor, Sarah Bunin. 2010. Ethnolinguistic repertoire: Shifting the analytic focus in language and ethnicity. *Journal of Sociolinguistics* 14(2):159–183.

Blommaert, Jan. 2013. *Ethnography, superdiversity, and linguistic landscapes: Chronicles of complexity*. Clevedon, UK: Multilingual Matters.

Blommaert, Jan, James Collins, and Stef Slembrouck. 2005. Spaces of multilingualism. *Language & Communication* 25(3):197–216.

Blommaert, Jan, and Ben Rampton. 2011. Language and superdiversity. *Diversities* 13(2):1–22.

Bloomfield, Leonard. 1927. Literate and illiterate speech. *American Speech* 2(10):432–439.

Bonfiglio, Thomas. 2002. *Race and the rise of standard American*. Berlin: Mouton de Gruyter.

Bonfiglio, Thomas. 2010. *Mother tongues and nations: The invention of the native speaker*. Berlin: Mouton de Gruyter.

Bonilla-Silva, Eduardo. 2004. From bi-racial to tri-racial: Towards a new system of racial stratification in the USA. *Ethnic and Racial Studies* 27(6):931–950.

———. 2011. The invisible weight of whiteness: The racial grammar of everyday life in contemporary America. *Ethnic and Racial Studies* 35(2):173–194.

———. 2014 [2003]. *Racism without racists: Color-blind racism and the persistence of racial inequality in the United States*. Lanham, MD: Rowman and Littlefield Publishers, Inc.

Bourdieu, Pierre. 1991. *Language and symbolic power*. Cambridge, MA: Harvard University Press.

Bourdieu, Pierre, and Jean-Claude Passeron. 1977. *Reproduction in education, society, and culture*. London: Sage.

Briggs, Laura. 2003. *Reproducing empire: Race, sex, science, and U.S. imperialism in Puerto Rico*. Berkeley: University of California Press.

Brown, Wendy. 2006. *Regulating aversion: Tolerance in the age of identity and empire*. Princeton, NJ: Princeton University Press.

Bucholtz, Mary. 2003. Sociolinguistic nostalgia and the authentication of identity. *Journal of Sociolinguistics* 7(3):398–416.

———. 2009. From stance to style: Gender, interaction, and indexicality in Mexican immigrant youth slang. In *Stance: Sociolinguistic perspectives*, ed. Alexandra Jaffe, 146–170. Oxford: Oxford University Press.

————. 2011. *White kids: Language, race, and styles of youth identity.* New York: Cambridge University Press.

Bucholtz, Mary, and Kira Hall. 2005. Identity and interaction: A sociocultural linguistic approach. *Discourse Studies* 7(4-5): 585–614.

Candelario, Ginetta E. B. 2007. *Black behind the ears: Dominican racial identity from museums to beauty shops.* Durham, NC: Duke University Press.

Carbado, Devon. 2005. Racial naturalization. *American Quarterly* 57(3):633–658.

Carter, Phillip. 2014. National narratives, institutional ideologies, and local talk: The discursive production of Spanish in a "new" U.S. Latino community. *Language in Society* 43(2):209–240.

Cassilas, Dolores Ines. 2014. *Sounds of belonging: U.S. Spanish-language radio and public advocacy.* New York: New York University Press.

Chabram-Dernersesian, Angie. 1999. Chicana! Rican? No, Chicana-Riqueña!: Refashioning the transnational connection. In *Between woman and nation,* ed. Caren Kaplan, Norma Alarcón, and Minoo Moallem, 264–295. Durham, NC: Duke University Press.

————. 2009. "Growing up Mexi-Rican: Remembered snapshots of life in La Puente. *Latino Studies* 7(3):378–392.

Chavez, Alex. 2017. *Sounds of crossing: Music, migration, and the aural poetics of Huapango Arribeño.* Durham, NC: Duke University Press.

Chavez, Leo. 2008. *The Latino threat: Constructing immigrants, citizens, and the nation.* Stanford, CA: Stanford University Press.

Chow, Rey. 2002. *The protestant ethnic and the spirit of capitalism.* New York: Columbia University Press.

Chumley, Lily Hope, and Nicholas Harkness. 2013. Introduction: Qualia. *Anthropological Theory* 13(1/2):3–11.

Chun, Elaine. 2009. Ideologies of legitimate mockery: Margaret Cho's revoicings of mock Asian. In *Beyond yellow English: Towards a linguistic anthropology of Asian Pacific America,* ed. Angela Reyes and Adrienne Lo, 261–287. New York: Oxford University Press.

————. 2011. Reading race beyond black and white. *Discourse & Society* 22(4):403–421.

Chun, Elaine, and Adrienne Lo. 2016. Language and racialization. In *The Routledge handbook of linguistic anthropology,* ed. Nancy Bonvillain, 109–123. New York: Routledge.

Cintron, Ralph. 1997. *Angel's town: Chero ways, gang life, and the rhetorics of the everyday.* Boston: Beacon Press.

Collins, Patricia Hill. 2000. *Black feminist thought: Knowledge, consciousness, and the politics of empowerment.* New York: Routledge.

Crawford, James. 2007. Hard sell: Why is bilingual education so unpopular with the American public? In *Bilingual education: An introductory reader,* ed. Ofelia García and Colin Baker, 145–161. Clevedon, UK: Multilingual Matters.

Cruz, Wilfredo. 2007. *City of dreams: Latino immigration to Chicago.* Lanham, MD: University Press of America.

Cummins, Jim. 2000. *Language, power, and pedagogy: Bilingual children in the crossfire.* Clevedon, UK: Multilingual Matters.

Dávila, Arlene. 1997. *Sponsored identities: Cultural politics in Puerto Rico.* Philadelphia: Temple University Press.

———. 2008. *Latino spin: Public image and the whitewashing of race.* New York: New York University Press.

———. 2012 [2001]. *Latinos, inc.: The marketing and making of a People.* Berkeley: University of California Press.

De Genova, Nicholas. 2004. The legal production of Mexican/migrant "illegality." *Latino Studies* 2(2):160–185.

———. 2005. *Working the boundaries: Race, space, and "illegality" in Mexican Chicago.* Durham, NC: Duke University Press.

De Genova, Nicholas, and Ana Y. Ramos-Zayas. 2003. *Latino crossings: Mexicans, Puerto Ricans, and the politics of race and citizenship.* New York: Routledge.

Delpit, Lisa. 1995. *Other people's children: Cultural conflict in the classroom.* New York: The New Press.

Del Valle, Jose. 2011. Política del lenguaje y geopolítica: España, la RAE, y la población Latina de Estados Unidos. In *El Dardo en la Academia*, ed. Silvia Senz y Montse Alberte, 551–590. Barcelona: Melusina.

———. 2014. The politics of normativity and globalization: Which Spanish in the classroom? *The Modern Language Journal* 98(1):358–372.

Devine, John. 1996. *Maximum security: The culture of violence in inner-city schools.* Chicago: The University of Chicago Press.

Dick, Hilary Parsons, and Kristina Wirtz. 2011. Racializing discourses. *Journal of Linguistic Anthropology* 21(S1):E2-E10.

di Leonardo, Micaela. 1994. White ethnicities, identity politics, and baby bear's chair. *Social Text* 41:165–191.

Dewey, John. 1916. *Democracy and education.* New York: Free Press.

Du Bois, W. E. B. 1903. *The souls of black folk.* New York: Penguin Books.

Duchêne, Alexandre, and Monica Heller, eds. 2012. *Language in late capitalism: Pride and Profit.* New York: Routledge.

Duranti, Alessandro. 1997. *Linguistic anthropology.* New York: Cambridge University Press.

———. 2004. Agency in language. In *A companion to linguistic anthropology*, ed. Alessandro Duranti, 451–473. Malden, MA: Blackwell Publishing.

Duranti, Alessandro, and Elinor Ochs. 1997. Syncretic literacy in a Samoan American family. In *Discourse, tools, and reasoning: Essays on situated cognition*, ed. Lauren Resnick, Roger Saljo, and Clotilde Pontecorvo, 169–202. Berlin: Springer-Verlag.

Eckert, Penelope. 1989. *Jocks & burnouts: Social categories and identity in the high school.* New York: Teacher College Press.

———. 2000. *Linguistic variation as social practice*. Malden, MA: Blackwell Publishing.

Eisenlohr, Patrick. 2004. Language revitalization and new technologies: Cultures of electronic mediation and the refiguring of communities. *Annual Review of Anthropology* 33:21–45.

Fader, Ayala. 2009. *Mitzvah girls: Bringing up the next generation of Hasidic Jews in Brooklyn*. Princeton, NJ: Princeton University Press.

Fanon, Frantz. 1967. *Black skin, white masks*. New York: Grove Press.

Farr, Marcia, ed. 2004. *Latino language and literacy in ethnolinguistic Chicago*. New York: Routledge.

———. 2006. *Rancheros in Chicagoacán: Language and identity in a transnational community*. Austin: University of Texas Press.

———. 2011. Urban pluralingualism: Language practices, policies, and ideologies in Chicago. *Journal of Pragmatics* 43(5), 1161–1172.

Fergus, Edward, Pedro Noguera, and Margary Martin. 2010. Construction of race and ethnicity for and by Latinos. In *Handbook of Latinos and education: Theory, research, and practices*, ed. Enrique G. Murillo, Jr., Sofia A. Villenas, Ruth Trinidad Galván, Juan Sánchez Muñoz, Corinne Martínez, and Margarita Machado-Casas, 170–181. New York: Routledge.

Fernández, Lilia. 2012. *Brown in the windy city: Mexicans and Puerto Ricans in postwar Chicago*. Chicago: University of Chicago Press.

Fikes, Kesha. 2009. *Managing African Portugal: The citizen-migrant distinction*. Durham, NC: Duke University Press.

Fine, Michelle. 1988. Sexuality, schooling, and adolescent females: The missing discourse of desire. *Harvard Educational Review* 58(1):29–54.

——— 1991. *Framing dropouts*. Albany: State University of New York Press.

Fine, Michelle, and Sara I. McLelland. 2006. Sexuality education and desire: Still missing after all these years. *Harvard Educational Review* 76(3):297–338.

Fishman, Joshua. 1981. Language policy: past, present, and future. In *Language in the USA*, ed. Charles A. Ferguson and Shirley Brice Heath, 516–526. New York: Cambridge University Press.

Fishman, Joshua, and John Lovas. 1970. Bilingual education in sociolinguistic perspective. *TESOL Quarterly* 4(3):215–222.

Flores, Juan. 2009. *The diaspora strikes back: Caribeño tales of learning and turning*. New York: Taylor and Francis.

Flores, Nelson. 2013. The unexamined relationship between neoliberalism and plurilingualism: A cautionary tale. *TESOL Quarterly* 47(4):500–520.

———. 2014. Creating republican machines: Language governmentality in the United States. *Linguistics and Education* 25:1–11.

Flores, Nelson, and Ofelia García. 2017. A critical review of bilingual education in the United States: From basements and pride to boutiques and profit. *Annual Review of Applied Linguistics* 37:14–29.

Flores, Nelson, and Jonathan Rosa. 2015. Undoing appropriateness: Raciolinguistic ideologies and language diversity in education. *Harvard Educational Review* 85(2):149–171.

Flores-González, Nilda. 1999. The racialization of Latinos: The meaning of Latino identity for the second generation. *Latino Studies Journal* 10(3):3–31.

———. 2002. *School kids/street kids: Identity development in Latino students.* New York: Teachers College Press.

———. 2017. *Citizens but not Americans: Race and belonging among Latino millennials.* New York: New York University Press.

Foucault, Michel. 1991. Governmentality. In *The Foucault effect: Studies in governmentality*, ed. G. Burchell, C. Gordon, and P. Miller, 87–104. London: Harvester Wheatsheaf.

Fought, Carmen. 2003. *Chicano English in context.* New York: Palgrave Macmillan.

Freire, Paulo. 1970. *Pedagogy of the oppressed.* New York: Continuum International Publishing Group.

Gal, Susan. 1988. The political economy of code choice. In *Codeswitching: Linguistic and anthropological perspectives*, ed. Monica Heller, 245–264. Berlin: Mouton de Gruyter.

———. 1989. Language and political economy. *Annual Review of Anthropology* 18:345–367.

———. 2002. A semiotics of the public/private distinction. *Differences* 13(1):77–95.

———. 2005. Language ideologies compared: Metaphors of public/private. *Journal of Linguistic Anthropology* 15(1):23–37.

———. 2006. Contradictions of standard language in Europe: Implications for the study of practices and publics. *Social Anthropology* 13(2):163–181.

———. 2012. Sociolinguistic regimes and the management of "diversity." In *Language in late capitalism: Pride and profit*, ed. Monica Heller and Alexandre Duchene, 22–37. New York: Routledge.

Garcia, Antero. 2017. *Good reception: Teens, teachers, and mobile media in a Los Angeles Classroom.* Cambridge, MA: MIT Press.

García, Ofelia. 2009. *Bilingual education in the 21st century: A global perspective.* Malden, MA: Wiley-Blackwell.

———. 2014. U.S. Spanish and education: Global and local intersections. *Review of research in education* 38(1):58–80.

García, Ofelia, and Leah Mason. 2009. Where in the world is U.S. Spanish? Creating a space of opportunity for U.S. Latinos. In *Language and poverty*, ed. Wayne Harbert, Sally McConnell-Ginet, Amanda Miller, and John Whitman, 78–101. Clevedon, UK: Multilingual Matters.

García, Ofelia, and Rosario Torres-Guevara. 2010. Monoglossic ideologies and language policies in the education of U.S. Latinas/os. In *Handbook of Latinos and education: Theory, research, and practices*, ed. Enrique G. Murillo, Jr., Sofia A. Villenas,

Ruth Trinidad Galván, Juan Sánchez Muñoz, Corinne Martínez, and Margarita Machado-Casas, 182–194. New York: Routledge.

Garrett, Paul. 2012. Dying young: The decline of pidgins, creoles, and other contact languages. In *The anthropology of extinction: Essays on culture and species death*, ed. Genese Marie Sodikoff, 143–163. Bloomington: Indiana University Press.

Garza, Aimee V., and Lindy Crawford. 2005. Hegemonic multiculturalism: English immersion, ideology, and subtractive schooling. *Bilingual Research Journal* 29(3):599–619.

Ghosh Johnson, Subhadra Elka. 2005. *Mexiqueño? Issues of identity and ideology in a case study of dialect contact*. Doctoral Dissertation, University of Pittsburgh.

Gilroy, Paul. 2000. *Against race*. Cambridge, MA: Harvard University Press.

Glazer, Nathan. 1997. *We are all multiculturalists now*. Cambridge, MA: Harvard University Press.

Godreau, Isar. 2008. Slippery semantics: Race talk and everyday uses of racial terminology in Puerto Rico. *CENTRO Journal* 20(2):5–33.

Goffman, Erving. 1963. *Stigma: Notes on the management of spoiled identity*. Englewood Cliffs, NJ: Prentice-Hall.

———. 1974. *Frame analysis: An essay on the organization of experiences*. Boston: Northeastern University Press.

———. 1981. *Forms of talk*. Philadelphia: University of Pennsylvania Press.

Gonzales, Roberto G. 2015. *Lives in limbo: Undocumented and coming of age in America*. Berkeley, CA: University of California Press.

González, Juan. 2001. *Harvest of empire: A history of Latinos in America*. New York: Penguin Books.

González, Norma. 2006. *I am my language: Discourses of women and children in the borderlands*. Tucson: University of Arizona Press.

Gregory, Eve, Dinah Volk, and Susi Long. 2013. Syncretism and syncretic literacies. *Journal of Early Childhood Literacy* 13(3):309–321.

Gumperz, John. 1982. *Discourse strategies*. Cambridge, UK: Cambridge University Press.

Gupta, Akhil, and James Ferguson. 1992. Beyond "culture": Space, identity, and the politics of difference." *Cultural Anthropology* 7(1):6–23.

Hanks, William. 1996. *Language and communicative practices*. Boulder, CO: Westview Press.

Harris-Lacewell, Melissa. 2004. *Barbershops, bibles, and BET: Everyday talk and black political thought*. Princeton, NJ: Princeton University Press.

Heath, Shirley Brice. 1982. What no bedtime story means: Narrative skills at home and school. *Language in society* 11(1):49–76.

———. 1983. *Ways with words: Language, life, and work in communities and classrooms*. New York, NY: Cambridge University Press.

Heller, Monica. 2006 [1999]. *Linguistic minorities and modernity: A sociolinguistic ethnography*. New York, NY: Longman.

Heller, Monica, and Bonnie McElhinny. 2017. *Language, colonialism, and capitalism: Towards a critical history.* Toronto: University of Toronto Press.

Herder, Johann Gottfried. 1968. *Reflections on the philosophy of the history of mankind.* Chicago: University of Chicago Press.

Hernández, David. 2008. Pursuant to deportation: Latinos and immigrant detention. *Latino Studies.* 6(1-2):35–63.

Hernandez, Jillian. 2009. "Miss, you look like a bratz doll": On chonga girls and sexual-aesthetic excess. *NWSA Journal* 21(3):63–90.

Hesse, Barnor. 2016. Counter-racial formation theory. In *Conceptual aphasia in Black: Displacing racial formation*, eds. P. Khalil Saucier and Tryon P. Woods, vii–x. Lanham, MD: Lexington Books.

Higginbotham, Evelyn Brooks. 1993. *Righteous discontent: The women's movement in the black Baptist church, 1880–1920.* Cambridge, MA: Harvard University Press.

Hill, Jane H. 1993. Is it really "no problemo"?: Junk Spanish and Anglo racism. *Texas Linguistics Forum* 33:1–12.

———. 1998. Language, race, and white public space. *American Anthropologist* 100(3):680–689.

———. 2005. Intertextuality as source and evidence for indirect indexical meanings. *Journal of Linguistic Anthropology* 15(1):113–124.

———. 2008. *The everyday language of white racism.* Malden, MA: Wiley-Blackwell.

Holston, James. 1998. Space of insurgent citizenship. In *Making the invisible visible: A multicultural planning history*, ed. Leonie Sandercock, 37–56. Berkeley, CA: University of California Press.

Hull, Glynda, and Katherine Schultz. 2002. *School's out! Bridging out-of-school literacies with classroom practice.* New York: Teachers College Press.

Hutchinson, Sydney. 2007. *From quebradita to duranguense: Dance in Mexican American Youth Culture.* Tucson, AZ: The University of Arizona Press.

Inoue, Miyako. 2003a. Speech without a speaking body: "Japanese women's language" in translation. *Language and Communication* 23(3):315–330.

———. 2003b. The listening subject of Japanese modernity and his auditory double: Citing, sighting, and siting the modern Japanese woman. *Cultural Anthropology* 18(2):156–193.

———. 2006. *Vicarious language: Gender and linguistic modernity in Japan.* Berkeley: University of California Press.

Irvine, Judith T. 1989. When talk isn't cheap: Language and political economy. *American Ethnologist* 16(2):248–267.

———. 2005. Knots and tears in the interdiscursive fabric." *Journal of Linguistic Anthropology* 15(1):72–80.

———. 2006. Speech and language community. In Encyclopedia of language and linguistics, 2nd Edition, ed. Keith Brown, 689–698. Oxford: Elsevier Publishers.

Irvine, Judith T., and Susan Gal. 2000. Language ideology and linguistic differentiation. In *Regimes of language: Ideologies, Polities, and Identities*, ed. Paul V. Kroskrity, 35–84. Santa Fe: School of American Research Press.

Jacobs-Huey, Lanita. 2006. *From the Kitchen to the Parlor: Language and becoming in African American women's hair care*. New York: Oxford University Press.

Jaffe, Alexandra. 2009. The Sociolinguistic Stance. In *Stance: Sociolinguistic perspectives*, ed. Alexandra Jaffe, 3–28. New York: Oxford University Press.

Jaspers, Jürgen. 2005. Linguistic sabotage in a context of monolingualism and standardization. *Language & Communication* 25(3):279–297.

Jocson, Korina M. 2005. Examining hybrid literacies of critical youth poets. *International Journal of Learning* 12(8):49–55.

Johnson, Laura Ruth. 2008. A re-storying framework: The intersection of community and family narratives in Puerto Rican Chicago. *Thresholds in Education* 34(1):41–47.

Kim, Catherine Y., Daniel J. Losen, and Damon T. Hewitt. 2010. *The school-to-prison pipeline: Structuring legal reform*. New York: New York University Press.

Kockelman, Paul. 2004. Stance and subjectivity. *Journal of Linguistic Anthropology* 14(2):127–150.

Kramsch, Claire. 2009. *The multilingual subject*. New York: Oxford University Press.

Ladson-Billings, Gloria. 1994. *The dreamkeepers: Successful teachers of African American children*. San Francisco: Jossey-Bass.

Leeman, Jennifer. 2004. Racializing language: A history of linguistic ideologies in the US census. *Journal of Language and Politics* 3(3):507–534.

Leeman, Jennifer. 2012. Investigating language ideologies in Spanish as a heritage language. In *Spanish as a heritage language in the US: State of the science*, ed. Sarah Beaudrie and Marta Fairclough, 43–59. Washington, DC: Georgetown University Press.

Lipman, Pauline. 2008. Education and the new urban workforce in a global city. In *City kids, city schools: More reports from the front row*, ed. William Ayers, Gloria Ladson-Billings, Gregory Michie, and Pedro A. Noguera. New York: The New Press.

———. 2011. *The new political economy of urban education: Neoliberalism, race, and the right to the city*. New York: Routledge.

Lipski, John M. 2008. *Varieties of Spanish in the United States*. Washington, DC: Georgetown University Press.

Lo, Adrienne. 1999. Codeswitching, speech community membership, and the construction of ethnic identity. *Journal of Sociolinguistics* 3(4):461–479.

Lo, Adrienne, and Angela Reyes. 2009. On yellow English and other perilous terms. In *Beyond yellow English: Toward a linguistic anthropology of Asian Pacific America*, ed. Angela Reyes and Adrienne Lo, pp. 3–17. New York: Oxford University Press.

Lopez, David, and Yen Espiritu. 1990. Panethnicity in the United States: A theoretical framework. *Ethnic and Racial Studies* 13:198–224.

López, Ian Haney. 2006. *White by law: The legal construction of race*. New York: New York University Press.

Lopez, Nancy. 2003. *Hopeful girls, troubled boys: Race and gender disparity in urban education*. New York: Routledge.

Luker, Kristin. 1996. *Dubious conceptions: The politics of teenage pregnancy*. Cambridge, MA: Harvard University Press.

Macías, Reynaldo F. 2014. Spanish as the second national language of the United States: Fact, future, fiction, or hope? *Review of Research in Education* 38(1):33–57.

MacSwan, Jeff, Kellie Rolstad, and Gene V. Glass. 2002. Do some school-age children have no language? Some problems of construct validity in the pre-LAS Español. *Bilingual Research Journal* 26(2): 395–420.

Mahiri, Jabari, ed. 2004. *What they don't learn in school: Literacy in the lives of urban youth*. New York: Peter Lang Publishing.

Makoni, Sinfree, and Alastair Pennycook, eds. 2007. *Disinventing and reconstituting languages*. Clevedon, UK: Multilingual Matters.

Males, Mike. 2010. *Teenage sex and pregnancy: Modern myths, unsexy realities*. Santa Barbara, CA: ABC-CLIO, LLC.

Malinowski, Bronislaw. 1922. *Argonauts of the Western Pacific: An account of native enterprise and adventure in the archipelagoes of Melanesian New Guinea*. New York: E. P. Dutton & Co.

Managan, Kathe. 2008. Anthropological linguistic perspectives on writing Guadeloupean Kréyòl: Struggles for recognition of the language and struggles over authority. In *Studies in French applied linguistics*, ed. Dalila Ayoun, 223–253. Amsterdam: John Benjamins.

Márquez, John. 2012a. Latinos as the "living dead": Raciality, expendability, and border militarization." *Latino Studies*. 10(4):473–498.

Márquez, John. 2012b. The Black Mohicans: Representations of everyday violence in postracial urban America. *American Quarterly* 64(3):625–651.

Martínez, Glenn A. 2006. *Mexican Americans and language: Del dicho al hecho*. Tucson: University of Arizona Press.

Martínez, Ramón. 2010. Spanglish as literacy tool: Toward an understanding of the potential role of Spanish-English code-swtiching in the development of academic literacy." *Research in the Teaching of English* 45(2):124–149.

———. 2013. Reading the world in Spanglish: Hybrid language practices and ideological contestation in a sixth-grade English language arts classroom. *Linguistics & Education* 24(3):276–288.

Martínez, Ramón, and P. Zitlali Morales. 2014. ¿Puras groserias?: Rethinking the role of profanity and graphic humor in Latin@ students bilingual wordplay. *Anthropology & Education Quarterly* 45(4):337–354.

Martin-Jones, Marilyn, and Suzanne Romaine. 1986. Semilingualism: A half-baked theory of communicative competence. *Applied Linguistics* 7(1): 26–38.

Marx, David, Sei Jin Ko, and Ray A. Friedman. 2009. The "Obama effect": How a salient role model reduces race-based performance differences. *Journal of Experimental Social Psychology* 45(4):953–956.

Mason Carris, Lauren. 2011. La voz gringa: Latino stylization of linguistic (in)authenticity as social critique. *Discourse & Society* 22(4):474–490.

Mendoza-Denton, Norma. 2008. *Homegirls: Language and cultural practice among Latina youth gangs.* Malden, MA: Blackwell Publishing.

Michaels, Walter Benn. 1992. Race into culture. *Critical Inquiry* 18(4):655–685.

Monzó, Lilia D., and Robert Rueda. 2009. Passing for English fluent: Latino immigrant children masking language proficiency. *Anthropology and Education Quarterly* 40(1):20–40.

Mora, Cristina. 2014. *Making Hispanics: How activists, bureaucrats, and media constructed a new American.* Chicago: University of Chicago Press.

Morales, Ed. 2002. *Living in Spanglish.* New York: St. Martin's Griffin.

Mumm, Jesse. 2014. *When the white people come: Gentrification and race in Puerto Rican Chicago.* Doctoral Dissertation, Northwestern University.

Munn, Nancy D. 1986. *The fame of Gawa: A symbolic study of value transformation in a Massim (Papua New Guinea) Society.* Durham, NC: Duke University Press.

Negron-Muntaner, Frances. 2004. *Boricua pop: Puerto Ricans and the Latinization of American culture.* New York: New York University Press.

Ngai, Mae. 2004. *Impossible subjects: Illegal aliens and the making of modern America.* Princeton, NJ: Princeton University Press.

Nieto, Sonia. 2002. *Language, culture, and teaching: Critical perspectives for a new century.* New York: Routledge.

Nocella II, Anthony J., Priay Parmar, and David Stoval, eds. 2014. *From education to incarceration: Dismantling the school-to-prison pipeline.* New York: Peter Lang Publishing.

Noguera, Pedro A. 2003. Schools, prisons, and social implications of punishment: Rethinking disciplinary practices. *Theory Into Practice* 42(4):341–350.

O'Brien, Eileen. 2008. *The racial middle: Latinos and Asian Americans living beyond the racial divide.* New York: New York University Press.

Ocampo, Anthony. 2014. Are second-generation Filipinos "Becoming" Asian American or Latino?: Historical colonialism, culture, and panethnicity. *Ethnic and Racial Studies* 37(3):425–445.

Olmedo. Irma A. 2005. The bilingual echo: Children as language mediators in a dual-language school. In *Latino language and literacy in ethnolinguistic Chicago*, ed. Marcia Farr, 135–155. Mahwah, NJ: Lawrence Erlbaum Associates, Inc.

Otheguy, Ricardo, and Ana Celia Zentella. 2012. *Spanish in New York: Language contact, dialectal leveling, and structural continuity.* New York: Oxford University Press.

Padilla, Elena. 1947. *Puerto Rican immigrants in New York and Chicago: A study in comparative assimilation.* Master's Thesis, The University of Chicago.

Padilla, Felix M. 1985. *Latino ethnic consciousness.* South Bend, IN: University of Notre Dame.

Pallares, Amalia. 2010. Representing "la familia": Family separation and immigrant activism. In ¡Marcha!: Latino Chicago and the national immigrant movement, ed. Amalia Pallares and Nilda Flores-González, 215–236. Chicago: University of Illinois Press.

Paris, Django. 2011. Language across difference: Ethnicity, communication, and youth identities in changing urban schools. New York: Cambridge University Press.

Pattillo, Mary. 2007. Black on the block: The politics of race and class in the city. Chicago: The University of Chicago Press.

Penney, Joel. 2012. "We don't wear tight clothes": Gay panic and queer style in contemporary hip hop. Popular Music and Society 35(3):321–332.

Perea, Juan F. 1997. The black/white binary paradigm of race: The "normal science" of American racial thought." California Law Review 85(5):1213–1258.

Pérez, Gina. 2003. "Puertorriqueñas rencorosas y Mejicanas sufridas": Gendered ethnic identity formation in Chicago's Latino communities. Journal of Latin American Anthropology 8:96–125.

———. 2004. The Near Northwest Side story: Migration, displacement, and Puerto Rican families. Berkeley: University of California Press.

———. 2006. How a scholarship girl becomes a soldier: The militarization of Latina/o youth in Chicago public schools. Identities: Global Studies in Culture and Power 13(1):53–72.

———. 2015. Citizen, student, soldier: Latina/o Youth, JROTC, and the American Dream. New York: New York University Press.

Phillipson, Robert. 1992. Linguistic imperialism. New York: Oxford University Press.

Plant, E. Ashby, Patricia G. Devine, William T.L. Cox, Corey Columb, Saul L. Miller, Joanna Goplen, and B. Michelle Peruche. 2009. The Obama effect: Decreasing implicit prejudice and stereotyping. Journal of Experimental Social Psychology 45(4):961–964.

Plascencia, Luis. 2009. The "undocumented" Mexican migrant question: Re-examining the framing of law and illegalization in the United States. Urban Anthropology 38(2-4):375–434.

Pollock, Mica. 2004a. Colormute: Race talk dilemmas in an American school. Princeton, NJ: Princeton University Press.

———. 2004b. "Race Bending: 'Mixed' Youth Practicing Strategic Racialization in California." Anthropology and Education Quarterly 35(1):30–52.

Potowski, Kim. 2005. Latino children's Spanish use in a Chicago dual-immersion classroom. In Latino language and literacy in ethnolinguistic Chicago, ed. Marcia Farr, 157–185. Mahwah, NJ: Lawrence Erlbaum Associates, Inc.

Potowski, Kim and Janine Matts. 2008. MexiRicans: Interethnic language and identity. Journal of Language, Identity, and Education 7:137–160.

Povinelli, Elizabeth A. 2001. Radical worlds: The anthropology of incommensurability and inconceivability. Annual Review of Anthropology 30:319–34.

———. 2002. *The cunning of recognition: Indigenous alterities and the making of Australian multiculturalism*. Durham, NC: Duke University Press.

———. 2011. *Economies of abandonment: Social belonging and endurance in late liberalism*. Durham, NC: Duke University Press.

———. 2012. "The will to be otherwise/the effort of endurance." *The South Atlantic Quarterly* 111(3):453–475.

Ralph, Laurence. 2014. *Renegade dreams: Living through injury in gangland Chicago*. Chicago: The University of Chicago Press.

Ramírez, Leonard. 2011. *Chicanas of 18th street: Narratives of a movement from Latino Chicago*. Champaign, IL: University of Illinois Press.

Ramos, Julio. 2001. *Divergent modernities: Culture and politics in 19th century Latin America*. Durham, NC: Duke University Press.

Ramos-Zayas, Ana Yolanda. 2003. *National performances: The politics of class, race, and space in Puerto Rican Chicago*. Chicago: The University of Chicago Press.

———. 2004. Delinquent citizenship, national performances: Racialization, surveillance, and the "politics of worthiness" in Puerto Rican Chicago. *Latino Studies* 2(1):26–44.

Rampton, Ben. 1995. *Crossing: Language and ethnicity among adolescents*. London: Longman.

———. 1998. Language crossing and the redefinition of reality. In *Codeswitching in conversation*, ed. Peter Auer, 290–317. London: Routledge.

———. 1999. Sociolinguistics and cultural studies: New ethnicities, liminality, and interaction. *Social Semiotics* 9(3):355–373.

———. 2002. Ritual and foreign language practices at school. *Language in Society* 31(4):491–525.

———. 2006. *Language in late modernity: Interaction in an urban school*. New York: Cambridge University Press.

Reyes, Angela. 2002. "Are you losing your culture?": Poetics, indexicality, and Asian American identity *Discourse Studies* 4(2):183–199.

———. 2007. *The other Asian: Language, identity, and stereotype among Southeast Asian American youth*. Mahwah, NJ: Lawrence Erlbaum Associates, Inc.

———. 2014. Linguistic anthropology in 2013: Super-new-big. *American Anthropologist* 116(2):366–378.

Richland, Justin B. 2007. Pragmatic paradoxes and ironies of indigeneity at the "edge" of Hopi sovereignty. *American Ethnologist* 34(3)540–557.

Ricourt, Milagros, and Ruby Danta. 2003. *Hispanas de Queens: Latino panethnicity in a New York City neighborhood*. Ithaca, NY: Cornell University Press.

Rinaldo, Rachel. 2002. Space of resistance: The Puerto Rican Cultural Center and Humboldt Park. *Cultural Critique* 50:135–174.

Rios, Victor M. 2011. *Punished: Policing the lives of Black and Latino boys*. New York: New York University Press.

Rios, Michael, and Leonardo Vazquez, eds. 2012. *Diálogos: Placemaking in Latino communities*. New York: Routledge.

Rivera, Raquel Z., Wayne Marshall, and Deborah Pacini Hernandez. 2009. *Reggaeton*. Durham, NC: Duke University Press.

Rivera-Servera, Ramón H. 2012. *Performing Latinidad: Queer sexualities and global imaginaries*. Ann Arbor: University of Michigan Press.

Rodriguez, Luis. 2005 [1993]. *Always running—la vida loca: Gang days in L.A.* New York: Touchstone.

Rodriguez, Richard. 1982. *Hunger of memory: The education of Richard Rodriguez*. Boston: D. R. Godine.

Rodríguez-Muñiz, Michael. 2010. Grappling with Latinidad: Puerto Rican activism in Chicago's immigrant rights movement. In *¡Marcha!: Latino Chicago and the national immigrant movement*, ed. Amalia Pallares and Nilda Flores-González, 237–255. Chicago: University of Illinois Press.

———. 2015. *Temporal politics of the future: National Latino civil rights advocacy, demographic knowledge, and the "browning" of America*. Doctoral Dissertation, Brown University.

Rosa, Jonathan. 2012. "Contesting representations of immigration: The "drop the i-word" campaign from the perspective of linguistic anthropology." *Anthropology News* 53(8):s13–s14.

———. 2014a. Learning ethnolinguistic borders: Language and diaspora in the socialization of U.S. Latinas/os. In *Diaspora studies in education: Towards a framework for understanding the experiences of transnational communities*, ed. Rosalie Rolón Dow and Jason G. Irizarry, 39–60. New York: Peter Lang.

———. 2014b. Language as a sign of immigration? *American Anthropologist* 116(1):11–12.

———. 2016. Racializing language, regimenting Latinas/os: Chronotope, social tense, and American raciolinguistic futures. *Language & Communication* 46:106–117.

———. 2018. Community as a campus: From "problems" to possibilities in Latinx communities. In *Civic engagement in diverse Latinx communities: Learning from social justice partnerships in action*, ed. Mari Castañeda and Joseph Krupczynski, 111–123. New York: Peter Lang.

Rosa, Jonathan, and Nelson Flores. 2017. Unsettling race and language: Toward a raciolinguistic perspective. *Language in Society* 46(5):621–647.

Rosaldo, Renato. 1994. Cultural citizenship and educational democracy. *Cultural Anthropology* 9(3):402–411.

Rosas, Gilberto. 2012. *Barrio libre: Criminalizing states and delinquent refusals of the new frontier*. Durham, NC: Duke University Press.

Roth-Gordon, Jennifer. 2013. Racial malleability and the sensory regime of politically conscious Brazilian hip hop. *Journal of Latin American and Caribbean Anthropology* 18(2):294–313.

Rúa, Mérida. 2001. Colao subjectivities: PortoMex and MexiRican perspectives on language and identity. *CENTRO Journal* 13(2):117–133.

———. 2012. *A grounded identidad: Making new lives in Chicago's Puerto Rican neighborhoods*. New York: Oxford University Press.

Rubin, Beth C., and Pedro A. Noguera. 2004. Tracking detracking: Sorting through the dilemmas and possibilities of detracking in practice. *Equity & Excellence in Education* 37(1):92–101.

Rymes, Betsy. 2001. *Conversational borderlands: Language and identity in an alternative urban high school.* New York: Teachers College Press.

———. 2011. Deference, denial, and beyond: A repertoire approach to mass media and schooling. *Review of Research in Education* 35(1):208–238.

Sanchez, George. 1993. *Becoming Mexican American: Ethnicity, culture, and identity in Chicano Los Angeles, 1900–1945.* New York: Oxford University Press.

Sanchez, Reymundo. 2000. *My bloody life: The making of a Latin King.* Chicago: Chicago Review Press.

———. 2003. *Once a king, always a king: The unmaking of a Latin King.* Chicago: Chicago Review Press.

Santa Ana, Otto. 2002. *Brown tide rising: Metaphors of Latinos in contemporary American public discourse.* Austin: University of Texas Press.

———. 2004. Chronology of events, court decisions, and legislation affecting language minority children in American public education. In *Tongue tied: The lives of multilingual children in public education,* ed. by Otto Santa Ana, 86–105. Lanham, MD: Rowman & Littlefield Publishers, Inc.

Sarroub, Loukia. 2005. *All American Yemeni girls: Being Muslim in a public school.* Philadelphia: University of Pennsylvania Press.

Schieffelin, Bambi, and Rachelle Doucet. 1994. The "real" Haitian Creole: Ideology, metalingusitics, and orthographic choice. *American Ethnologist* 21(1):176–200.

Shankar, Shalini. 2008. *Desi land: Teen culture, class, and success in Silicon Valley.* Durham, NC: Duke University Press.

———. 2013. Racial naturalization, advertising, and model consumers for a new millennium. *Journal of Asian American Studies* 16(2):159–188.

———. 2015. *Advertising diversity: Ad agencies and the creation of Asian American consumers.* Durham, NC: Duke University Press.

Shankar, Shalini, and Jillian Cavanaugh. 2012. Language and materiality in global capitalism. *Annual Review of Anthropology* 41:355–369.

Shedd, Carla. 2015. *Unequal city: Race, school, and perceptions of injustice.* New York: Russell Sage Foundation.

Shipps, Dorothy. 2006. *School reform, corporate style: Chicago, 1880–2000.* Lawrence, Kansas: University of Kansas Press.

Silverstein, Michael. 1976. Shifters, linguistic categories, and cultural description. In *Meaning in anthropology,* ed. Keith Basso and H. Selby, 11–55. Albuquerque: University of New Mexico Press.

———. 1996 [1987]. Monoglot "standard" in America: Standardization and metaphors of linguistic hegemony. In *The matrix of language: Contemporary linguistic anthropology,* ed. Donald Lawrence Brenneis and Ronald K. S. Macaulay, 284–306. Boulder: Westview Press.

———. 1999. NIMBY goes linguistic: Conflicted "voicings" from the culture of local language communities. In *Proceedings of the Chicago Linguistic Society 35, Part 2, Papers from the panels*. Chicago: Chicago Linguistic Society.

———. 2003a. Indexical order and the dialectics of sociolinguistic life. *Language & Communication* 23(3-4):193–229.

———. 2003b. The whens and wheres—as well as hows—of ethnolinguistic recognition. *Public Culture* 15(3): 531–557.

———. 2004. "Cultural" concepts and the language-culture nexus. *Current Anthropology* 45(5):621–652.

———. 2005. Axes of evals: Token versus type interdiscursivity. *Journal of Linguistic Anthropology* 15(1):6–22.

Simpson, Aura. 2014. *Mohawk interruptus: Political life across the borders of settler states*. Durham, NC: Duke University Press.

Skutnabb-Kangas, Tove. 1988. Multilingualism and the education of minority children. In *Minority education: From shame to struggle*, ed. Tove Skutnabb-Kangas and Jim Cummins, 9–44. Clevedon, UK: Multilingual Matters.

Slobe, Tyanna. 2018. Style, stance, and social meaning in mock white girl. *Language in Society* 47(4):541–567.

Smitherman, Geneva. 1994. *Black talk: Words and phrases from the hood to the amen corner*. Boston: Houghton Mifflin Company.

Smulyan, Lisa. 2000. *Balancing acts: Women principals at work*. Albany: State University of New York Press.

Stavans, Ilan. 2003. *Spanglish: The making of a new American language*. New York: Rayo.

Thije, Jan D. ten, and Ludger Zeevaert. 2007. *Receptive multilingualism: Linguistic analyses, language policies, and didactic concepts*. Philadelphia: John Benjamins.

Todd-Breland, Elizabeth. 2018. *A political education: Black politics and education reform in Chicago since the 1960s*. Chapel Hill, NC: University of North Carolina Press, to appear.

Torres, Lourdes, and Kim Potowski. 2008. A comparative study of bilingual discourse, markers in Chicago Mexican, Puerto Rican, and MexiRican Spanish. *International Journal of Bilingualism* 12(4):263–279.

Torres-Saillant, Silvio. 2003. Inventing the race: Latinos and the ethnoracial pentagon. *Latino Studies* 1(1):123–151.

Tough, Paul. 2012. *How children succeed: Grit, curiosity, and the hidden power of character*. New York: Houghton Mifflin Harcourt.

Tuck, Eve. 2012. *Urban youth and school pushout: Gateways, get-aways, and the GED*. New York: Routledge.

Tuck, Eve, and K. Wayne Yang. 2012. Decolonization is not a metaphor. *Decolonization: Indigeneity, Education, & Society* 1(1):1–40.

Urban, Greg. 2001. *Metaculture: How culture moves through the world*. Minneapolis: University of Minnesota Press.

Urciuoli, Bonnie. 1994. Acceptable difference: The cultural evolution of the model ethnic American citizen. *PoLAR: Political and Legal Anthropology Review* 17(2):19–36.

———. 1996. *Exposing prejudice: Puerto Rican experiences of language, race, and class.* Boulder, CO: Westview Press.

———. 2001. The complex diversity of languages in the U.S. In *Cultural diversity in the United States: A critical reader*, ed. I. Susser and T. Carl, 190–204. Malden, MA: Blackwell Publishing.

———. 2008. Whose Spanish? The tension between linguistic correctness and cultural identity. In *Bilingualism and identity: Spanish at the crossroads with other languages*, ed. Mercedes Niño-Murcia and Jason Rothman, 257–277. Philadelphia: John Benjamins Publishing Company.

———. 2009. Talking/not talking about race: The enregisterments of culture in higher education discourses. *Journal of Linguistic Anthropology* 19(1):21–39.

———. 2016. The compromised pragmatics of diversity. *Language & Communciation* 51:30–39.

Urla, Jacqueline. 2012. *Reclaiming Basque: Language, nation, and cultural activism.* Reno, NV: University of Nevada Press.

Valdés, Guadalupe. 1996. *Con respeto: Bridging the distances between culturally diverse families and schools.* New York: Teachers College Press.

———. 1997. Dual language immersion programs: A cautionary note concerning the education of language-minority students. *Harvard Educational Review* 67:321–429.

———. 2000. *Learning and not learning English.* New York, NY: Teachers College Press.

Valenzuela, Angela. 1999. *Subtractive schooling: U.S. Mexican youth and the politics of caring.* Albany: State University of New York Press.

Varenne, Hervé, and Ray McDermott. 2003. *Successful failure: The school America builds.* Boulder: Westview Press.

Vasconcelos, José. 1997. *The cosmic race/La raza cósmica* (D. T. Jaén, Trans.). Baltimore: Johns Hopkins University Press.

Vázquez, David J. 2011. *Triangulations: Narrative strategies for navigating Latino identity.* Minneapolis: University of Minnesota Press.

Veltman, Calvin. 2000. The American linguistic mosaic: Understanding language shift in the United States. In *New immigrants in the United States: Readings for second language educators*, ed. Sandra Lee McKay and Sau-ling Cynthia Wong, 58–98. Cambridge, UK: Cambridge University Press.

Viego, Antonio. 2007. *Dead subjects: Toward a politics of loss in Latino studies.* Durham: Duke University Press.

Washington, Booker T. 1901. *Up from slavery.* New York: Doubleday.

Whitman, David. 2008. *Sweating the small stuff: Inner-city schools and the new paternalism.* Washington: Thomas B. Fordham Institute Press.

Wiley, Terrance G. 2007. Accessing language rights in education: A brief history of the U.S. context. In *Bilingual Education*, ed. Ofelia García and Colin Baker, 89–107. Clevedon, UK: Multilingual Matters Ltd.

Williams, Brackette F. 1989. A class act: Anthropology and the race to nation across ethnic terrain. *Annual Review of Anthropology* 18:401–444.

Willis, Paul. 1977. *Learning to labour*. Farnborough, UK: Saxon House.

Wirtz, Kristina. 2014. *Performing Afro-Cuba: Image, voice, spectacle in the making of race and history*. Chicago: University of Chicago Press.

Woolard, Kathryn A. 1989. Sentences in the language prison: The rhetorical structuring of an American language policy debate. *American Ethnologist* 16:268–278.

———. 1998. Simultaneity and bivalency as strategies in bilingualism. *Journal of Linguistic Anthropology* 8(1): 3–29.

Wortham, Stanton. 2006. *Learning identity: The joint emergence of social identification and academic learning*. Cambridge, UK: Cambridge University Press.

———. 2008. Linguistic anthropology of education. *Annual Review of Anthropology* 37:37–51.

Wortham, Stanton, Enrique G. MurilloJr., and Edmund T. Hamann, eds. 2002. *Education in the new Latino diaspora: Policy and the politics of identity*. Westport, CT: Greenwood.

Wortham, Stanton, and Angela Reyes. 2015. *Discourse analysis beyond the speech event*. New York: Routledge.

Zentella, Ana Celia. 1990. Lexical leveling in four New York City Spanish dialects: Linguistic and social factors. *Hispania* 73:1094–1105.

———. 1996. The chiquitafication of U.S. Latinos and their languages, or: Why we need an anthropolitical linguistics. *Texas Linguistics Forum* 36:1–18.

———. 1997. *Growing up bilingual: Puerto Rican children in New York*. Malden, MA: Blackwell Publishing.

———. 2003. "José, Can You See?" Latin@ responses to racist discourse. In *Bilingual aesthetics,* ed. by Doris Sommer, 51–66. Durham, NC: Duke University Press.

———. ed. 2005. *Building on strength: Language and literacy in Latino families and communities*. New York: Teachers College Press.

———. 2007. "Dime con quién hablas, y te dire quién eres": Linguistic (in)security and Latina/o identity. In *A Companion to Latina/o studies*, ed. Juan Flores and Renato Rosaldo, 25–38. Malden, MA: Blackwell Publishing.

———. 2009 [2002]. Latin@ languages and identities. In *Latinos: Remaking America*, ed. Marcelo M. Suárez-Orozco and Mariela M. Páez, 21–35. Berkeley: University of California Press.

INDEX

Tables and figures are indicated by an italic t and f following the page number

Printed in the USA/Agawam, MA
August 6, 2021

779128.016